WOMEN ON GUARD

Discrimination and Harassment in Corrections

Ontario corrections has recently been plagued by allegations of gender-based discrimination and harassment, particularly with respect to female guards in prisons for men, where women now account for over 20 per cent of the workforce. This book presents two case studies, the first of a training centre for correctional staff, and the second of a jail. Women's experiences of discrimination and harassment are extensively documented, with an emphasis on the systemic aspects of related problems. The book also documents management's lack of success in redressing discrimination and harassment, and how its focus on operational rather than policy matters contributed to this.

Three women from the jail studied in this book successfully pursued their grievances of discrimination and harassment before the Grievance Settlement Board of Ontario. Beth Symes, a lawyer retained by the Ontario Public Service Employees Union, represented the women. In the epilogue to this book, she joins Maeve McMahon in discussing the ground-breaking features of the arbitration decision in addressing systemic issues, as well as the reactions to the decision by union, management, and the grievors.

MAEVE McMAHON is an associate professor in the Department of Law, Carleton University. In the early 1990s she served as a policy adviser and executive assistant to the Ontario Minister of Correctional Services.

WOMEN ON GUARD

Discrimination and Harassment in Corrections

Maeve McMahon

UNIVERSITY OF TORONTO PRESS
Toronto Buffalo London

© University of Toronto Press Incorporated 1999
Toronto Buffalo London
Printed in Canada

ISBN 0-8020-4146-9 (cloth)
ISBN 0-8020-7996-2 (paper)

Printed on acid-free paper

Canadian Cataloguing in Publication Data

McMahon, Maeve W. (Maeve Winifred), 1957–
  Women on Guard : discrimination and harassment in corrections

  Includes bibliographical references.
  ISBN 0-8020-4146-9 (bound)   ISBN 0-8020-7996-2 (pbk.)

  1. Women correctional personnel – Ontario – Hamilton.   2. Women
  correctional personnel – Ontario .   3. Sexual harassment of women –
  Ontario – Hamilton.   4. Sexual harassment of women – Ontario.
  5. Bell Cairn Staff Training Centre.   6. Wakefield Jail.   I. Title.

  HV9509.O5M35 1999   365′.9713′082   C98-931167-8

University of Toronto Press acknowledges the support to its publishing
program of the Canada Council for the Arts and the Ontario Arts Council.

For my parents, Deirdre and Sean McMahon

Contents

ACKNOWLEDGMENTS   IX

1 Women Working in Corrections and in Prisons for Men   3

Introduction   3
The Hidden World of Prisons   4
The Need for Research   6
The Genesis of This Book   7
An Outline of This Book   12

2 A History of Women Working in Corrections and in Prisons for Men   16

The Situation Prior to the 1970s   16
The Introduction of Female Correctional Officers in Prisons
    for Men   18
Developments Facilitating the Entry of Women into Prisons
    for Men   21
The Extent, and Limitations, of Women's Involvement in
    Corrections   24

3 Gender-Based Discrimination and Harassment: From Policy Initiatives to Problems at Bell Cairn   28

Government Policies toward Equity and Harassment
    Prevention   28
Correctional Strategies toward Equity for Female Officers   29

Disjunctures between Rhetoric and Reality in the Ministry   31
Ministry Initiatives in Preventing Harassment in the
    Early 1990s   32
Allegations of Sexual Harassment and Gang-Rape at
    Bell Cairn   35
Initial Perceptions of a Problem with Rowdiness at
    Bell Cairn   36
Incidents at Bell Cairn: Growing Recognition of Sexual
    Harassment   41
Problems in the Ministry's Response to Events at Bell Cairn   47
Actions, and Problems, Subsequent to the Bell Cairn
    Scandal   49

4 **Discrimination and Harassment at the Wakefield Jail:**
   A Research Perspective   55

Research on Women Working in Prisons for Men   55
The Wakefield Jail as a Case Study   56
The Male Culture of Prisons   61
The Male Culture at the Wakefield Jail   64
Micro-inequities   66
Micro-inequities at the Wakefield Jail   67
Gender Discrimination   69
Gender Discrimination at the Wakefield Jail   76
Sexual Harassment   74
Sexual Harassment at the Wakefield Jail   76
The Wakefield Jail as a Poisoned Environment   84
Women's Feelings Following Discrimination and
    Harassment   86

5 **Impediments to Reporting Discrimination and**
   Harassment   89

Research on Impediments to Reporting   89
Management Staff's Contribution to, and Exacerbation of,
    Problems   93
Why Did Women Not Complain, Or Not Complain
    Sooner?   100

Problems and Reprisals Following the Initiation of
   Complaints   104

6 **Responding to, and Ending, Discrimination and**
   Harassment   110
Strategies toward Dealing with Discrimination and
   Harassment   110
Recognizing Operational Matters as Policy Issues   112
Implementing Meaningful Responses and Penalties   115
Providing Effective Training for Staff   120
Improving Hiring, Promotion, and Support Systems
   for Women   124

7 **Conclusion**   130
Harassment and Discrimination as 1990s Issues   130
The Need for Systemic Solutions   134

Epilogue: The Arbitration Decision about the Wakefield
   Grievances   136
A Decision at Last   136
Legal Foundation of the Grievance Settlement Board's
   Decision 137
Findings of the Board about Individual Grievances   139
The Board's Innovative Imposition of Systemic Remedies   142
Individual Remedies for the Grievors   145
The Grievors' Reactions to the Decision   146
Reactions at the Jail   152
Challenges Facing the Union and the Ministry   153
Postscript   154

APPENDIX Workplace Discrimination and Harassment Prevention:
   Policy Directive and Guideline, Ontario Government 1992   155

NOTES   177

REFERENCES   203

INDEX   211

Acknowledgments

This research has taken a long and winding route, and has involved contact with many people. Owing, however, first, to the sensitive nature of the topic of sexual discrimination and harassment, second, the fact that a pseudonym is used for the jail discussed in this book, and third, many individuals' preferences to discuss issues informally, anonymously, or 'off-the-record,' it is not possible to identify all of those who have assisted here. Let me first, then, generically thank everybody who helped me with this research.

My greatest debt of gratitude is to the three women from the Wakefield Jail who grieved their case, and whom I discuss under the pseudonyms Nora Diamond, Diana Hooper, and Karla Preston. They have each, in their own individual ways, encouraged me to pursue this research and publish this book. Their openness in this regard, their willingness to share their views and experiences, and their tolerance of my intruding on them with requests for information and clarification have all been crucial in making this research possible. My heartfelt thanks go to them all. I also thank the grievors' lawyer, Beth Symes, for involving me in their case, and for co-authoring the epilogue of this book with me.

My knowledge of issues of sexual discrimination and harassment in corrections has been enhanced by discussions with many people. I thank officials of the Ontario Public Services Employees Union, and especially their president, Leah Casselman, as well as Pam Doig, Barry Scanlon, Beverley Johnson, and Denis Boyer. Two female correctional officers – Audrey E. Williams and Margaret Slatern –

selected by OPSEU gave the manuscript a close reading, and their comments and encouragement were very helpful. Extended discussion with Margaret did much to improve my understanding of discrimination and harassment experienced by women correctional officers across the province. The individual who was the union's representative at the Wakefield Jail while this book was being completed was also most helpful in clarifying important points. My interview with Francis Lankin, a member of Ontario's legislature, and, in the late 1970s, a correctional officer at the Don Jail in Toronto, provided an insightful view of her experience as one of the first female officers working in a prison for men in Ontario.

Various officials of the Ontario Ministry of the Solicitor General and Correctional Services helpfully discussed gender issues in corrections with me. Ross Virgo of Communications kindly provided specific items of information. My knowledge of the correctional context generally also gained from my own experience as a member of the minister's staff between late 1990 and the spring of 1992. I wish to thank my then colleagues Elisa Amsterdam, Carolyn Nantais, Julia Powditch, and Rudy Ticzon, for stimulating debates about corrections and politics, and for their continued interest in discussing penal reform long after we had all moved on to other positions. Elisa's assistance in sending me relevant newspaper articles when I was in far-off places was most helpful. The late Ron Cavalucci inspired us all with his humanitarian concern combined with political acuity.

My initial steps in this research were undertaken with Kelly Hannah Moffat, who was then a doctoral student at the University of Toronto, and is now an assistant professor at Brock University. Kelly's assistance was invaluable in reviewing the literature, and in developing the analytical framework of the research. It was also most enjoyable discussing the issues with her, and doing several conference presentations together. I particularly appreciate Kelly's ongoing interest in the research, even after her own immediate involvement had ceased. Finally, I thank Kelly for suggesting an apt title for this book – *Women on Guard.*

Communicating the findings of one's research is always useful in advancing it. This research benefited from the comments and suggestions of participants at several conferences of the Correctional

Service of Canada in 1992, and at the British Criminology Conference in 1997. I also thank participants at the Conference of the European Group for the Study of Deviance and Social Control held in Ireland in 1995 – notably Karen Leander and Ida Koch – for their helpful discussions and critiques. The research was aided by comments by several readers. I thank Professor Mary Jane Mossman of the Osgoode Hall Law School, York University, for both reading and discussing this work with me. The responses of two anonymous reviewers appointed by the University of Toronto Press were very useful in the final stages of the work.

My understanding of the situation of women working in prisons for men internationally has been enhanced by visits to prisons in places other than Ontario. As these visits tended to be informal (organized, for example, in conjunction with a conference being held locally), and as my discussions with staff were 'off-the-record,' I cannot name individual institutions or people. The prison guards, managers, and governors, will know themselves, however, and I offer them sincere thanks for their forthright, and sometimes heated, discussions. It is a pleasure to be able to thank some of those people who assisted in organizing these visits, namely Professor Nils Christie of Oslo University, and Asbjørn Langås, director of the Norwegian Department of Justice; Elías Carranza of ILANUD in Costa Rica; Professor Viktoras Justickis of the Lithuanian Law Academy, and Dr. Antanas Dapsys of the Law Institute, Lithuanian Ministry of Justice; Geoff Huggins of the Prison Service in northern Ireland; Frank Dunne and John Lonergan of the Department of Justice, Republic of Ireland; Tim Wilson of HM Prison Service in England; and Professor Eduard Raska and Ms. Riina Soosaar of the Estonian National Defence and Public Service Academy. K.-J. Lång, director of the Finnish Prison Service, also went well beyond the call of duty in helping me to organize one of these visits.

My work on this project commenced when I was with the Centre of Criminology at the University of Toronto. I thank the faculty and staff there for their assistance, and especially Cathy Matthews and Jane Gladstone, then with the Centre's library. More recently, Tom Finlay of the Centre of Criminology library has been very helpful. Most of the research has been carried out at the Department of

Law, Carleton University. I warmly thank our chair, Professor Brettel Dawson, for consistently encouraging me in my research endeavours, and for facilitating me in any way she can. I thank my colleague Professor Diana Majury for advancing me on this research path, and my colleague Professor Michael MacNeil for his helpful comments on one section of the manuscript. Graduate students Marnie MacDonald and Rosemary Nagy ably provided research assistance, and I am also grateful to Laurie Campbell of the Carleton University library. Support staff at the Department of Law – Margaret Wood, Joan Clarke, Heather Park, and Barb Higgins – patiently provided administrative assistance. At the library of the Ministry of the Solicitor General in Ottawa I thank Heather Moore, Noëlla Marvin, and Leonard Bonavero for helping me out on many occasions.

This research benefited from some research grants. The initial work was made possible through a Canada Research Fellowship, funded by the Social Sciences and Humanities Research Council of Canada, and by the University of Toronto. Its completion was facilitated by several GR-6 grants, funded by the Social Sciences and Humanities Research Council of Canada, and by Carleton University.

One could not wish for a better publisher than the University of Toronto Press. I thank Virgil Duff, executive editor, Anne Forte, managing editor, and Margaret Williams, assistant editor, for their efficiency, editorial guidance, and enthusiasm for this project. William Wood did an excellent job of copyediting. Barbara Schon efficiently prepared the index. It is a pleasure to work with such good-humoured people!

Some of the early writing of this book was done in the depths of winter at Denbigh, Ontario. I thank my friends Jan Anderson and Nico Trocme, and all of the 'Denbigh-ites,' for generously sharing their retreat with me at a time when it was much needed. More generally, I thank my family and friends in Ireland, Canada, and elsewhere – especially for their understanding and support when my research interrupted our social lives. Val and Charles Kinghorn and Kathryn Drysdale are among the many who have been tolerant in this regard! Discussions with my mother – Deirdre McMahon – of her observations on informal strategies for dealing with sexual discrimination and harassment in the workplace helped me clarify some of my own opinions on this issue. She has also generously provided much practical assistance to my research endeavours over the years, and this, along with her moral support, has been much appreciated by me. My sister, Deirdre Downes, and her wonderful family provided a welcome twenty-four-hour babysitting service, which enabled me to do some writing at a crucial point. Her consistent readiness to help me, and indeed that of all of my immediate family, is a great support.

Experiences of discrimination and harassment are extremely disturbing. While nothing compares to going through these experiences, I have found that writing about them – when one is acutely sensitive to the pain the research subjects have suffered – also poses emotional, ethical, practical, and personal difficulties. I thank Michael Kinghorn for helping me through these difficulties, and for engaging in lengthy discussions and debates about sexual discrimination and harassment. I also thank Michael for designing and forging the sculpture that adorns the cover of this book. To our lovely son, Declan, I say: your birth 'due date' proved more effective than any deadline!

WOMEN ON GUARD

Discrimination and Harassment in Corrections

1 Women Working in Corrections and in Prisons for Men

Introduction

> When I started work in a maximum security institution in 1964, one of the inmates had not seen a woman in 30 years. I shall never forget what this change in the status quo meant for the inmates and guards – and for myself. (Maryrose Lette, National Parole Board, in 1975, quoted in Correctional Service of Canada 1975, 10)

> One of the real kinds of isolation faced by an inmate is isolation from women. How can he go back into society and behave normally towards women if he has not been able even to communicate with a woman for months or years[?] (Psychologist quoted in Correctional Service of Canada 1980, 5)

The provincial prison system in the Canadian province of Ontario is almost two hundred years old. Since its inception, the vast majority of prison/correctional officers have been men. In explaining this, some people might point to the predominance of males among offenders. Specifically, it might be argued that given that men have constituted the vast majority of offenders, it logically follows that the majority of correctional workers should also be male. But even a cursory look at the situation of female offenders casts doubt on such logic. For, not only recently, but also historically, male officers have worked with female prisoners.[1] In general, while it has not been unusual to find males working with female prisoners, one would rarely find women working in prisons for men, particularly as correctional officers.

It is only the past few decades in Ontario that have seen the introduction of a substantial number of women working in prisons for men. The change that this has involved has had qualitative as well as quantitative aspects. Those few women who previously worked in Ontario prisons for men typically worked in clerical positions, or as nurses and treatment staff. In short, they were engaged in traditionally female occupations.

By contrast, from the 1970s, women have entered the traditionally male occupation of correctional officer. Where in 1975, the total number of female correctional officers in Ontario provincial prisons stood at 174, and where only 16 of them worked in male institutions (Campbell 1990), by 1998 there were 1,020 female correctional officers, of whom about 969 were working in prisons for men (Personal communication, Ross Virgo, Communications, Ministry of Correctional Services, July 1998. Note: a small proportion of female correctional officers in prisons for men were working in female units within those prisons).

As this book will document, the introduction of female correctional officers into prisons for men has been fraught with tension. This is unsurprising, as the more general story of women's entry into traditionally male occupations – including, for example, law, science, mining, autoworking, construction, policing, and the military – has also been one with sub-plots of hostility, conflict, abuse, and harassment, being experienced by the women (e.g., Aggarwal 1992; Binken and Bach 1977; Deaux and Ullman 1983; Epstein 1981; Gruber and Bjorn 1982; Hartel and VonVille 1995; Hunt 1986; Kanter 1977; Lafontaine and Tredeau 1986; Martin 1980; Meyer and Lee 1978; Price and Gavin 1982; Riemer 1979; Rustad 1982; Westley 1982; White 1975).

A substantial amount of information has now been gathered about women's experiences in traditionally male occupations. But there has been a dearth of information about, and analysis of, the experience of female employees in prisons for men. Indeed, in Canada today, analysis of the situation of female correctional officers in prisons for men is still at an embryonic stage.[2]

The Hidden World of Prisons

Corrections is the least visible branch of the criminal justice system. (Arbour 1996, xi)

Why has there been so little inquiry into the experiences of female correctional officers, particularly in Canada? In part, this lack of information may arise from the distinctive occupational and social world of prisons themselves. While it has been difficult for members of the public not to notice the growing proportion of women working as drivers of public transport vehicles, and as lawyers, doctors, dentists, professors, journalists, accountants, and so on, it has been easy for the growing number of female correctional officers to go relatively unnoticed.

By definition, the work of prison officers takes place behind high walls, security fences, and other barriers to public entry.[3] In contrast to the occupation of policing, with which every member of the public will have some contact (if only in the form of traffic regulation), only a relatively small proportion of the public will come into contact with correctional officers as they do their work. In short, the hidden nature of the prison system is one reason why members of the public are relatively uninformed about the everyday world and work of correctional officers, both male and female.

In addition to the spatial segregation, other factors have also contributed to the lack of knowledge about correctional officers. In a democratic society that values personal freedom and autonomy, those whose work consists primarily of the custody and control of others can experience occupational ambiguity and insecurity with respect to their social status. As a result of the stigma that they perceive to be attached to their jobs by the community, some correctional officers have been disinclined to personally advertise the specifics of their jobs, and have preferred to identify themselves as 'working for the government.'

The oath of secrecy traditionally taken by correctional officers has also reinforced their isolation from local communities and their tendency to socialize primarily with their peers. As Marron (1996, 154) has observed with respect to federal correctional officers in

Canada: 'tired of being harangued by neighbours about the failures of the prison system, and unable to talk about the realities of their work, [correctional officers] are likely to prefer the company of their co-workers ...' While there are signs that this insecurity and isolation of correctional officers may now be declining as the professional status of their occupation is growing, their traditional reticence in communicating about their work, and the legal constraints to which correctional officers are subject, also help to explain why the world of prisons, and the everyday life of workers there, have had a hidden character.[4]

Public knowledge of the everyday world of correctional officers is further hindered in that prisons are relatively rarely the subject of media attention. While the news media frequently focus on what is happening with respect to crime, policing, and the courts, attention to what is happening in prisons is far less common. Moreover, when the news media do focus on prisons, it is typically in the context of a major problem being experienced in running the system (as, for example, when a major riot takes place).[5] As Marron (157, 158) puts it: 'The successes of the prison system are often hard to measure, and there is little of interest that one can say about them ... The failures are what captures everyone's attention.' This tendency to focus on the problems, as opposed to accomplishments, of prisons perpetuates the phenomenon of the prison system being largely hidden from the public view. Also, when senior prison administrators perceive that public attention is associated with criticism, a tendency to shield the system from scrutiny is reinforced.[6]

The Need for Research

Why should attention to the situation of female correctional workers, and especially female officers working in prisons for men, be considered important?

• Females working as correctional officers in prisons for men are entering a traditionally male occupation, a situation that, in itself, involves a variety of hazards. Moreover, these women are working in a particularly male environment, given that their co-workers as well as the inmates with whom they work are male.

- Females working in prisons for men are working in an occupational environment which has traditionally been shielded from public scrutiny.
- Females working in prisons for men are working in an environment where the culture has been an authoritarian one. This applies not only to the manner in which prison officers have interacted with prisoners, but also – given the paramilitary organization of staffing that has prevailed – to the manner in which supervisors have interacted with their subordinates.

In short, women working in prisons for men can be considered vulnerable in many ways: they are in an environment that is overwhelmingly male, where staff have been treated in authoritarian and paramilitaristic ways, and where their everyday work is shielded from public view. Under these circumstances, it is important to examine their experiences, not only from social scientific perspectives, but also in light of government's commitment to providing, defending, and advancing women's rights, including equity in the workplace.

The Genesis of This Book

No research exists in a vacuum, and the current research is no exception. A few words therefore, on the genesis of this book – especially given the hidden nature of the everyday world of corrections – may be of interest to the reader.

Between 1990 and 1992 I had the opportunity to take leave from the university to work with the Ontario Ministry of Correctional Services for two seven–month periods.[7] During the first phase, I was policy advisor to the minister of correctional services, and during the second period, I was executive assistant (chief-of-staff) to the minister, who was also solicitor general for the province. Both of these positions were political, rather than civil service, appointments. As an academic with a long-standing interest in justice issues, and especially correctional ones, the positions offered me an exciting opportunity not only to work at a senior level of the system, but also to complement my academic knowledge of the justice field with first-hand experience of the dynamics of criminal justice policy, and of the complex intersection of policy, operational, bureaucratic, fiscal, and political issues that these dynamics entail.[8]

During the second period of my sojourn (from September 1991 until March 1992), the deputy minister – that is, the most senior civil servant – at the Ministry of Correctional Services was a woman, Dina Palozzi. Ms Palozzi was the first woman to be appointed to this position in Ontario corrections. Given her progressive approach and forthright manner, it was a pleasure to work alongside her. With such a communicative deputy minister, and with the mountains of information that typically flow into a minister's office on any given day, I felt confident that the minister, and his staff, were very well informed about current events and issues within the ministry.

My confidence was shaken. That our knowledge of developments within the ministry was by no means comprehensive became apparent soon after my departure from the minister's office. Several months later, in mid-July 1992, a major scandal broke. At the heart of the scandal were allegations that two female employees of the ministry had been 'gang-raped' by their male colleagues at the Bell Cairn Staff Training School for correctional workers (i.e., prison/correctional officers and probation and parole officers) in Hamilton, Ontario. The gang-rapes allegedly took place about six weeks earlier. It was further alleged that sexual harassment of women had been prevalent at the Bell Cairn Staff Training Centre since it had opened the previous fall – including the entire period of September to March when I had been the minister's executive assistant.

The news[9] of these allegations was very disturbing. In the first place, allegations of gang-rape, whatever the context, and wherever the place, are extremely disturbing in themselves. But it was also upsetting news to me that sexual harassment could have taken place for such a long period without coming to the attention of the deputy minister, or the minister and his staff. It was also upsetting that although Dina Palozzi was committed to equity issues generally, and was intolerant of sexist attitudes and behaviour, she was soon removed from her position as deputy minister of correctional services. In my eyes at least, she had become another 'victim' of the scandalous events.

Over time my reaction to the scandal and ensuing developments coalesced into two sets of research questions. The first questions focus on organizational, bureaucratic, and procedural issues. They draw from the observation that knowledge of ongoing sexual harassment at Bell Cairn did not percolate into the deputy minister's office until the early summer of 1992, over six months after the problems had commenced. A basic question is: Why did detailed information about the sexual harassment at Bell Cairn not reach the deputy minister's office until the situation had reached crisis proportions? Looking at the situation more abstractly, another question can be raised: What do events at Bell Cairn reveal about the social construction, definition, and especially the management, of problems within the ministry?

While the above questions are concerned with what might be described as 'process,' the second set of questions focus more on issues of 'content,' and especially the content of women's experience working in corrections. Specifically, for me, the dramatic allegations with respect to gang-rape served to raise some basic and broader questions: What is the situation of women working in corrections more generally, and especially in the male-dominated environments of prisons for men? Were the allegations concerning Bell Cairn in any way typical, or should they be seen as an aberration?

Under the normal course of events, attempting to conduct research addressing these questions could be extremely difficult. Research on gender relations among correctional workers that does exist is overwhelmingly survey-based. Qualitative research, including case studies of gender relations in individual institutions, is lacking. This lack is likely due to the more general paucity of research attention to issues concerning female correctional workers. This paucity, in turn, is due to the hidden nature of prisons already discussed, and to the accompanying difficulties of gaining permission for research access to prisons and other correctional institutions.

Fortunately, however, a combination of events directed my attention to the formulation of the above research questions, and also provided conditions and information through which I could begin to address them. In the first place, official reactions to the scandal at Bell Cairn included Ontario Premier Bob Rae's instruction that internal ministry documents concerning events at Bell Cairn be publicly released. These documents included letters and memos written by supervisors of correctional staff who had experienced harassment while taking courses at Bell Cairn, by staff of Bell Cairn responding to these outsiders' expressions of concern, by staff of Bell Cairn documenting ongoing problems, and by ministry investigators, and middle- and senior-level managers, as they became aware of problems at Bell Cairn. The ensuing *Chronology of Events: Bell Cairn Staff Training Centre,* released by the Ministry of Correctional Services in July 1992, also included documentation of details of the incidents finally being brought to the attention of the deputy minister in the weeks before the 'gang-rape' scandal broke, and of the ministry's perspective on them, and of actions taken, at that time.

The immediate impetus to the instruction that this information be released was, no doubt, the government's frustration with the amount of information, and sometimes disinformation, which was already being 'leaked' to members of the media, opposition politicians, and other interested parties. Instructing that relevant memos and other information be publicly released would forestall further leaks, and would also help to stem the flow of rumours concerning what had actually happened.

While this impetus to the release of the *Chronology of Events* was clearly a political one, from an academic point of view it also constituted a unique research opportunity. Put simply, such detailed information about a current controversy is more usually kept confidential, and thereby shielded from public view. For this reason, detailed case studies of controversial events, and internal ministry reactions to them, are often not possible until decades later, when related documents become available through government archives.[10] In the case of Bell Cairn, however, I was able to examine the ministry's perception of various events soon after they had actually occurred. Having acquired a copy of the *Chronology of Events*, I was able to initiate research on what had transpired at Bell Cairn between September 1991 and June 1992.

Meanwhile, invitations to speak at several conferences involving female correctional officers in the Correctional Service of Canada provided me with the opportunity to discuss with them research observations in the literature on the situation of women working in corrections. The interest expressed by these federal correctional officers encouraged me to undertake further research should the opportunity arise.

Such an opportunity arose in 1995,[11] when I was contacted by Beth Symes, a lawyer retained by the Ontario Public Service Employees Union to represent three women from the Wakefield Jail[12] with respect to their grievances, which were undergoing arbitration before the Ontario Crown Employees Grievance Settlement Board (hereafter Grievance Settlement Board). The women's grievances arose from gender-based discrimination and harassment that had taken place at the jail over a lengthy period. The Wakefield Jail is administered by the Ontario Ministry of Correctional Services,[13] and is located in a small town, far from Ontario's major urban centres. It is one of Ontario's smaller jails. Built in 1928, the jail had a forty-bed capacity. In early 1995, the staff consisted of a superintendent, five lieutenants, seventeen correctional officers, six to eight casual correctional officers, four cooks (one full-time, one part-time, and two casual), and several administrative staff.

Ms Symes asked me to prepare a report on the topic of women working in prisons for men, with particular attention to the situation of women at the Wakefield Jail. To this end, she provided me with related documents,[14] and I duly completed a report. Again, from an academic point of view, these documents gathered in conjunction with the Grievance Settlement Board hearings constituted a valuable database on an under-researched topic. Together with the *Chronology of Events* concerning incidents at the Bell Cairn Staff Training School, they comprise the primary sources upon which the following analysis is based.

In sum, two sets of incidents have acted as the stimulus of this book: those at the Bell Cairn Staff Training Centre and at the Wakefield Jail. It is important to state that what is unusual about each of these sets of incidents is not that they took place. For, as the available research literature suggests, gender-based discrimination and harassment are a common feature of the experience of women working in traditionally male occupations, with corrections being no exception. Rather, what is unusual is that such detailed documentation of each set of incidents is available for research scrutiny.

Further, it is also important to state that while the incidents at Bell Cairn and at the Wakefield Jail are individually and cumulatively disturbing, the resulting documentation of events arguably has some positive effect. While the incidents have been negative experiences for the women involved, documentation of their context, and of responses to them, can also be viewed as positive in that:

- It offers an opportunity to describe and acknowledge the discrimination, harassment, humiliation, and angst, as well as the physiological and psychological damage, experienced by some of the women affected.[15]
- It offers an opportunity to describe more general problems of gender-based discrimination and harassment experienced by women working in corrections, and especially those working in prisons for men.
- It offers an opportunity to acknowledge the efforts that have been made to date – by the Ontario government, and by the Ministry of Correctional Services – in acknowledging and responding to gender-based discrimination and harassment. It also offers an opportunity to reflect on how these agencies, along with the Ontario Public Services Employees Union, can work together in the future in recognizing, remedying, and ending gender-based discrimination and harassment.

It is my hope that documenting these events in the Ontario context will be useful to policy-makers, victims, and researchers elsewhere as they work toward describing, understanding, challenging, and redressing problems of gender-based discrimination and harassment.

An Outline of This Book

The second chapter of this book provides a historical perspective on women working in corrections and in prisons for men in Ontario. The third chapter documents growing sensitivity to gender-based discrimination and harassment on the part of the Ministry of Correctional Services. It also documents some of the policy and educational steps taken as they reflect this growing sensitivity. That good intentions do not necessarily, or rapidly, translate into satisfactory accomplishments becomes apparent when analysing some of the problems, and the eventual scandal, at the ministry's Bell Cairn Staff Training Centre for correctional workers. In turn, a discussion of the limitations of, and problems with, responses to the Bell Cairn incidents highlights an important point: intense activity, and the proliferation of procedures aimed at accountability, do not of themselves guarantee effective responses to harassment. Rather, both problems of gender-based discrimination and harassment, and effective routes toward dealing with these problems, must be recognized as complex and nuanced.

The fourth chapter examines incidents at the Wakefield Jail. This examination is situated in the context of existing literature about women working in prisons for men. By reviewing the relevant literature (most of which has been developed in the United States), this chapter reveals that much of the (mis)treatment to which women at the Wakefield Jail have been subjected by their male colleagues can be considered paradigmatic of the situation of women working in prisons for men. Virtually every problem that has been documented in the literature has been evident in the specific case of the Wakefield Jail. Specifically, this chapter documents how the Wakefield Jail has evidenced a *male culture*, and how female workers at the Wakefield Jail have experienced *micro-inequities* and *gender discrimination*. In turn, some of the women at the Wakefield Jail have experienced *sexual harassment*. Overall, despite various initiatives on the part of the Ministry of Correctional Services, the Wakefield Jail could be considered a prototype of the 'poisoned environment' that the Ontario government's Workplace Discrimination and Harassment Prevention policy of the early 1990s aimed to preclude. Indeed, given the repeated, and clearly unwanted, physical and sexual intrusions experienced by some women, the Wakefield Jail could be considered as reflecting an exceptionally poisoned environment.

The fifth chapter addresses problems in reporting gender-based discrimination and harassment. In the case of Wakefield Jail – as in many other situations involving harassment – women have been questioned as to why they did not complain, or why they did not complain sooner. A review of the literature reveals some of the generalized problems in reporting experienced by women in prisons for men. That these problems have also been experienced by the women at the Wakefield Jail is illuminated by an examination of their own explanations for not complaining. It is argued that management's contribution to, and exacerbation of, problems of discrimination and harassment has constituted a major impediment to reporting by women.

The sixth chapter discusses the difficult issues of how gender-based discrimination and harassment can be more effectively responded to, prevented, and ended. While this discussion focuses on the particular case of the Wakefield Jail, many of the principles identified, and points made, are pertinent for correctional institutions more generally. Overall, what *should not* be done is considered as important as what *should* be done. New management procedures aimed at accountability, and the imposition of penalties, are not sufficient when taken in isolation. It is contended that any new procedures must be meaningful. They must work not only on paper, and not only from the top down. They must also work from the bottom up, and must additionally radiate from the middle levels of the organization. They must offer women, and men, more than a modicum of dignity and respect. They must not engage in the equivalent of witch-hunts of a select or unfortunate few, while ignoring, or glossing over, the transgressions of many. It is the macho culture of prisons for men as a whole that must be challenged and transcended, by management and unions working in tandem. More specifically, this chapter suggests how meaningful, cooperative responses to gender-based discrimination and harassment might take place. Problems, remedies, and recommendations are discussed with respect to:

- recognizing that operational matters involve policy issues
- implementing meaningful responses and penalties
- providing effective training for staff
- improving hiring, promotion, and support systems for women

The seventh and concluding chapter reflects on wider preoccupations, debates, and controversies about issues of discrimination and harassment in the 1990s. Neither outright dismissal of claims of sexual harassment in the context of the wider backlash against feminist and equity issues nor naive affirmation that sexual harassment has taken place without informed investigation are helpful in charting and dealing with the realities of the problem. Moreover, as the study of women working in corrections in Ontario presented here reveals, when gender-based discrimination and harassment become a systemic problem, the only viable solutions are also systemic ones.

2 A History of Women Working in Corrections and in Prisons for Men

The Situation Prior to the 1970s

> Corrections has traditionally been a male domain, managed by men for men. (Ministry of Correctional Services 1983a, 7)

To date, knowledge of the history of women working in prisons for men in the Ontario provincial system[1] is skimpy. Nonetheless, a review of available sources reaffirms the general observation that female correctional officers were noticeable primarily by their absence until the mid to late 1970s.

Prior to the mid 1970s, those few women who did work in prisons for men were engaged in traditionally female occupations. For example, women were employed in positions as nurses.[2] Women also worked in clerical roles.

When the immediate post–Second World War period is examined, it can be seen that Ontario prisons were not only run by males, but were run in a particularly authoritarian way. The prisons – like prisons in many other Western jurisdictions – were run along paramilitary lines. According to Don Sinclair, who worked in Ontario corrections at increasingly senior positions between 1956 and 1974, the institutions were run in a quasi-military manner (interview with the author). As Mann (1967, 30) has described, one aspect of this military orientation was the practice whereby, 'in lieu of other criteria, promotions to the higher positions in the Ontario [corrections] field until the late 1950s tended to favour men with military training and outlook.' The appointment of Colonel Hedley Basher as a superintendent, and later as deputy minister in the 1950s, was 'typical' of this tendency.

The regime at Guelph Reformatory, for example, illustrates the militaristic orientation of Ontario prisons. As Sinclair has observed, the staff 'just took orders. Their ranks were run the same as military ranks; they were called corporals, and sergeants ... it was very like being in the army.' According to Mann, in the early 1960s, at Guelph (30–1):

> The impact of the institution's physical structure upon the inmates is highly reinforced by the military-type characteristics of the supervisory and administrative personnel. Guards and officials with few exceptions are regularly dressed in military-type khaki apparel, are accorded military title and are expected to deport themselves with military precision and formality ... With disciplined military men at the top and other military accoutrements including titles and uniforms, it is natural that inmates will be handled by the barking of orders and the external disciplines of a military-type system.

Apart from the small numbers of women who worked as treatment and clerical workers, the other major category of women to permeate the male enclave of Ontario prisons prior to the 1970s were termed 'matrons.' These matrons performed traditionally female tasks, and also worked with the female section of the prison population. In the words of a historical retrospective by the Ministry of Correctional Services (1983a, 7), matrons 'were responsible for the care of the female inmates, and depending on the size of the institution, for the cooking, clothing, making of the beds, etc.' This ministry narrative indicates that there was an element of forced labour in the work of some of the matrons in that they received their positions, and were compelled to work, by virtue of being married to the governor or superintendent of the jail. As the ministry narrative elaborates (7–8):

> [Matrons] were often part of a husband and wife team, their husband being the Governor or Superintendent of the jail. They were required

to live in residence. Mr. E.W. Martin, former Superintendent at the old Kingston Jail, recalls that in 1947, when offered the position as Superintendent he had indicated to the Deputy Minister, Mr. Neelands, that his wife did not wish to be the Matron. Mr. Neelands, in his Scottish accent, told him 'Laddie, this is a package deal, your wife has to become the Matron and you have to live in residence to become Governor of the Jail.' These wives of jailers were often on call 24 hours a day and had to raise their families in that environment.

Larger institutions, such as the Don Jail in Toronto, had several matrons. According to the ministry narrative, these matrons 'tended to be motherly types' (8). They worked largely with females, most of whom, in the Don Jail – as elsewhere – were incarcerated 'due to alcoholism and prostitution.'[3]

Overall, the number of matrons was relatively small. As of March 1966, there were 35 matrons in Ontario prisons. And in 1971, matron positions for the wives of jail superintendents were abolished when the ministry 'announced that husband and wife could no longer work together in the same institution' (8, 9).

The Introduction of Female Correctional Officers in Prisons for Men

The first prison for men to take an initiative in hiring female correctional officers was the Alex Brown Clinic/Ontario Correctional Institute in Brampton. This institution began hiring female correctional officers in the early 1970s. By the mid-1970s, a number of other institutions were also hiring female correctional officers.[4] By the end of the 1970s, female correctional officers were working with male inmates in at least 24 institutions (Ministry of Correctional Services 1983a, 10, Table 3).

Table 2.1 documents the introduction of female correctional officers in prisons for men for select years.[5] The table also documents the total number of female correctional officers in the ministry (i.e., females working at the Vanier Centre for women are also included). These figures are derived from a variety of sources, which are not always fully in accord with one another (Anon. 1982;

Table 2.1
Female Correctional Officers in Ontario

Year	Female Corr. Off. in Male Institutions	Total Female Corr. Off.
1975	16	174
1977	110	249
1980	154	313
1983	224	352
1985	329	382
1989	550	596
1990	567	619
1992	569	679
1998	969	1,020

Bronskill 1980; Campbell 1990; Employment Systems Review Task Force 1994; Ministry of Correctional Services 1983a; Ombudsman of Ontario 1977). They are provided here primarily to document the general trend.

Overall, and primarily through their growing representation among correctional staff in prisons for men, the number of female correctional officers has grown proportionately. In the early 1980s, women accounted for approximately 8.5 per cent of all correctional officers in the ministry. In 1990, they accounted for about 18 per cent, and by 1992, they accounted for 21 per cent.[6] Data provided by Ross Virgo of the ministry reveals that, as of June 1998, women accounted for 23.7 per cent of all correctional officers (of 4,296 correctional officer positions, 1,020 were held by women).

In addition to entering the occupation of correctional officer in prisons for men, in the mid-1970s a few women also began to secure some representation at management level within institutions for men. Specifically, the historical retrospective by the ministry reports that in 1976 a woman was appointed shift supervisor in a male institution; in 1979–80, the first female deputy superintendent of a jail was appointed, and, in 1982, a female was appointed superintendent of a male adult prison (Ministry of Correctional Services 1983a, 18).

A Note on Women in Probation and Parole

By the end of the 1970s, in addition to entering institutions for males, women had advanced in other areas of the work of the Ministry of Correctional Services. For example, probation had again been a traditionally male preserve. A brief review of the evolution of probation reveals that women's entry to this profession occurred at about the same time as their entry into that of correctional officer.

While a small probation service had long existed in Ontario, its development took off with the appointment of Dan Coughlan as director in the early 1950s. In 1950, there were only fourteen probation officers in Ontario. By 1960, the number had increased to 150 officers, and subsequently continued to grow rapidly (Oliver and Whittingham 1987, 245). Coughlan had himself been trained as a social worker, and was a former probation officer with the juvenile and family court. Coughlan had also served in both the British merchant marine and the Canadian navy. In addition, Coughlan had been ordained as an Anglican priest (246). Coughlan's leadership of the probation service was marked by a missionary zeal.

The limitations on the employment of women in the probation service derived partly from Coughlan's monopoly on appointments, and, in particular, on his preference for selecting clergymen and veterans over other candidates (Oliver and Whittingham 1987, 245; Outerbridge 1979). Although the number of probation officers was increasing, 'very few females were hired in this field' (Ministry of Correctional Services 1983a, 12). Moreover, 'traditionally, the few women probation officers supervised female offenders and juveniles' (12). Women were rarely given the opportunity to work with adult male offenders.

The early 1970s saw both the transfer of the probation service from the aegis of the attorney general to that of Correctional Services, and the retirement of Dan Coughlan. Subsequently, women were more successful in securing positions as probation officers. In 1975, there were 39 female probation officers, and by 1983, they numbered 139 (14). By the early 1980s, female probation officers had also seen progress in terms of equality between their roles and those of the male officers, as they were 'expected to carry out the same responsibilities and perform the same tasks as their male counterparts' (14). Indeed, in terms of entering the profession, women had moved beyond equality: in 1983 women accounted for 55 per cent of new entrants to the probation service. This trend continued, and, by 1990, women accounted for 66 per cent of new entrants, and for 53 per cent of the total number of probation and parole officers (Ministry of Correctional Services 1983a; Employment Equity Program 1990).

Where parole is concerned, the pattern of women's involvement was similar. Until at least the 1950s, the Ontario Parole Board apparently had fewer than ten members, and limited responsibilities. Female appointments appear to have been made specifically to facilitate cases involving women and girls (Ministry of Correctional Services 1983a, 14–15). Women usually accounted for one or two out of the total of seven or eight members of the Board (15).

In 1979, the mandate and responsibilities of the Parole Board were expanded. More women were also appointed, bringing females to a total of eleven out of twenty-nine members. Women also began to be appointed as vice-chairs, and, by 1980, the Parole Board had its first female chairperson (15, 18).

Developments Facilitating the Entry of Women into Prisons for Men

What factors explain the entrance of women in Ontario into the traditionally male occupation of correctional officer in prisons for men? The full story of their initial exclusion, and later of their growing involvement, remains to be told. Even with the limited information available, however, it seems that the process was somewhat different to that which took place in the United States. In the United States, as documented by Lynn Zimmer (1989) and others (e.g., Graham 1981; Jacobs 1981; Morton 1981), it was legislative changes, and most notably the passage of the 1972 Amendments to Title VII of the 1964 Civil Rights Act,[7] which cleared the way for women's employment in male correctional institutions. The Amendments to Title VII strengthened anti-discrimination provisions of the Civil Rights Act, and 'extended the obligation of nondiscrimination to public as well as private employers' (Zimmer 1989, 56). They also strengthened the legislation's powers of enforcement. As a result, where before 1972 in the United States 'no women worked as COs [Correctional Officers] in men's prisons,' by the late 1980s it could be observed that 'women supervise male inmates in every state prison system as well as the Federal Bureau of Prisons and most county jails' (209).

In Ontario, the introduction of women into prisons for men cannot be so directly traced to a specific piece of legislation. Rather, it appears to have come about through the Ontario government's, and the Ministry of Correctional Services's, proactive responses – especially as expressed in the Affirmative Action program – to a series of provincial and federal reports concerned with the status of women. Specifically, following from the *Report of the Royal Commission on the Status of Women*, published by the federal government in 1970, Premier Bill Davis of Ontario had an interministerial committee appointed to comment on the report, and to make recommendations for provincial action. In 1973, the interministerial committee published a report entitled 'Equal Opportunity for Women in Ontario: A Plan for Ontario.' In turn, the recommendations from the Ontario report facilitated the development of the Affirmative Action program, which sought to increase and diversify women's participation in the Ontario public service.

At the time of the publication of the interministerial committee's report, two-thirds of the employees in Correctional Services worked in the traditionally male occupations of correctional officer, probation officer, and parole officer. With the government's commitment to affirmative action, the recruitment of females as correctional officers, and as probation and parole officers, was promoted. Consequent to this, between 1975 and 1983, the overall representation of women within the ministry is said to have increased by 7.1 per cent.

At the same time, the overall profile of the ministry continued to be male dominated and traditional with respect to gender divisions (Ministry of Correctional Services 1983b, 2):

The Ministry of Correctional Services is a male dominated Ministry with 73.6% men and 26.4% women. Approximately one half (43.5%) of all the women in the Ministry are employed in the clerical and office service categories where they hold 91% of the jobs, while 73.2% of the men in the Ministry are employed as correctional officers or probation officers.

As noted, the story of the Ministry of Correctional Services's growing receptivity to hiring women in prisons for men has yet to be fully told. It is likely, however, that as well as indicating senior management's willingness to comply with affirmative action, the emphasis on the hiring of women from the mid-1970s may also have accorded with the ministry's correctional philosophy at that time.

Specifically, while the 1960s had seen a growing emphasis on implementing rehabilitation programs within the institutions (cf. Oliver 1985; McMahon 1992), from the late 1960s a growing commitment to the 'reintegration' of offenders was also evident (as reflected, for example, in the introduction of the Temporary Absence program, which allowed inmates to be temporarily absent from prisons for educational, work, humanitarian, and other reasons). In turn – and for a variety of complex fiscal, political, and ideological reasons (see McMahon 1992) – the 1970s saw an increasing emphasis on, and the implementation of, community-based programs (including, for example, half-way houses, community services orders and victim-offender reconciliation programs). Overall, one might state that the period from the late 1960s was one when ministry officials were trying to dissolve certain boundaries between their institutions and wider communities in Ontario. The introduction of women to the male prison setting accorded well with this ministry orientation. By late 1977, the Ombudsman of Ontario (1977, 412) could observe that:

> In recent years, the Ministry of Correctional Services has embarked upon a bold course of action which has resulted in the introduction of female correctional staff into previously all-male adult institutions. This new direction is an attempt to 'normalize' the prison environment and reduce artificial barriers which may mitigate against the offender's successful reintegration into the community. This introduction of this new element is even more noteworthy given the traditional nature of most correctional institutions and the long-established pattern of male-only staffing.

The introduction of women into prisons for men in Ontario may have accorded with the ministry's wish not only to fulfil objectives of affirmative action, but also to redirect the work going on within the prisons in more reintegrative, progressive, and community-oriented directions.[8]

The Extent, and Limitations, of Women's Involvement in Corrections

Overall, the period following the early 1970s has seen the transcending of some previously existing barriers to the recruitment of women as correctional officers in prisons for men. But there have also been continuing limitations on their involvement. Female correctional officers in prisons for men have continued to be under-represented, with respect to both hiring and promotion. More generally, women in the Ministry of Correctional Services have also been limited in various ways when compared to men.

In 1994, the Employment Systems Review Task Force published their report entitled *Open Minds/Open Doors*. The report, which was a joint venture on the part of ministry management and the representatives of the Ontario Public Service Employees Union, provides an excellent overview and discussion of the conditions within the ministry experienced by designated groups under the Employment Equity plan, which was in operation in the early 1990s (with designated groups including women, racial minorities, francophones, aboriginal peoples, and people with disabilities). The following quotes from the report highlight the extent, the nature, and the limitations of women's involvement within the ministry. As of March 1993, women accounted for 38 per cent of employees of the Ministry of Correctional Services. The report further observes that (Employment Systems Review 1994, 35–7):

- Overall, women are under-represented in the Ministry workforce. They are under-represented in each regional workforce, with the exception of Corporate and Head Offices (Toronto and North Bay).
- In the largest occupational group in the Ministry (i.e. Correctional Officers 1 & 2) women represented only 21% of employees in this job class. Between July 1989 and March 1992, 28% (165) of

the 591 new hires into the short-term contract correctional officer positions (i.e. 3 months and under) were women.

- Although 21% of Correctional Officers were female, only 9.7% of OM14–16 [i.e. Lieutenant/Operational Management] positions were held by women in March 1992, compared to 73.5% by the non-designated group.
- In the Institutional Management positions (AM14–AM23) [i.e. positions such as Deputy Superintendent], women held 13.6% of the positions.
- While women were over-represented in the Probation and Parole Service (54.9%), they were significantly under-represented in the Social Programs Administration category (32.4%).
- Thirty-four percent of all Ministry female employees were in the Office Administration Group. OAG positions represented 13% of the Ministry's total and women occupied 94.6% of these positions. However, general administration management positions were held by only 57.9% women.
- Women were significantly under-represented in the Senior Management Group [which includes Superintendents], holding 19.4% of said positions.
- Women with no other designated group status earned slightly more on average than other groups of women, but still earned 88% of the earnings of the non-designated group – about $5,400 less on average.
- On average, women with another designated group status earned 85% of the earnings of the non-designated group – approximately $6,700 less on average.
- Each group of women earned less than their male counterparts and this reflected their over-representation in the lower paying positions.
- Women held *none* of the positions in both Trades and Crafts (Bargaining Unit) and Skills and Trades (Management Compensation Plan).

The report additionally observes that, in the case of unclassified (and thereby the most insecure) positions, women were over-represented in accounting for 54.5 per cent of these positions (52).

It is important to note, moreover, that these data only include un-classified staff with contracts of over three months duration. Fully 1,066 unclassified staff with contracts of three months or less were not included in the survey (52). In short, casual and unclassified employees, who are most vulnerable, in that they are guaranteed neither hours nor ongoing work, remained unsurveyed.

Other indicators of the unsatisfactory situation of women within the ministry include the observations that, while women accounted for 47 per cent of all employees within the public service as a whole in 1992, they accounted for only 38 per cent of those in Correc-tional Services. Moreover, where women accounted for 28 per cent of senior management positions in the public service as a whole, in the Ministry of Correctional Service, as we have seen, they accounted for only 19.4 per cent (53). Finally, although the fact that women accounted for 50.3 per cent of all new hires in Correctional Services between July 1989 and May 1992 was good news, this was somewhat offset by data indicating that women accounted for 53.4 per cent of all exits.[9]

In summary, as this series of data reveals, there is still much to be done with respect to improving the situation of women within the Ministry of Correctional Services. In particular, female correctional officers can be seen as a group requiring special attention. As noted, women now account for only 23.7 per cent of all correctional officers, and for only 13 per cent of the correctional management OM–16 positions.[10]

While the occupational situation for women within the Ministry of Correctional Services, including their prospects for promotion, is problematic, the situation for women at the Wakefield Jail can be seen as particularly bad. Where women account for 13 per cent of correctional management positions in the ministry, none of women to be discussed at the Wakefield Jail occupied management posi-tions.

As for correctional officers, while females account for nearly a quarter of all officers, as of August 1997, Wakefield Jail only had one full-time female correctional officer (Micheline Pelletier), and one casual correctional officer (Kathy Poirier). Overall, female cor-rectional officers have only accounted for between one-sixth and one-twelfth of correctional officers at the Wakefield Jail at any given time between the mid-1980s and mid-1990s. And, of those women employed during that time (as cooks or correctional officers), a majority were in the most vulnerable – that is, casual – positions. In sum, as is clearly evidenced in the case of the Wakefield Jail, females can experience serious barriers to hiring and promotion in the Ministry of Correctional Services.

In addition to, and in conjunction with, the barriers they have experienced with respect to hiring and promotion, female correctional staff in Ontario have experienced multifarious forms of gender-based discrimination and harassment. The next chapter of this book examines growing awareness of such problems, both in the Ontario government in general, and in the Ministry of Correctional Services in particular. This examination – including a review of events at the ministry's Bell Cairn Staff Training Centre – will in turn assist in elaborating specific problems that have occurred in the case of the Wakefield Jail.

3 Gender-Based Discrimination and Harassment: From Policy Initiatives to Problems at Bell Cairn

Government Policies toward Equity and Harassment Prevention

In Ontario, as elsewhere in Canada, issues of gender-based harassment and discrimination in the workplace have recently received a marked growth in government and political attention. This growing sensitivity to problems faced by women has been associated with the increase in attention to the problems faced by a variety of marginalized groups. Accordingly, in 1987 Ontario's Affirmative Action program was extended through the government's introduction of the Employment Equity program. Under Employment Equity, attention was now to be given to the hiring and equitable treatment not only of women, but also of other groups considered vulnerable to exclusion and marginalization – namely, racial minorities, francophones, aboriginal people, and people with disabilities.

Prior to the Employment Equity program, and in addition to the Affirmative Action program, a variety of other legislative initiatives also contributed to equity and human rights. For example, the *Canadian Charter of Rights and Freedoms*, enacted in 1982, seeks to identify and entrench legal rights. In particular, Sections 15 (1) and 15 (2) of the *Charter* specify equality rights, and, in doing so, uphold affirmative-action programs, which address disadvantages arising from sex and other characteristics. Specific to Ontario, the *Human Rights Code* also affirms and upholds principles of equity.

Where attention to the specific issue of gender-based discrimination and harassment is concerned, an important step was taken by the Ontario government at the end of 1991. At that time, the government proclaimed the Workplace Discrimination and Harassment Prevention policy (WDHP). The following March, related directives and guidelines were issued, and became applicable government-wide.[1] The period following the introduction of this policy saw an acceleration in political and public concern, and debate, about discrimination and harassment in the workplace. Events that have taken place in the Ministry of Correctional Services – and specifically with respect to incidents at the Bell Cairn Staff Training School for correctional workers – provide an example of the problems intended to be addressed by the Workplace Discrimination and Harassment Prevention policy. These events will be discussed later in this chapter. First, a brief review of earlier ministry strategies toward occupational equity for female correctional officers in prison for men will be provided.

Correctional Strategies toward Equity for Female Officers

While the Ministry of Correctional Services may still have a long way to go in achieving equity for women, in some respects the ministry can also be considered a leader, both in Canada and internationally, in identifying and addressing issues of gender-based discrimination in corrections, and specifically with respect to issues of women working in prisons for men. Reportedly, the Ministry of Correctional Services 'was the first provincial ministry to employ women correctional officers to work in institutions for adult males' (Bronskill 1980, 2; Caron 1981, 7). By the end of 1982, where the percentage of women working with male inmates was still as low as 0–3 per cent in five Canadian provinces, in Ontario 8.5 per cent of correctional officers working with male inmates were women (Anon. 1982). As we have seen, by the early 1990s, over a fifth of correctional officers working with male inmates in Ontario were women.

In addition to initiating the hiring of women to work as correctional officers in prisons for men, senior management at the Ontario Ministry of Correctional Services also took other steps to facilitate female correctional officers undertaking a wide range of tasks within their positions. Specifically, in the fall of 1982, 'a committee was established to develop policy and make recommendations on the assignment of male and female correctional officers in [the] ministry's institutions' (Podrebarac 1984, 1).

The ministry's senior management approved the committee's recommendations in December of 1983. In March 1984, a memorandum by the deputy minister announced the Ministry's policy. According to the announcement (Podrebarac 1984, 1):

> It is public policy in Ontario to recognize the dignity and worth of every person, and to provide for equal rights and opportunities. It is the policy of the Ministry of Correctional Services to recruit, train and promote men and women as correctional officers without regard to their sex.

> The ministry is an Equal Opportunity Employer and fully recognizes the importance of actively supporting and implementing the Ontario Government's Affirmative Action Program through its management policies and practices. Sex discrimination in hiring and in the determination of post and duty assignment for correctional officers within an institution is therefore prohibited, except where gender is a bona fide qualification based on respect for the personal dignity and modesty of an inmate on the grounds of public decency.

In specifying the limitations to be imposed on cross-sex supervision on the grounds of modesty and public decency, the policy imposed restrictions on both male and female correctional officers with respect to supervising congregate showers, and to performing strip searches (except in cases of emergency). Where cross-sex frisk searches were concerned, however, the ministry provided female correctional officers greater latitude than male correctional officers on the grounds that (4):

> Current standards of public decency indicate different standards for male and female inmates and the need to afford greater protection to females in terms of personal dignity and modesty. Except in emergency situations, therefore, only female correctional officers will per-

form frisk searches on female inmates; however, both male and female correctional officers will perform frisk searches on male inmates.

In 1993, a decision by the Supreme Court of Canada endorsed and upheld the allowing of greater latitude to female correctional officers in undertaking cross-sex supervision. Specifically, in the *Conway* case – which was brought by a federal inmate challenging the constitutionality of frisk searching and surveillance by female correctional officers – the Court stated that (Supreme Court of Canada, *Philip Conway v. Her Majesty the Queen*,[2] 12 August 1993; emphasis added):

> It does not follow from the fact that female prison inmates are not subject to cross-gender frisk searches and surveillance that these practices result in discriminatory treatment of male inmates. Equality under Section 15 (1) of the *Charter* does not necessarily condone identical treatment; in fact, different treatment may be called for in certain cases to promote equality. Equality, in the present context, does not demand that practices which are forbidden where male officers guard female inmates must also be banned where female officers guard male inmates. *Given the historical, biological and sociological differences between men and women, it is clear that the effect of cross-gender searching is different and more threatening for women than for men.*

In addition, and similarly to the remarks of the Ombudsman of Ontario (1977) reported earlier, the Supreme Court stated that 'The important government objectives of inmate rehabilitation and security of the institution are promoted as a result of the humanizing effect of having women in these positions.'

Disjunctures between Rhetoric and Reality in the Ministry

Overall, initiatives by the Ontario Ministry of Correctional Services with respect to, first, hiring female correctional officers in prisons for men, and, second, facilitating women's access to the broad spectrum of tasks involved in the work of correctional officers, seemed to augur well for enhancing the occupational equity of women. Moreover, in the early 1990s, the Ministry of Correctional Services' commitment to the Workplace Harassment and Discrimination Prevention policy also carried the promise of improving the recognition, remedying, and prevention of related problems within the workplace.

For anyone familiar with the ongoing incidents of discrimination and harassment experienced by women at the Wakefield Jail between the mid-1980s and the mid-1990s, however, such statements and policies on the part of senior management seem very far removed from the everyday realities of relations between male and female correctional officers.

How could such disjunctures between officially stated policy and the actuality of discrimination and harassment exist? And how could such disjunctures continue to exist in the face of increasingly specific and publicized identification of potential problems of harassment and discrimination, and of the remedies available, by the Ministry of Correctional Services? Should the incidents at the Wakefield Jail be seen as an anomaly in, or as somehow typical of, the everyday culture within Ministry of Correctional Services institutions more generally?

Toward addressing these questions, and before going on to examine incidents at the Wakefield Jail, a review will be provided of management strategies in the early 1990s intended to deal with harassment, and their limited success. In discussing these limitations, the focus will be on a series of incidents that occurred at the ministry's Bell Cairn Staff Training Centre. For, as previously noted, apart from the information that has now become available about the Wakefield Jail, the incidents at Bell Cairn appear to be the only other case involving the Ministry of Correctional Services where there is sufficient information publicly available to examine both the evolution of, and responses to, related problems.

Ministry Initiatives in Preventing Harassment in the Early 1990s[3]

I am committed to a working environment that is harassment free. Any form of harassment or discrimination in the workplace cannot be tolerated. As deputy minister, I have both a moral and legal obligation to take appropriate action against any and all workplace harassment. All managers share this obligation whether or not the complainant wants to pursue the matter. The principles of decency and mutual respect must be fundamental to our working relationships. (Extract from a memo sent by the deputy minister to all ministry staff, 23 October 1991)

It is somewhat ironic that the ministry's staff training school, Bell Cairn, experienced repeated and serious problems with sexual harassment from the time of its opening in August 1991 until its temporary closure from July 1992. For this was also the period when there was a more concentrated commitment at the most senior level of the ministry to addressing harassment than ever before. This commitment largely arose from the government's introduction of the Workplace Discrimination and Harassment Prevention policy. It was given added impetus by the commitment of the newly appointed deputy minister, Dina Palozzi, to issues of equity and human rights.

In October 1991, soon after her appointment, the deputy minister sent a memo concerning harassment to all of the Ministry's staff. Through the memo, the deputy minister emphasized her commitment to a workplace free of sexual, racial, and personal harassment. She called attention to the Ontario government's Human Rights Code, which acknowledges that behaviour such as 'sexually explicit remarks, offensive language and racial slurs create a poisoned environment which is a form of harassment.' The Deputy identified her, and the entire management staff's, duty to take action against harassment, even in face of a complainant's reluctance to pursue the matter. And she advocated mutually respectful treatment on the part of all staff.

During the following months, other initiatives were also undertaken toward increasing awareness of harassment issues, and of mechanisms for dealing with it. These initiatives included the following:

• In January 1992, a poster on workplace harassment was produced by the ministry's communications branch, and distributed to all ministry offices and institutions.

- In January–February 1992, the ministry's staff newsletter contained an article about the government's new Workplace Discrimination and Harassment Prevention policy.

  The article explained that the policy defines harassment as 'any comment or conduct that is: based on race/color, ancestry, place of origin, ethnic origin, language, citizenship, sex, sexual orientation, age, marital status, disability, criminal charges or record; and [is] offensive to any employee and is known, or ought reasonably to be known, as unwelcome.'

  The article exhorted correctional employees not to tolerate harassment and provided advice as to how victims could respond.[4] The article again notified employees that supervisors and managers receiving complaints of discrimination or harassment were obligated to take action. It identified the ministry's specialist advisors on harassment, and specified the remedies available should a complaint be found to be justified.[5]

- In early spring 1992, posters and guides to the government policy on harassment for managers and complainants, were distributed to all ministry offices.

- In early April 1992, pamphlets on the government policy on harassment were distributed with all employees' pay cheques.

- On 14 April 1992, the deputy minister again sent a memo to all staff, highlighting the government's policy on harassment. In the memo, the deputy minister reiterated her support for the policy, and identified the availability of advisors and remedies.

- Training sessions for groups of ministry staff continued to be provided by the ministry's employment equity manager, and plans were in progress for all staff to receive relevant training commencing in the fall of 1992.

Despite the fact that late 1991 and early 1992 was a period characterized by such intense activity with respect to issues of harassment, this very period was also one when a series of harassing incidents were taking place at the ministry's Bell Cairn Staff Training School. Moreover, it was also one characterized by inadequate responses to related problems. A review of events at Bell Cairn illustrates these points. In turn, a review of the Bell Cairn scandal also helps to illu-

minate that the difficulties the ministry has experienced in responding to gender-related problems at the Wakefield Jail are by no means
unique.

Allegations of Sexual Harassment and Gang-Rape at Bell Cairn

> Several months ago, two female members of the ministry, while at-
> tending a course at the [Bell Cairn] college, were sexually assaulted
> by others attending the college ... A significant number of males as-
> saulting two females ...
>
> A decision was taken within the Ministry not to pursue it simply
> because the women allegedly involved would not file an official com-
> plaint because of their fears about peer pressure ...
>
> These women feel extremely vulnerable working in an atmosphere
> and environment dominated by male co-workers ... (Bob Runciman,
> opposition Member, Ontario Provincial Legislature,[6] quoted in the
> *Toronto Star*, 15 July 1992)

Anyone active in the field of corrections knows that there is a multi-
tude of occupational, professional, bureaucratic, and human-rights
issues worthy of greater attention in the public culture than they are
typically given. In corrections, as in other social contexts, it often
takes a dramatic event, coupled with a political crisis, to bring a
problematic situation to light. Thus, public identification of a problem is not necessarily concurrent with its emergence, but rather
provides a platform for highlighting related issues that have been
ignored in the public and political realms. In due course, and as
the immediate crisis ameliorates with a range of political and
bureaucratic initiatives having been undertaken, public attention
usually declines.

In Ontario corrections, such a convergence of dramatic events
occurred when opposition critic Bob Runciman raised questions
in the provincial legislature on 15 July 1992 about allegations that
two female employees had been sexually assaulted (or, as more
colloquially expressed, 'gang-raped') by their colleagues while at
the ministry's Bell Cairn Staff Training Centre. In turn, these
allegations were linked to those of more general, and ongoing,

problems with harassment at the centre. Some critics also seized of the opportunity to raise questions about sexual misconduct by male employees of the ministry more generally.[7]

With respect to political responsibility and accountability, critics alleged that there had been a 'passive cover-up' of incidents at Bell Cairn by senior ministry officials. They highlighted the minister's ignorance of the incidents, and, alleging that he had lost control over the ministry, called for his resignation.

We shall later examine the various responses that followed from the political scandal about Bell Cairn. First, however, and drawing from the *Chronology of Events* that Premier Bob Rae ordered the ministry to release, we shall chart the ministry's internal definition of, and responses to, the problems of harassment that were prevalent at Bell Cairn in the months preceding the scandal.

Initial Perceptions of a Problem with Rowdiness at Bell Cairn

The Bell Cairn Staff Training Centre for correctional employees, located in Hamilton, Ontario, was officially opened on 29 August 1991, and residential programs began in September.[8] The centre had accommodation for 72 people, and provided courses for correctional officers who work in prisons, as well as for probation and parole staff. Probation and parole officers' courses generally lasted one week. Courses for correctional officers lasted up to three weeks. Although the point is not emphasized in ministry discussions of conflicts between staff, it appears that many of the problems that ensued at the centre in 1991–92 involved not just men harassing women, but male correctional officers harassing female probation and parole officers.[9]

Signs of trouble at Bell Cairn became evident when it first began taking residents. Late in the month of September – less than a month after the centre had been fully operational – the manager of Bell Cairn received a letter from the area manager of probation and parole in Owen Sound. In her letter, the probation and parole manager expressed concern about one of her staff's experiences at Bell Cairn. The probation officer had experienced disruptions to her work, sleep, and comfort, arising from the inconsiderate and intimidating behaviour of correctional officers, some of whom were drunk. In documenting her colleague's distressing experience, the probation and parole manager attached a letter from the individual concerned. An extract from this provides a glimpse of the conditions prevailing during the first month of Bell Cairn's operation. According to the probation and parole officer:

> Early on in the evening of Sunday, September 22nd the level of noise, in the form of loud music and laughter, from room number 221 made it very difficult to study. At 11:30p.m. the Barnes security guard requested that as it was after 11:00p.m., for the music to be turned down. The security guard returned again on at least two separate occasions between 12:00a.m. and 1:00a.m. and requested of the group of correctional officers to again reduce the noise level. His requests were met with an increase in the volume of music and loud clapping. At 1:30a.m., I went out into the hallway and noted that the door to room 226 from which the noise was emanating was propped open, and proceeded to shut the door. The noise eventually subsided between 2:30 and 3:00a.m. ...
>
> [On the evening of September 23rd] at 11:30, myself and a fellow PPO [probation and parole officer] requested of the occupants of room 219 to reduce the noise level. The response was that they were on their way out. At approximately 1:15a.m., I was wakened by loud banging in the hallway. A group of correctional officers were banging on the doors of numerous rooms along the hallway and requesting for other correctional officers to join them. At approximately 2:00a.m. I went out into the hallway and requested a reduction in the noise. The group of 5 or 6 correctional officers appeared to be extremely intoxicated and were unresponsive to this request. I then called the security guard who also requested quiet. At 2:20 the telephone in my room rang and upon answering, I heard laughter in the background and hung up the phone. A [second] call at 2:30 prompted me to unplug the phone. This was proceeded [sic] by further loud banging which seemed to echo along the pipes. At this point, I felt extremely intimidated and harassed. (Extract from a letter from an Owen Sound probation and parole officer to the area manager, 26 September 1991)

In her covering letter to the manager of Bell Cairn, the probation
and parole manager expressed concern about policies dealing with
liquor consumption on the premises, and with responses to those
who drank to excess and became obnoxious. More generally, she
stated that:

> I personally feel concerned that this type of behaviour should not be
> tolerated anywhere, from any group, let alone at a Ministry of Correc-
> tional Services' facility for Ministry staff. What alarms me most about
> this incident is the fact that [the probation and parole officer] did
> not feel safe in a Ministry facility where the individuals responsible
> for this behaviour were Ministry personnel being trained in the areas
> of safety and security.

The reply to this correspondence by the manager of Bell Cairn
illustrates some of the inadequacies in the facility's preparedness
for dealing with such incidents. The manager replied (emphasis
added):

> Thank you for your letter of September 26, 1991. I regret that [the
> probation and parole officer] had a difficult experience while at Bell
> Cairn.

> You are quite right, the kind of inappropriate behaviour described is
> unacceptable. *Please be assured that the individuals involved have been dealt
> with.*

> As I'm sure you can appreciate, Bell Cairn is a brand new facility and
> we are experiencing some 'growing pains.' Some of the issues we are
> currently working through involve the discipline of participants, the
> use of liquor and the security of the building. I hope that we can
> count on input and back-up from the field in our efforts to make Bell
> Cairn a comfortable place for all staff.

As can be seen, while this reply is relatively sympathetic, it is strik-
ingly short on details of specific actions being taken with respect to

the correctional officers involved. However satisfactory the actions taken may have been,[10] the facility's communication of them appears limited.

Several days later, the manager of Bell Cairn received another letter. The letter was again from an area manager of probation and parole, this time in Kitchener. The probation and parole manager similarly complained about probation and parole staff experiencing difficulty sleeping because of 'unruly Correctional Officers.' He also said that their exams had been 'interrupted several times by Correctional Officers walking into the room even though the door was marked examination in progress ...' (letter dated 3 October 1991).

The Bell Cairn manager's response to this letter was arguably less than satisfactory. She tersely replied that trainers had informed her that 'there was no instance when correctional officers walked into ongoing exams.' Where noise, sleep disruption, and ineffectiveness of security staff were concerned, she again uninformatively stated that:

> The correctional officers involved were dealt with on the day following the incident. We are concerned about the comfort of all participants and *intend* to deal with incidents of this kind promptly. We have also been working with our security staff to develop protocols and the proper communication of problems. (Response by the manager of Bell Cairn, dated 8 October 1991; emphasis added)

Here, the word 'intend' is significant as, taken together with the lack of specific information with respect to the specific correctional officers concerned, the impression is fostered that, prior to the opening of the facility, no clear policies had been developed on potential problems that might occur, and the responses (including penalties) that should follow.

Also early in October of 1991, another female complained that she had 'received a harassing telephone call in her room' (Ministry of Correctional Services 1992, 4). Ministry actions subsequent to this incident indicate how their response was out of step with the evolving problems. Specifically, soon after the incident, the ministry's manager of investigation and security visited Bell Cairn. A report concerning his visit reveals that his observations dealt with peripheral matters. Thus he observed that the building was not a particularly attractive target for break-ins; that an expensive security system was probably unnecessary; that a magnetic system should be installed to ensure that security staff were doing their rounds; that all fire doors should have security locks; that the front door should have a speaker outside, and a lock which could be operated from the reception area; and that lighting should be improved at the rear of the building.

Most of these items are pertinent to protecting the building from potential intruders. But the complaints that had been made to date arose from *within* the building, and concerned residents rather than outsiders. Meanwhile, the only mention of phones is the security manager's opinion that there would not be a problem in shutting them off at night.[11] Most notably, the report by the manager of investigation and security makes no mention of the gendered basis of the problems that had already begun to emerge.

With no specific action having been taken to deal with them, the emergent problems continued unabated. According to the ministry, the period between September of 1991 and January of 1992 was one of episodic incidents 'involving noise, conflict between participant groups, abuse of alcohol and unruly behaviour' (Ministry of Correctional Services 1992, 5). 'Difficulties' experienced by the Ministry in dealing with these incidents included (5):

- Vague complaints from managers about staff feeling uneasy/unsafe at Bell Cairn.
- Security staff not informing managers of problems in a timely or complete way.
- Receiving information about incidents second-hand by way of rumours from the field or after time had elapsed. This information was often vague and did not include sufficient information to identify perpetrators.
- The contract of the company providing security service came to an

end, they were not successful in the tendering process, and a new security firm was hired. This meant that procedures had to be taught to a new group of staff.

In attempting to respond to these problems, in January 1992, the ministry updated its pamphlet entitled *Welcome to Bell Cairn Staff Training Centre*, which was given to course participants on arrival. The ministry also provided discipline protocols entitled *Procedures for Residents Causing Problems Outside of Class*, and *Procedures [for] Disruptive Course Participants*.

In retrospect, the most notable feature of the information given to participants is that, while it dealt with issues of noise, rowdiness, abusive behaviour towards staff and residents, damage to rooms, and limits on the places where alcohol could be consumed, and while these documents generally emphasized respect for peoples' need for quiet to sleep and study, there was absolutely no mention of issues of sexual harassment and abuse. In short, despite the fact that it was females who had disproportionately (and possible exclusively) been making complaints, until at least January 1992, the official documentation of existing and potential problems at Bell Cairn lacked any reference to gender-specific areas of concern.

Incidents at Bell Cairn: Growing Recognition of Sexual Harassment

Female probation officers from this region continue to feel harassed and unsafe in the Bell Cairn residence. (Memo from a regional manager, Western Region, to the regional director, Western Region, Ministry of Correctional Services, 29 June 1992)

It is difficult to say whether the ministry officials' primary definition of problems at Bell Cairn in terms of rowdiness stemmed from the nature of the problems during the first four months of the centre's existence, or from a reluctance to recognize the gender-related aspects of at least some of the problems among participants. Whatever the reason, in the middle of January 1992 – at the very time when the new discipline protocols with their emphasis on noisiness and potential damage to property were being circulated – female course participants were subject to behaviour on the part of their male correctional officer colleagues that clearly constituted sexual harassment. These problems were apparently not documented within the ministry until a group of women affected returned to Bell Cairn for another course late in February. At that time, they talked to a senior staff development officer about their experiences during their January and current courses. The officer in turn related the following 'synopsis of complaints' to the manager of Bell Cairn:

1. Obscene and unwelcome telephone calls received at all hours of the night by at least two female participants – primarily during the week of January 13.
2. High levels of noise (radios, shouting, obscenities, partying) on several evenings (extending into early morning) during both weeks of training.
3. One female participant indicated that she feared for her safety when walking the halls of the residence due to the inebriated condition of participants enroled in correctional officer courses. She would always call other colleagues so she would not have to leave her room alone.
4. Inappropriate sexist remarks concerning their anatomy experienced by at least two female participants while walking past members of the I.C.I.T. [Institutional Crisis Intervention Team] team in the halls enroute [sic] the classroom during the day (during the week of P.O. [Probation Officer] Basic Training).
5. One unidentified male was heard knocking on several doors (during week two) looking for sex.
6. The *most serious* complaint was from one female participant, who while standing in the residence lounge experienced the following:
   • Lewd remarks.
   • One (older C.O.) came up behind her and stroked her hair. When she asked him to stop, he came around to her side and said 'I just want to see if you are real.' At that point he began touching her arm. The participant believes she would recognize this officer.
   • He then rejoined a colleague. It is my understanding that the

colleague – not the original officer, came up behind her and began stroking the back of her leg (behind the knee). The participant then left the area.[12] (Extract from a memo from a senior staff development officer to the manager of Bell Cairn, February 1992)

That additional incidents involving women were occurring is also evident in a memo written during the same week in February. The memo was written by the manager of Bell Cairn to the ministry's manager of investigation and security. Here, the manager reported on two incidents that had occurred on the night of February 20:

> In the first case, a CO [Correctional Officer] had been ostracized by some of her classmates for not participating in their partying and because they thought she had reported a smoking incident. She found both of her rear tires had been flattened overnight. Fortunately, we were able to re-inflate the tires. She has agreed to document the kinds of behaviours she experienced during the week.
>
> Secondly, another CO allowed her boyfriend access to her room. She did not sign him in and he was still here at 3:00am. Apparently he became quite intoxicated and belligerent and aggravated some of the participants to the point where a fight might have broken out. He was asked to leave, and when he refused, the police were called. They removed the person and held him overnight for detoxification. (Extract from memo from the manager of Bell Cairn to the manager of investigation and security, 21 February 1992)

A subsequent memo (dated 24 February 1992), by a senior Staff development officer, provides more details about this incident. Prior to being escorted from Bell Cairn by the police, the individual was verbally abusive to his correctional officer partner, and 'threw her against the wall.' The individual also physically threatened the staff development officer and other correctional officers present. The female correctional officer later expressed concern that 'this incident would get back to her institution and affect her job.' Her concern appears to have been justified as the ministry's *Chronology of Events* reveals that the woman's superintendent 'was notified of the incident and asked to counsel this individual' (Ministry of Correctional Services 1992, 7).

Of all the incidents alluded to in the ministry memos, this is the one where most detail about the actual event and the follow-up are provided. It is perhaps not coincidental that, in this instance, the abusive male was *not* a resident of Bell Cairn or an employee of the ministry. The fact that an outsider was involved may also help to explain why the police were called in this case and not in the others.

It is also notable that, in the other incidents discussed to date involving perpetrators who were male employees of the ministry, there is no mention of information being passed on to their home institutions. Yet in this instance, involving a female employee who was a victim, the information *was* passed on. Moreover, given that the woman's supervisor was asked to 'counsel' her,[13] the purpose of the communication from Bell Cairn was clearly to see that the woman was penalized for any infraction involved in allowing her boyfriend into her room, rather than to ask her supervisor to provide any support pursuant to the verbal and physical abuse she had suffered. This response on the part of management at Bell Cairn would hardly have encouraged other women to submit complaints. It suggests a tendency toward blaming, rather than supporting, the victim.

Nevertheless, although Bell Cairn's responses to situations such as the above were arguably problematic, recognition of the gendered aspects of the incidents was becoming more evident, including at senior management level of the ministry. By early March, the assistant deputy minister of operations saw fit to send a memo to all regional directors in an effort to have them speak to the superintendents of institutions. In turn, the superintendents were to speak to correctional officers attending Bell Cairn. The assistant deputy minister expressed his concern by saying: 'The staff at Bell Cairn are having increasing difficulty with some Correctional Officers being rowdy and extremely disruptive during courses held at Bell Cairn. I am told that the behaviour of some male Correctional Officers towards women staff at the Ministry who are attending courses at Bell Cairn borders on being abusive and perhaps even assaultive.'

The assistant deputy minister noted that the security staff hired to oversee the facility at night 'are ineffective in containing the rowdyism.' He advised that the matter would be discussed at the March meeting of the operations division management committee. The assistant deputy minister also conveyed the manager of Bell Cairn's prophetic views: 'I am particularly concerned by the fact that [the manager of Bell Cairn] tells me that the problem has been getting worse over the last few months and that she is worried that it may get out of hand in the near future.'

Thus, six months after Bell Cairn had opened to residents, although the Ministry continued to emphasize the 'rowdy' aspect of participants' behaviour, it had begun to more explicitly focus on the gender aspects of the problems occurring. About this time (March 1992), preventative actions being taken included the drafting of a new *Code of Behaviour*. In contrast to the earlier protocols, with their focus on issues of noise and the need to generally respect property, liquor regulations, and others' needs for quiet to work and sleep, the new code clearly specified unacceptable behaviours, with 'sexual or personal harassment' being the first item listed. The complete list of unacceptable behaviours was as follows: '1. Sexual or personal harassment; 2. Assault; 3. Fighting; 4. Drunkenness; 5. Failure to abide by the noise curfew; 6. Unauthorized or improper use of the facility and its equipment; 7. Abusive language; 8. Wilful damage or theft; 9. Failure to follow the direction of security staff; 10. Being under the influence of an illegal drug, or being in possession of an illegal drug; 11. Possession of alcohol in restricted areas; 12. Smoking in non-smoking areas; 13. Disruptive behaviour in the classroom.

Yet, while recognition of the gendered aspects of problems that were occurring was a step forward, the ministry's statements with respect to potential penalties continued to be inadequate. The *Code of Behaviour* simply stated that: 'Infractions will be dealt with by management staff, according to the merits of each case.'

Meanwhile, those regional managers who – as directed by the assistant deputy minister – did contact superintendents appeared to be limited to exhorting them to remind correctional officers of their professional status. No specific consequences were identified other than making statements such as: 'Inappropriate behaviour will not be tolerated by training staff, the Region or the Ministry' (Memo from a regional director to superintendents, 9 March 1992). In short, statements about potential penalties were vague. They by no means indicated that violations of the *Code* would definitely be taken seriously.

Meanwhile, ministry reaction to such problems as had already occurred were also limited. Where general, as well as more specific allegations of harassment were concerned, by 5 March, the ministry's manager of security and investigation 'did not feel that sufficient information was available to warrant a full investigation' (Ministry of Correctional Services 1992, 8).

Over the following few months, various meetings and discussions took place among ministry officials. Decisions were made, for example, about returning participants to their home institutions for discipline if necessary. Plans were also advanced for hiring a night manager, and various attempts were made to enhance the quality of security services being provided. Notably, however, while the deputy minister was 'made aware of these incidents verbally in a general sense, [she] did not know the details of each incident at the time' (Ministry of Correctional Services 1992, 2). Nor was the minister informed.[14]

To put it mildly, such responsive actions as were taken in the month of March and thereafter did not secure the desired effect. In April, incidents involving male correctional officers disrupting the human-rights segment of a course, and harassing a female participant, took place.[15] Course evaluations by participants indicated that incidents were continuing, but many were not receiving any formal attention.

Most dramatically, on 1 June, another 'unruly' party occurred at Bell Cairn. Subsequent discussions among staff at the centre yielded additional disturbing information. When the deputy minister paid a routine visit to the centre on 5 June, she was made aware of the recent revelations. Further discussions and meetings took place, and the manager of Bell Cairn was advised to inform regional directors of the latest incidents and allegations. Her ensuing memo provides some details of what had happened (and, when its content was leaked beyond the ministry, became a key document in the ensuing scandal):

You may have heard that there was another unruly party at Bell Cairn on Monday, June 1, 1992. While there have been rumours circulating that the lounge was 'trashed,' this is incorrect. It was left in a mess and there was some extremely tasteless decorating done with intimate female attire. Understandably, there was also excessive noise, both inside and outside the building, continuing into the early morning hours ... During the course of this, a social worker counselling two female ministry staff advised us that they had been seriously sexually assaulted in the residence while here on [a] course.[16] In each instance more than one male was involved.[17]

Unfortunately these victims do not feel safe in bringing this situation to the courts because of feared retaliation from their peers. The names of the victims were not shared as that is confidential information. Of course, the staff at Bell Cairn were appalled that these women did not feel safe enough to talk to any of the staff here, or to notify security ...

On 2 July, a senior-level meeting of ministry officials was held. Significantly, neither the head office nor regional coordinators of the ministry's Workplace Discrimination and Harassment Prevention policies were present at the meeting. With respect to the alleged sexual assaults, the immediate dilemma was how to respond to the situation, given that the women victimized did not want to come forward. Various unsuccessful efforts to secure their cooperation had already been made, and plans were formulated to continue encouraging them to facilitate the ministry in pursuing the matter. The ministry had limited opportunity to put these plans into action, however. For, by the middle of July, allegations of the 'gang-rapes' and other problems had become public, and responses to events at Bell Cairn now began to involve actors, and institutions, beyond the ministry.

Problems in the Ministry's Response to Events at Bell Cairn

Some of the problems in the ministry's response to events at Bell Cairn have already been alluded to. Perhaps the most basic problem was that the ministry's initial definition of problems did not acknowledge their gender-based component. Although complaints, typically, and perhaps exclusively, were made by women, this fact was not initially highlighted in ministry memos.

Other problems in the ministry's dealings with events at Bell Cairn can be summarized as follows:

- The facility appears to have opened without procedures in place to deal with the kinds of problems that immediately arose.
- The Bell Cairn staff lacked authority over, and ability to discipline, course participants. They did not have an adequate response to troublesome situations. This inadequacy was exacerbated after class hours given, firstly, the reliance on a private security firm whose relationship to participants' home institutions was even further removed than that of the centre staff; and, secondly, the ambiguous status of residents who, although on ministry property, may have been technically off-duty.
- Although awareness of the sexual/gender component of incidents appeared to be growing prior to the most dramatic allegations, and was reflected in the new code of discipline, both monitoring and follow-through on incidents continued to be limited, and problematic.
- With respect to the allegations of sexual assault, the victims' desire for confidentiality came into conflict with, and was given precedence over, requirements under Ontario's Workplace Discrimination and Harassment Prevention policy that cases of harassment must be pursued. Moreover, staff working in the Workplace Harassment and Discrimination Prevention unit in the ministry were apparently not involved in some key meetings that sought to develop responses to incidents at Bell Cairn.
- Management officials' definition of the problems as operational (i.e., as involving managerial and administrative matters, such as the physical security of the building) rather than policy (i.e., gender-related) matters resulted in relevant information being withheld from the minister.[18]

Overall, the management of evolving problems at Bell Cairn was such that, not only was the ministry ineffective in providing assistance to actual and potential victims of sexual harassment and abuse, but it was also ineffective in ensuring its own ability to be politically accountable for its actions. As such, when rumours and memos were leaked to opposition members and the press in July 1992, the ministry was immediately vulnerable to charges of having engaged in a 'passive' cover-up, with this, along with the allegations of sexual assault, becoming the subject of a provincial inquiry.

Actions, and Problems, Subsequent to the Bell Cairn Scandal

Subsequent to the Bell Cairn scandal, a variety of actions were taken. The deputy minister was transferred out of corrections. Bell Cairn was temporarily closed. A police investigation into the alleged assaults was initiated. Within several days, Judge Inger Hansen had been appointed to conduct a Provincial Inquiry into Bell Cairn. By the time the legislature reconvened after the summer recess, the ministry had not only a new deputy minister, but also a new minister. Meanwhile, offices of the ministry pertinent to harassment issues had been strengthened and expanded. The ministry now had a Workplace Harassment Unit, a Contentious Issues Unit, an Independent Investigations Unit, and eight advisors to provide confidential advice on sexual harassment and discrimination.

This is a striking – and costly – flurry of activity. Yet, and as already alluded to, intense activity is no guarantee that issues will be resolved. Indeed, when it is considered that incidents at Bell Cairn, particularly the allegations of gang-rape, were the stimulus to much of this activity, and most specifically to the police investigation and the Provincial Inquiry, the outcomes appear quite meagre. In the first place, the police investigation did not result in any charges.[19] Less than nine months after the scandal, at least one journalist felt confident in asserting that 'there was no gang rape' (Palango 1993). Whatever rumours and information may have circulated within the ministry, no further information about the particular party where sexual assaults allegedly took place had been made publicly available. Such a lack of public information is disappointing in view of the seriousness of the allegations involved.

Where the *Report of the Bell Cairn Inquiry* by Judge Inger Hansen is concerned, insights into what happened at Bell Cairn are arguably lacking. In part, this is due to the legal restrictions under which such inquiries typically operate. As explained by Judge Hansen, the terms of reference of the inquiry, and of provincial inquiries more generally, effectively preclude drawing conclusions about the civil or criminal liability of any individual or organization. In accordance with this, the terms of reference instructed that the inquiry would 'neither identify individuals alleged to have committed offences, nor reach conclusions about matters which are currently subject to police investigation' (Hansen 1993, iii).

In short, the terms of reference precluded any reporting into the allegations that were the very stimulus to the inquiry. As Judge Hansen expresses it: 'Describing facts and finding specific wrongs ... would be against the law' (xiv). In light of this, it is not surprising to learn that, in Judge Hansen's words, 'this Report does not demonstrate the quantity of the information which was collected' (v). Although the report provides some general information on problems at Bell Cairn, these sections are arguably far less informative about specific events and incidents than such information as had already been released by the Ministry of Correctional Services in the *Chronology of Events.*

While commissions are typically limited in their fact- and fault-finding mandate in relation to specific incidents and allegations, their strength often lies in their ability to document the organizational and policy context of problems (cf. Roach 1995). But it can again be argued that Judge Hansen's report did not take full advantage in this respect. This limitation of the report is not immediately evident. Therefore, I shall here first point to those problems in the ministry culture which *are* identified by Judge Hansen, and then elaborate on the important sub-features of these problems – specifically, gender-related ones – which the report not only fails to adequately address, but also about which it makes some potentially misleading statements.

On the positive side, Judge Hansen's report does acknowledge and point to the existence of a 'poisoned environment' within the ministry and Bell Cairn. As explained by Judge Hansen, pursuant to the Workplace Discrimination and Harassment Prevention policy, a 'poisoned environment' includes 'an environment where an employee is subject to sexually oriented remarks, behaviour or surroundings that create an intimidating, hostile or offensive work environment, or surroundings which are conducive to sexual harassment' (Hansen 1993, 26). In Judge Hansen's words (viii, xv):

> This report concludes that there is a systemic problem within the Ontario Ministry of Correctional Services caused by the so-called culture. That culture inhibits the full implementation of the Government's policy on Workplace Discrimination and Harassment Prevention (WHDP) ... My conclusions are that the Ministry's culture, as evidenced by circumstances and attitudes, perpetuated a work environment in which individuals were at risk of harassment and intimidation.

Moreover, Judge Hansen reported that, in addition to the information provided to the inquiry at the outset (including the *Chronology of Events*), the inquiry 'heard many examples of events that could give rise to complaints under the Workplace Discrimination and Harassment Policy (WHDP) and might have contributed to a "poisoned environment"' (26).[20]

The limitation of the report's observations on this existence of a 'poisoned environment' is that it does not elucidate on how women are disproportionately affected and victimized by it. Rather, the report tends to equate the harassment experienced by men with that experienced by women. This is disturbing. For example, the report states that '[s]exual harassment is generally thought of as something done by men to women. However, men also reported incidents. Within the Ministry's culture, the masculinity of a male who rejects an advance from a woman may be questioned. Without detracting from the problems that women experience in reporting sexual harassment and sexual assault, it should also be noted that men experience similar challenges' (22).

While some men in the ministry may experience sexual harassment, and while this is an issue that certainly merits further attention, the report's summing up of the situation is problematic. Sexual harassment is not just a phenomenon that is 'generally thought of

as something done by men to women.' Rather, it is widely known –
and has been well documented (e.g., Beirne and Messerschmidt
1995, 135–8) – that the rate at which men sexually harass women far
exceeds the rate at which men experience sexual harassment by
women. In turn, sexual harassment is often a reflection, and a result
of, a more generalized power imbalance that favours men over
women. In short, women are far more likely than men to experience sexual harassment.[21] It would have been useful if Hansen's
report had provided some information about the differing scale of
the problem as described by men and women to the Inquiry. It would
also have been useful if the report had explored power imbalances
with respect to gender, and their effects in rendering women particularly vulnerable to sexual harassment. A discussion of the research literature on sexual harassment of women working in
corrections would have further illuminated organizational and cul-
tural features of related problems in this particular workplace.

Unfortunately, no such insights are provided in the report. Rather,
information about problems experienced by women is accompanied by, and thereby merged with, those experienced by men. For
example, it is observed that (26):

> Men reported groping of their genital area by females, conversations
> with sexual overtones, the showing of pornographic videos in the
> lounge, and having been invited to have sex. Women reported being
> followed, being leered at, unwanted touching, harassing telephone
> calls, gender-based insults, and being approached for sex. Walking
> through the halls at Bell Cairn was described by women as 'running
> the gauntlet' and several women reported planning their activities to
> walk through the halls with a friend. Participants spoke of frequent
> heavy drinking and partying and games of strip poker in the lounge.

In short, the report side-steps the issue of women's far greater
vulnerability to sexual harassment. One indication of this is the fact
that the recommendations included in the report (35–7) do not
once mention women as a specific group. By this merging and equating of women's and men's experiences, under the terminology of
'participants' at Bell Cairn, and 'employees' of the ministry, the re-

port loses opportunities for social education that such commissions (Roach 1995) can provide.

The Bell Cairn Staff Training Centre was reopened at the end of May 1993, with the report's recommendations having been implemented.[22] Within the ministry more generally, action was taken to advance Workplace Discrimination and Harassment Prevention training. How effective these and other initiatives taken by the Ministry of Correctional Services pursuant to the Bell Cairn scandal have been, however, has yet to be fully documented. According to the Employment Systems Review Task Force (1994, 94), the 'Bell Cairn incident ... did result in an immediate heightened awareness by staff of the Workplace Discrimination and Harassment Prevention policy, attributable probably to ongoing mass media coverage and subsequent training offered by the Ministry.' But questions remain as to whether this has translated into any substantial impact on peoples' behaviour.

Some clues about the effectiveness of the ministry's response can be found in the report *Building a Partnership for Change: A Report on the Evaluation of WHDP Policy Training*, carried out by the consulting firms Dowrich Management Services and Key Learning Group (1995). The evaluation reported that, by the late spring of 1994, over 8,000 employees of the Ministry of Correctional Services had received one-day training with respect to the WHDP policy by two-member teams of management and union personnel.

In conducting the evaluation, the firms took random samples of the course participants and used several approaches – including analyses of reaction sheets filled out by course participants, of a follow-up self-administered questionnaire survey, and of face-to-face interviews.[23] The evaluation also undertook focus groups with employment-equity designated, and other, groups.

Arising from this research, the evaluation reported that staff knowledge of the policy, and of related issues and rights, had improved (Dowrich Management Services 1995, 4). It also reported that '[t]he more blatant inappropriate behaviour evident before the training commenced has now subsided, and the demeaning and insensitive sexist and racist humour has significantly declined in many work areas' (6). At the same time, the evaluation suggested that no fun-

damental change had taken place, and that problems were continuing (6–8):

- There is a sense ... that the 'zero tolerance' message is still being
  undermined, evidenced by some reports of condonation by persons in authority, and continuing fear of reprisals by staff who are
  vulnerable.
- The level of awareness and increase in knowledge by all staff, have
  not yet been converted into demonstrable positive changes, in terms
  of how staff view their places of work.
- There is evidence of a tentativeness, on the part of employees in
  reporting major gains (positive changes) in the culture of the
  organization ...
- Most members of vulnerable groups continue to feel that they are
  required to be more 'realistic' and put up with the abrasive and
  demeaning behaviour which they encounter from time to time. This
  is primarily a concern of those in an institutional setting ...
- There are still some obstacles to the achievement of a discrimination and harassment free workplace ... There are some clear sig-
  nals [of change] that staff are looking for but have not yet seen, in
  sufficient measure, to raise their level of confidence, regarding
  workplace improvements.

Overall, the Bell Cairn incidents and their aftermath indicate that
gender-related problems in corrections are complex and nuanced.
These events also indicate that a proliferation of activity, both pre-
ventive and remedial, by no means guarantees a satisfactory resolution to problems. These points are further illustrated in the next
chapter's examination of events at the Wakefield Jail. Examining
related incidents primarily from the women's point of view, and in
light of broader knowledge available from research literatures, assists in more specifically elaborating on, firstly, the discrimination
and harassment to which women working in prisons for men are
vulnerable, and secondly, the problems encountered, and gener-
ated, in responding to gender-based discrimination and harassment
in corrections.

4 Discrimination and Harassment at the Wakefield Jail: A Research Perspective

Research on Women Working in Prisons for Men[1]

The evidence suggests that the sexism of the prison system is total. (Owen 1985, 155)

All of the current research indicates some hostility of male COs [Correctional Officers] towards women officers. (Horne 1985, 51)

In Canada, the topic of women working in prisons for men is not one that has received a great deal of research attention. The bulk of research has been done in the United States. To date, much of that literature tends to focus, first, on legislative developments that have facilitated women working in male prisons, and legal problems that have ensued (for example, the pitting of inmates' rights to privacy against women's right to undertake all of the duties normally involved in prison work); and, secondly, on presenting survey data that analyse the views of male and female correctional staff concerning women working in prisons for men.[2] Most of these studies lack a qualitative analysis of the everyday dynamics of harassment and discrimination. Nonetheless, despite this limitation, such literature as is available provides many useful insights on the nature of women's relationships with their male correctional-officer colleagues.

Usually, when one explores literature addressing specific topics in corrections, a wide variety of perspectives and debates rapidly become apparent. For example, literature on topics such as the purpose of punishment, on the effects of treatment and rehabilitation programs, or on the relationships between the use of community correctional programs and the size of prison populations, yield a striking diversity of opinions.[3] By contrast, existing literature on the situation of women working in prisons for men displays a remarkable consensus. Whether written by men or by women, whether focusing on experiences in the United States, Canada, Australia, or elsewhere, the literature repeatedly reveals that women working in prisons for men are subject to discriminatory and harassing behaviour by some of their male colleagues. Such behaviour on the part of the male colleagues ranges from trivial and irritating actions – which can be cumulatively very disturbing – to more explicit forms of sexual harassment.

This chapter first provides some background information about the emergence of complaints at the Wakefield Jail. It then describes the *male culture* of prisons for men, which sets the stage whereby gender-based discrimination and harassment can become taken for granted among male staff. Following this, various problems experienced by women, and specifically *micro-inequities, gender discrimination*, and *sexual harassment*, are documented. In discussing each of these phenomena, an overview of research findings is presented, and is followed by an elaboration of related events and incidents at the Wakefield Jail. Please note: all names mentioned are pseudonyms.

The Wakefield Jail as a Case Study

As noted above, the everyday dynamics of discrimination and harassment in correctional institutions often remain obscure within the existing literature. By contrast, the information about gender-related conflicts at the Wakefield Jail to be explored offers a rare opportunity to examine a series of incidents within one institution over a relatively lengthy period of time (the mid-1980s to the late 1990s). The information available about the Wakefield Jail also demonstrates how seemingly trivial individual events can be interwoven with more serious forms of sexual harassment, and how both can combine in yielding a 'poisoned environment.' Further, this availability of longitudinal information provides insights into how different groups of individuals (namely female employees, male employees, the union, and management) have reacted, and responded, to related problems.

Since the mid-1980s, the Wakefield Jail has had fewer than fifty employees (including supervisory, line, kitchen, nursing, and administrative staff), and an inmate capacity of forty or less (in the mid-1990s, the jail was operating below capacity).[4] The first female correctional officer to be hired at the jail was Diana Hooper, who was hired part-time in 1984, and full-time from 1986. From that time, other females were also hired as correctional officers. In total, six additional women had been hired as correctional officers by the mid-1990s, three of them on a classified, and three of them on a casual, basis. Overall, the proportion of female correctional officer employees seems to have been less than that found in Ontario more generally (where, as we have seen, in the early 1980s women accounted for approximately 8.5 per cent of all correctional officers in the ministry, and by 1992 they accounted for 21 per cent). Specifically, between the mid-1980s and the mid-1990s there appears to have never been more than four female correctional officers employed at Wakefield at any given moment. And, as noted earlier, at the time of the completion of this study in 1997, the jail had only two female correctional officers: one classified, and one casual.[5]

Other women employed at the jail during the period under consideration have been in more traditionally female positions, including nurses and cooks. Similarly to the female correctional officers, their positions have also been vulnerable, in that they have often been hired on a casual, rather than a classified, basis. For example, as of 1994, the jail had four cooks. The only male cook was hired on a full-time basis, while the three female cooks were either casual or part-time. Meanwhile, the two nursing positions have been part-time ones. It appears that it is only in specifically administrative positions that women's jobs have been more secure. As of 1997, for example, the jail had three women working in the office (two full-time and one part-time), all of whom held classified positions. The jail also had one female classification officer in a classified position.

Women's difficult situation at the Wakefield Jail has been evident in their lack of access to management positions. Where, in the ministry as a whole, women occupied 10 per cent of institutional management positions by the early 1990s, none of the female correctional officers employed during the period under consideration were able to advance to a management position.[6] Moreover, and as will be discussed later, when Diana Hooper was asked on occasion to fill in a lieutenant position in the course of a shift, she experienced negative repercussions from some colleagues.

When it is considered that the Wakefield Jail is a small institution, and one (like any prison) requiring twenty-four-hour staffing by correctional officers working in shifts, it can be seen that those females employed by the jail often had to work in isolation in an otherwise male environment. It would not be a rare event for a woman to be the *only* female correctional officer on duty. The tendency to schedule no more than one woman to a shift reinforced their vulnerability to gender-based discrimination and harassment.

While discriminatory and harassing incidents were occurring at the Wakefield Jail from at least the time of the hiring of the first female correctional officer in 1984, it was not until October 1992 that women at the jail began to become aware of one another's experiences, and thereby of the generalized aspects of offensive behaviour on the part of some of their colleagues. Indeed, Sharon West – a casual correctional officer who worked at the Wakefield Jail from 1988–90 – and who had experienced some of the most serious sexual harassment that took place there, suffered alone. Her ultimate response to the harassment she experienced by several colleagues was to resign. It was only when other complaints began to surface, and when the ministry's Independent Investigations Unit contacted Ms West as a possible witness, that the details of her own experiences of harassment were discovered and investigated.

As noted, the existence of discrimination and harassment at the Wakefield Jail began to come to light from the fall of 1992. This occurred when Karla Preston, a casual cook at the jail, initiated a complaint. During the previous year, Ms Preston had been receiving counselling to help her deal with the harassment she had been experiencing, and specifically that by then Superintendent Fred Ferguson. Encouraged by her doctor not only to confront Superintendent Ferguson, but to take action toward making a formal complaint, Karla Preston made several calls to the Independent Investigations Unit of the Ministry of Correctional Services in late September and early October. Indeed, it was not Karla Preston herself, but her doctor, who placed the first call. Moreover, when Karla Preston initially spoke by phone to staff of the Independent Investigations Unit, she was reluctant to identify herself or the jail concerned. After a few telephone conversations, however, she had identified herself, and the complaint investigation process was set in motion.

Pursuant to this initial complaint, a ministry investigator visited the Wakefield Jail in October. Those with whom she spoke included correctional officers Nora Diamond and Diana Hooper. Both women had also been experiencing problems with their colleagues' behaviour (Diana Hooper since soon after her hiring in 1984, and Nora Diamond soon after she commenced working at the Wakefield Jail in 1988). The initiative taken by Karla Preston acted as a stimulus for their also taking action. In the words of Diana Hooper (hearing notes,[7] 25 January 1995):

In October of 1992 I was approached by Karla Preston. I was working at the Jail, and Karla approached me. She was very upset and said that she had to speak to me privately. We spoke in the elevator and Karla expressed [sic] that she was being interviewed by the Investigation Unit, and she wanted to know if I would go with her for moral support. I did not know at this time that Karla was having problems at the Jail. She never told me. I did not tell her [about the discrimination and harassment that] I was facing. I went with Karla. Moore and Fielding were the investigators. I heard Karla give her story.

When we first entered the staff room, the two investigators were sitting across from us. We each sat down, and Karla answered questions. At two points I had to leave and cried in the bathroom. When I came back the last time they were almost done. Fielding was always looking at me, and asking if there was anything I wanted to add. I told them I was having problems ...

When I heard Karla [telling] her story, I did not really hear a lot of what was being said. I was thinking that I wanted to come forward, but was not sure if I could. I was trying to grin and bear the situation, because I [was] thinking it would get better – but it was not. I was worried about whether I was strong enough to file a complaint. Finally I decided I had to for peace of mind.

This reluctance to formally complain evidenced by Karla Preston and Diana Hooper is a typical response to sexual discrimination and harassment, and will be discussed in the next chapter. By the end of October, however, Karla Preston, Diana Hooper, and Nora Diamond had all filed complaints. In addition to investigating these, the Independent Investigations Unit of the Ministry of Correctional Services also addressed those arising from interviews with former employee Sharon West.

In 1993, Nora Diamond, Diana Hooper, and Karla Preston took their complaints further by submitting grievances under the Collective Agreement between the Government of Ontario and the Ontario Public Service Employees Union. Their cases were sent for arbitration before the Grievance Settlement Board of Ontario. Between October 1994 and September 1995, a total of thirty-seven days of hearings were held. The three grievors testified, and each of the women who had worked at the jail since 1985 were also called as witnesses. Testimony also included that by other staff members of the Wakefield Jail and of the Ontario Ministry of Correctional Services, and by other relevant individuals (including the family doctor of one of the grievors and another's psychiatrist, as well as Sheila Henriksen of the Correctional Service of Canada, whose research on discrimination and harassment in the federal system has been cited elsewhere in this book). Over 100 exhibits were submitted to the Board, and, as noted earlier, these, along with notes from the hearings, constitute the data base for the following analysis.

Overall, while the core focus of the proceedings was on the actions of the respondents originally named by Nora Diamond, Diana Hooper, and Karla Preston, much information also emerged about offensive behaviour by other colleagues at the jail, including anonymous behaviour.[8] Some of this broader information came from the grievors' female colleagues at the jail who also testified. Although the latter had not made formal complaints or grieved, they also had numerous observations on offensive, discriminatory, and harassing behaviour by colleagues – including not only those named in formal complaints, but also other male colleagues.

Taken together, the grievors' and non-grievors' accounts provide a holistic picture of sexual discrimination and harassment at the Wakefield Jail, one that reveals its multifarious forms. We now turn to an examination of this picture in light of broader knowledge about gender-based discrimination and harassment reflected in relevant research literature.

The Male Culture of Prisons

> In hindsight, it is clear that the major objection to women filling the CX [security] ranks came not from inmates, but from staff. (Taylor 1986, 51, discussing the Correctional Service of Canada)

Within the literature (most of it from the United States) on women working in prisons for men, one very telling piece of research posed an open-ended question asking what caused the majority of women's problems as correctional officers. One might have thought that, in the context of the clientele of male prisons, which are often portrayed as containing perverse, unsavoury, and dangerous prisoners,[9] women would have identified the inmates as a major source of their problems. This was not the case. Rather, the striking finding was than only 3 per cent of the female officers identified the inmates as their major problem, but fully 41 per cent of the respondents identified their co-workers as the largest problem they faced (Hunter 1986, 13; Jurik and Halemba 1984).[10]

Indeed, female correctional officers' relations with male inmates appear to be generally quite positive. The literature reports that inmates tend to be very favourable to the presence of women in prisons: women are seen to humanize the atmosphere, be less abusive, and be more willing to talk than their male colleagues. Moreover, contrary to beliefs that women in male prisons may be vulnerable to attack by the inmates, the research suggests that women are less likely than men to be assaulted by them (Horne 1985; 50; Shawver and Dickover 1986, 32; see also Lovrich and Stohr 1993; Petersen 1982, 449; and Walters 1992, 176). For their part, most female correctional officers 'feel that the inmates were kinder, more helpful, and more accepting of their presence than were their male coworkers' (Zimmer 1982, 79).[11]

This relatively positive account of the attitudes of male inmates to female workers in prisons stands in stark contrast to the perceptions reported on the part of male correctional officers. Many of the observations here also apply in the case of women working in other traditionally male occupations (such as business, construction, law, policing, coal mining, steelworking, and autoworking). But it might also be true that correctional officers are particularly slow in adapting to having women as colleagues. Put simply, work in prisons for men has traditionally been viewed as a primarily masculine domain, and the involvement of women is seen as a threat to this long-standing identity. For example, Horne (1985, 51) has observed that, prior to the early 1970s, prisons for men were essentially all-male environments. He reports:

> Female CO's were intruders into this male world. Their presence threatened the homogeneity of the guard force and the belief that masculinity was a necessary requirement for the job. Male CO's responded to this threat with adamant opposition to women's presence – opposition that was justified (in their minds) by claims that their personal security and the security of the prisons were being compromised ... more than a decade after the first women were hired as CO's for men's prisons, male CO opposition [remained] strong.

Zimmer (1986, 52) has similarly observed:

> There are male COs who hold to this type of image of the 'macho man' prison guard. Certainly Hollywood and the mass media have helped to shape and perpetuate this macho image also. If women can enter one of the most masculine of all jobs (at least that is the image) and perform effectively, then the male CO is forced to question his own self-image because the status attached to the role of a correctional officer will no longer automatically be that of a 'real man.'

In the case of prisons, male resistance to women's involvement may be intensified given that not only has the traditionally male nature of the occupation fostered a male occupational culture and camaraderie, but that the ensuing guard subculture has tended to be a generally conservative one, and, with respect to gender issues, supportive of conventional views of a woman's place (Owen 1985: 155). Again, Zimmer (1989, 64) insightfully comments on correctional officers' stereotypical perceptions:

> The opposition of male COs to the hiring of women grows largely out of their deeply held beliefs about natural differences between the sexes, about women's 'proper' role in society, and about the nature of guard work and the qualities necessary for successful job performance. To most men, the hiring of women as COs violates common sense. They believe the job of CO requires strength, machismo and the willingness to get into a physical confrontation without stopping to think about the consequences; and, they believe these qualities are absent in women. Even male officers who do not display these masculine characteristics may be given derogatory nicknames (like 'girl') and discouraged from continued employment. (Crouch, 1980)

With respect to correctional officers' perception of the inherently masculine character of their occupation, one of the ironies that arises – and which I have not seen discussed elsewhere in the literature[12] – is that, despite the male officers' self-image of their job as involving aggressiveness and strength, in practice most of the actual tasks they undertake parallel those traditionally undertaken by women in the home: correctional officers supervise their charges in getting out of bed in the morning, in tidying and cleaning their living-spaces, in eating breakfast, and in doing their chores and work. They also devote much energy to preventing petty squabbles from developing and escalating. Perhaps the issue is not so much whether the incoming women can perform in a job that has been seen as inherently male, but rather: does the presence and effectiveness of females serve to reveal that most correctional officer tasks bear a remarkable similarity to those traditionally seen as having inherently female aspects?

The Male Culture at the Wakefield Jail

The first major signifier of the male culture at the Wakefield Jail has been the dearth of women. As noted, as of April 1995, the jail had a superintendent, 5 lieutenants, 17 full-time correctional officers, and 6 to 8 casual correctional officers. This staff of between 29 and 31 people working with inmates included only 3 females. Moreover, in addition to representing only 10 per cent of correctional staff (and 0 per cent of managerial positions), it is notable that of the three female correctional officers, two were casual, and their positions were thereby insecure. In short, not only have women been strongly under-represented at the Wakefield Jail, but, with management and supervisory staff all being male, their access to work and sufficient hours on which to make a livable income have been strongly dependent on decisions made by men.

One of the ways in which the male culture of the Wakefield Jail was continually evident is through the relentless stream of comments made by men to women. These comments have clearly indicated men's belief that female correctional officers do not belong in a prison for men, and that they do not have the strength that the men consider necessary for the job. Men at the Wakefield Jail have also told women that they would not provide them support in dangerous situations. Nor would they support women should they be given a supervisory position.

The belief of male colleagues that female correctional officers do not belong in a prison for men was frequently reported by the women. According to Nora Diamond:[13] 'Once when I was leaving the institution at the end of a shift, an officer, named Gerry Kennedy, said there are many places for female correctional officers, and pointed to the administrative side of the institution. And [he] said there was not a place for women correctional officers.'

According to Sharon West: 'The attitude of the males was very old fashioned – that [women] didn't belong, that they would get hurt, [and] that they didn't have the power to restrain inmates if there was a fight or anything.'

According to Patricia Murray: 'On two occasions I was present when male officers said there was no place for females in corrections, and both of these comments occurred during human rights training.' She also reported that 'Gerry Kennedy didn't feel that women belonged in corrections.' Meanwhile, Diana Hooper reported that Lt Laroche told her 'O'Reilly said he did not want to work with two females.'

The hostility directed at the women has often taken non-verbal forms. For example, Patricia Murray reported that: 'While working George Gagnon would basically avoid me. He would go to his post and ignore me. When you are on a shift for 12 hours this is unusual.' Kerry Beauchamp similarly reported: 'I felt resentment from some [male] officers.' And Diana Hooper stated: 'The staff's behaviour intimidated me.'

The dangers that women were supposedly facing, and the fact that they could not rely on support from male colleagues, were alluded to by Sharon West and Nora Diamond. Sharon West reported: 'The male officers would say that they would have to carry out the females in body bags. This was said by Mr. Kennedy and Mr. Payne ... [They said] inmates were going to end up hurting [the women] severely. I was scared for my life. I was always alert. I always had my back to the wall.'

Nora Diamond reported: 'Gerald Kennedy talked about his experience in corrections where you needed the brawn, muscle power ... O'Reilly said we were weaker – not equal ... [A] male officer (Joe Robert) indicated ... that women weren't really so strong. "Whether it is a ball game or on the job," he said, "you think you're strong. But if you hit an emergency button, know that I won't be the first one coming."'

The lack of support on which women could count should they attain supervisory positions was described by Diana Hooper. She reported that on one occasion, Superintendent Fred Ferguson talked to her about being acting lieutenant, and mentioned a human-rights program in the ministry. Another colleague present, correctional officer Harding, 'said the boys would not support me if I became Acting Lieutenant, and they would not work for me.'[14]

Many of the male correctional officers at the Wakefield Jail were not only unaccepting of female correctional officers, but some also expressed traditional views concerning women and their place more generally. For example, several women referred to their colleague Gerry Kennedy's insistence on addressing women as 'dames.' He even addressed a Workplace Harassment and Discrimination Prevention instructor in this way. Diana Hooper reported that not only did Gerry Kennedy think 'we were not capable of doing the job, and he wanted male backup, not a woman,' but he also 'thought women did not belong in corrections, but in the kitchen.'

With respect to the unwelcoming culture of the Wakefield Jail, it is important to note that this has been the case not only in the mid- to late-1980s when some of the women were hired, but also in the 1990s, even after the initiation of formal complaints under the Workplace Discrimination and Harassment Prevention policy. For example, Micheline Pelletier, who was hired in July 1993 as a correctional officer, has remarked: 'I was not happy with my new job. I felt lonely, like a fish out of water ... [T]here was a lot of tension. People were leery of me coming into the job ... [The language] was not good, [it was] abusive ... [There was] a lot of swearing.'

Micro-inequities

> It has been said that when a man makes a stupid mistake, we say, 'What a stupid man.' But, when a woman makes a stupid mistake, we say 'How stupid women are.' (Correctional Service of Canada pamphlet, 1980)

The research literature on women working in prisons for men reveals that male expressions of hostility take a variety of more or less tangible forms. Where the latter are concerned, some authors refer to what they term 'micro-inequities.' Micro-inequities are 'forms of discrimination and harassment that are real, but too subtle to prove in a court of law' (Zimmer 1989, 70). As Zimmer elaborates:

> It is impossible to quantify and compare the amount of information and assistance given by experienced male officers to the men and women they train. It is impossible to quantify and compare the degrees of hostility in the nicknames given to male and female employees. There is much that goes on between women and men that makes

it difficult for women to become equal partners in the workplace; some of it does not fit within current definitions of sex discrimination and some of it is simply too subtle to bring into the courtroom.

A Canadian study by Szockyj (1989, 325) similarly observes that 'the comment "When a male staff member makes a mistake then it's forgotten, but if a woman makes a mistake then it's talked about for weeks" was typical of the opinions expressed by female officers.' Overall, the existence of micro-inequities perpetrated by their male colleagues appears to be a pervasive, yet amorphous, component of the female correctional officer's experience.

Micro-inequities at the Wakefield Jail

Accounts by the women about their experiences at the Wakefield Jail suggest that micro-inequities, and perceptions of such inequities, have been an ongoing characteristic of their everyday work lives.

According to Nora Diamond, for example, she felt excluded from the outset. When she started her job, there 'wasn't exactly a welcoming committee. [The male correctional officers] kept to their own little groups, [and] had their own chats ...' Karla Preston (who was hired as a casual cook in 1989, and had unsuccessfully applied on several occasions for a position as a correctional officer) also felt such exclusion, as evidenced in her remarks: 'We were not given the same opportunities ... We are being held back ... We are not being brought in as we should be ... [We are] constantly hearing belittling remarks to keep us in our place.'

As Zimmer (1989) has observed, the nature of micro-inequities makes them difficult to document. Those micro-inequities noted by women at the Wakefield Jail include Nora Diamond's perception that she was denied access to French-language training. She was also upset about being sent on a three-week training course at Bell Cairn with less than a $40 advance for food, and finding on arrival that staff from other institutions had received advances of hundreds of dollars. Proving that these were indeed cases of discrimination is beyond the scope of this research. Nonetheless, where access to French-language training is concerned, if Nora Diamond was not entitled to it, this information could have been clearly conveyed and explained to her. Allowing, and even encouraging, her to make repeated unsuccessful applications could in itself be construed as a form of harassment by omission.

Meanwhile, where sending Nora Diamond on a lengthy course without an adequate financial advance is concerned, although discrimination cannot be clearly proven, many questions can be raised about management's omission. According to management, not pre-paying Nora Diamond was an oversight arising from the belief that meals would be provided at Bell Cairn.[15] One might ask why this was not verified prior to the trip. One might also question the contrast between the lack of expense money advanced to Nora Diamond as compared to the more than adequate advance for gas given to the male correctional officer with whom she was travelling. It is understandable that an inequity might be perceived in this case – especially when immediately prior to the departure of the two correctional officers, their superior was making statements about how they would have to share a room during the course (a joke that neither officer appreciated).

Consistent with research findings generally, one of the most common forms of micro-inequities experienced by the female correctional officers at the Wakefield Jail has been that of a relentless focus on, and searches for, potential mistakes by them. Even the part-time cook Kerry Beauchamp, who was not one of the complainants, observed that: 'I felt that if I did something wrong it was always brought to my attention – and full-time male officers got away with murder ... I didn't feel [Lt Mallon] treated male officers the same way he reprimanded me for a number of minor incidents, and male officers were continuously overlooked for doing less, and worse, things.'

Correctional officer Melissa Jackson, another non-complainant, similarly commented on how, at the Wakefield Jail, Lt Laroche questioned her log books, and called her 'irresponsible' and 'undependable.'

Among the male correctional officers, Lt O'Reilly appears to have continually harassed several women. He did this by constantly engaging in what the women describe as 'nitpicking.' Thus, Nora Diamond reported that O'Reilly continually 'nitpicked' and 'counselled' her. Specifically, she was picked on by O'Reilly about entries in the logbook, about cooking popcorn and the smell it was making (although male officers cooked bacon and eggs), and about using the oven to keep warm. She was counselled by O'Reilly in front of an inmate, and without union representation. O'Reilly also followed Nora Diamond around while she was doing her rounds (something other supervisors do not do). In keeping records, if Nora Diamond wrote 1:05, O'Reilly would write 1:02. As described by Nora Diamond, no matter what she did, O'Reilly could find error: 'I have been counselled because my [time] punches are too close together, too far apart, because you are not punching it hard enough ... I never had problems with anyone else about my punching.'

Diana Hooper also described O'Reilly's focus on her mistakes. O'Reilly, she said, made 'comments to other staff that I was always making mistakes.' Yet, she continued, she 'never heard O'Reilly making a comment about a male correctional officer making a mistake.'

O'Reilly's harassment of Diana Hooper involved not only his following her around, but, she reported, he 'got on hands and knees when checking my corridor to see if [there was] any dust.' By contrast, when a male correctional officer was on duty, O'Reilly 'does not even go into the cell.' This intense checking by O'Reilly, said Hooper, 'happened multiple times.' It is understandable that under such circumstances, women would feel that their male colleagues' competence was being taken for granted, while their job performances have been constantly under scrutiny, and subject to question.

No doubt some male correctional officers have also, at least occasionally, experienced a focus on petty errors – potential and real – by their managers and supervisors. But in the case of female correctional officers, the demoralizing effects of such nitpicking have been exacerbated by the more generally unwelcoming and male culture of the Wakefield Jail. The effects of such petty harassment were also made worse when they were combined with the more specifically gender-focused forms of discrimination and harassment we shall now examine.

Gender Discrimination

A more tangible form of impediment faced by female officers can be described in terms of gender discrimination. Much of the U.S. literature reveals that, on the basis of privacy legislation as well as on more informal perceptions of what is appropriate, female correctional officers, from the training period onwards, tend to get different assignments than men in the workplace. Most generally, women can find themselves assigned to posts involving minimal contact with inmates. While this phenomenon may sometimes have a kindly intended, chivalrous basis, and while it may be appreciated by some women, it also has the deleterious effect of denying women experiences afforded to men, and has the longer-term effect of impeding their prospects for promotion. As investigations in Michigan during the 1980s concluded, 'female officers ... are encouraged to become incompetent officers,' and women 'were being put in situations that set them up for failure' (Abramajtys 1982, 11; 1987, 6, quoted in Zimmer 1989, 68).

Gender Discrimination at the Wakefield Jail

At the Wakefield Jail, gender discrimination appears to have taken three major forms. These are limitations on the hours of work made available to females; the allocation of different tasks to female correctional officers; and the exclusion of female correctional officers from certain tasks and assignments.

Where limitations on the hours of work made available to females are concerned, it is striking that five women (four correctional officers and one cook) have felt that they were at a disadvantage in getting hours and shifts. In the case of the correctional officers, this disadvantage was perceived as being at least partly related to some male colleagues' belief that two women make for a 'weak shift.' The scheduling of one woman on a shift, therefore, was seen as greatly reducing the prospects that another woman would be considered for a shift at that time. Hours were believed to be further limited given the belief of some colleagues that having even one woman present made for a 'weak shift.' Thus, Sharon West claimed that, because it was felt that females made for a weak shift, 'I was denied shifts.'

Some of the women have further claimed that their hours were limited because of O'Reilly's clear opposition to working with, and therefore scheduling, women. For example, Diana Hooper reported that (in October 1987) O'Reilly told her that women make a weak shift. Moreover, when Melissa Jackson and Diana Hooper were scheduled to both work a day shift, O'Reilly called in sick. Later that day, O'Reilly arrived at the Wakefield Jail in street clothes, and told Joe Robert that the reason he had called in sick was because he did not want to work with two females.

Diana Hooper also reported that in August 1989, when Lieutenant O'Reilly was in charge of the institution (because the superintendent was away), the acting IC [supervisor/'in charge'], correctional officer Fischer, was having difficulty getting staff. O'Reilly said to Fischer that he did not care who he called in, as long as it was not a female, and especially not Diana Hooper. Nonetheless, Diana Hooper was called in. When she arrived at the institution, she found that Joe Robert had been assigned as supervisor despite the fact that she had greater seniority than him. When she asked Fischer why Joe Robert was in charge, he recounted the conversation with O'Reilly.

Diana Hooper later took up this incident with the superintendent, Fred Ferguson. O'Reilly told Ferguson that he had been drinking that day, and did not remember making the statements that Fischer had attributed to him. Ferguson said it was Fischer's word against O'Reilly's, and nothing was resolved.[16]

Nora Diamond similarly reported problems in getting hours, and the role of O'Reilly in this. According to her, '[it] didn't take very long after beginning employment [before] I realized that I was receiving less hours than my male counterparts ... It was obvious that I wasn't receiving my fair shake of the hours ... Lt Page called me, and told me in confidence that he had been chastised by O'Reilly for scheduling females on O'Reilly's shift. [O'Reilly] said it made for a weak shift.' Nora Diamond also reported that O'Reilly was observed 'whiting out' hours at about 3 AM. Specifically, O'Reilly was said to be whiting out Nora Diamond's hours, and giving them to another male officer.

It is again beyond the scope of this research to determine the extent to which female correctional officers were discriminated against with respect to scheduling. But at the very least, the

women's perception that they were being discriminated against –
especially in light of the recurrent theme of their constituting weak
shifts – appears reasonable. Moreover, women's efforts to determine
if this was indeed occurring appear to have merely yielded further
harassment. For example, according to Melissa Jackson, when she
raised questions about hours and talked to casual correctional officers about them, 'Lt. Laroche proceeded to harass me for the next
two days regarding my log book, etc.'

Meanwhile, where casual cook Karla Preston is concerned, it is
significant that her problems with shifts began *after* she had received
counselling to assist her in dealing with the harassment she had
been experiencing, especially at the hands of Fred Ferguson (which
will be discussed below). Although Karla Preston had never refused
hours offered to her, and although she was anxious to work as many
hours as possible in order to support herself and her children, a
fourth cook was hired in January 1992. It is also notable that Karla
Preston's hours were further reduced in late 1993 – *after* her
Workplace Discrimination and Harassment Prevention complaint
had been dealt with, and the jail had been closed for two weeks
while staff underwent Workplace Discrimination and Harassment
Prevention training.

Yet again, it is beyond the scope of this research to determine the
extent to which limitations on, and the reduction of, Karla Preston's hours were a result of intended discrimination. But the wom-
en's perception that to identify and question harassment and
discrimination may result in its continuance – albeit in more subtle
and difficult-to-challenge forms – seems to be a reasonable one in
the circumstances.

As noted, the second form of gender discrimination at the
Wakefield Jail lies in the allocation of different tasks to women. As
with situations involving the allocation of hours, it has sometimes
been difficult for women to ascertain the extent to which such discrimination is intended and gender-related. For example, Micheline
Pelletier reported being passed over for an overtime opportunity
(transferring an inmate), and, the very next day, finding that hours
that had been allocated to her to do a medical escort had been
whited out, and that she was again being passed over. 'I was mad,'
she said, 'that was two days in a row.' She wondered 'if, as the only

female, he did not send me on the trip.' But she never directly asked. In this case, as in that of the allocation of hours, gender discrimination and micro-inequities overlap, and are difficult to challenge.

Other examples of differential assignments for women are more obvious. For example, on Melissa Jackson's first day at the Wakefield Jail in 1987, she was assigned to do laundry. Similarly, when Diana Hooper was first appointed in 1984, there were also times when she was assigned to do laundry. Such an assignment would not constitute discrimination if male correctional officers also undertook laundry. But, as Diana Hooper reported, male correctional officers were not stationed to do laundry. If they were involved in laundry, it was in supervising the inmates who were doing it.

From Diana Hooper's experience, it is clear that such a differential assignment was not by chance, but coincided with male colleagues' view of a woman's role. Thus, on another occasion during her first few years at the Wakefield Jail, an inmate was infected with crabs and the cell needed to be disinfected. Diana Hooper's colleague gave her all the supplies to do the job, saying, 'this is woman's work.'

More generally, Diana Hooper commented: 'I don't know how many times the officers would laugh, and say, "that is woman's work."' Where her male colleagues would supervise inmates in carrying out tasks such as washing windows, Diana Hooper would be assigned to wash windows *with* an inmate.

Diana Hooper's description of gender-based discrimination also indicates how women were in a proverbial situation of 'damned if you do, and damned if you don't.' To refuse an assignment would be to invite repercussions. Yet carrying it out could also lead to further troubles. For example, on one occasion, O'Reilly sent her to clean a male washroom. Subsequently, another officer complained when he went in to use it and Diana Hooper was there.

The third category of gender-based discrimination is that of the exclusion of women from certain tasks. In some of these cases, the differential assignment of women not only constitutes discrimination, but discrimination that directly contravenes the ministry's own stated policy. For example, on one occasion in March 1989, O'Reilly would not let Diana Hooper frisk an inmate who was being admitted. As Diana Hooper observed: 'he would not let me do the job I was qualified to do, and which was part of my job.' This discrimination by O'Reilly is difficult to reconcile with the ministry's policy on cross-gender supervision.

Other female correctional officers also reported being excluded from certain assignments. One notable instance was during times when an emergency was perceived to exist. Thus, Melissa Jackson reported that in emergency situations she would be sent to the control office, and 'the male would be sent out on the floor to handle the situation.'[17] On another occasion, when an inmate started yelling, screaming, and throwing things, Patricia Murray was sent off the floor to the duty office by Gerald Kennedy, and a male officer was sent 'to administer a chemical weapon – mace.' Sharon West similarly reported being excluded during perceived emergencies: 'If an incident happened, I would normally be sent to the office, and a Lieutenant would go out on the floor. I would be assigned to the duty office in order for them to provide more brute strength [to deal] with the situation.'

Not only is the tendency to exclude women from perceived emergencies discriminatory, but it also fails to recognize that there are ways other than strength that can often be more effective. This point was alluded to by Sharon West: '[Some] male officers would antagonize the inmates. But I would try to diffuse the situation by talking to the inmate, [and] use my humour ... On several occasions, I used my ability to talk an inmate out of a situation. It worked really well, rather than being a bully.'

Finally, several of the women have reported on situations that illuminate the 'glass ceiling' that can bar their occupational advancement. Quite simply, there have been occasions when women were senior, but were not given the opportunities this entails. For example, Melissa Jackson reported: 'there were times when I was senior, and I was not put in charge.' Such gender discrimination helps to explain both women's lack of success in securing senior positions at the Wakefield Jail, and their high turnover rate.

Sexual Harassment

In addition to documenting the existence of micro-inequities and

gender discrimination, the literature on female correctional officers also displays consensus on issues of sexual harassment. For example, female officers are subject to obscenities from their
'disgruntled male coworkers' (Horne 1985, 53), and to persistent
curiousity and rumours about their sexual lives (Petersen 1982,
452–3). As Zimmer (1989, 64–5) elaborates, such forms of sexual
harassment are often interwoven with 'verbal opposition' and 'discriminatory treatment':

> Women officers are teased and insulted. At various times, they are
> either ignored and shunned or noticed and talked about. They are
> made the butt of jokes and given derogatory nicknames. Speculation
> about their private lives is rampant and in some cases, rumours spread
> about sexual encounters with inmates. Their work is undermined and
> they are often reported by co-workers for minor rule violations that
> male workers ignore in each other. Any mistakes made by women
> become topics of conversations for weeks, even spreading from one
> prison to another. Women are excluded from informal information-
> sharing conversations on and off the job. The men they work with
> may fail to provide the training necessary for them to learn the job.
> Some men blatantly refuse to work with a woman; others try to drive
> women away with silence or verbal harassment.

Other authors have observed that, while guards' hostility towards
women may appear to lessen over time, in fact, it is just becoming
'less visible and overt. The less blatant hostility then manifests itself
in sexual rumours about the female COs, sexual harassment, and
the lack of acceptance into the established prison guard subculture'
(Horne 1985, 51).

The insidiousness of this harassment can difficult to convey. It
includes, for example, the saying applied to women in relation to
promotions: '"It is not who you know, but who you blow."' In the
face of such perceptions, women have to expend energy trying to
prove that they are not being promoted '"on their backs"' (Owen
1985, 158). It also includes having supervisors such as the one who
frequently failed to process disciplinary charges against inmates for
misconduct involving women, and commented that '"I'm not going

to process a critical incident every time a female officer gets her tits or ass grabbed"' (Abramajtys 1987, 13, quoted in Zimmer 1989, 65).

It further includes having to put up with male colleagues who repeatedly make offensive and sexist comments, and then criticize the female officers' lack of feminine characteristics. As one male officer commented (quoted in Owen 1985, 156): 'They come into work, their vocabulary's clean ... their walk, their whole manner-isms are feminine; two or three years later they sound like a steve-dore. They walk like they've got a grudge against the world, taking it out on everybody and they lose their attractiveness.'

Sexual Harassment at the Wakefield Jail

Accounts from the women at the Wakefield Jail reveal that they have repeatedly been subject to sexual harassment in the forms of teas-ing and insults, offensive and sexual comments, and speculation and rumours about their sexuality. Such behaviours in themselves would appear to confirm that the culture of the Wakefield Jail has constituted a 'poisoned environment' within the meaning of the Workplace Discrimination and Harassment Prevention policy. But, at the Wakefield Jail, given the additional and even more serious sexual harassment that women have been subjected to, it is apt to describe the environment as undoubtedly a poisoned one. As well as suffering insidious forms of harassment, some women have also been subject to unwelcome intrusions and sexual propositions, and to unwanted and sexual touching. Given the context of it clearly being unwanted, some of this sexual touching may fall within the realm of criminal offences of sexual assault. Meanwhile, other forms of aggressive physical attacks experienced by some women may come within the purview of criminal offences of assault.

Teasing and Insults

Women have been insulted and teased face to face. For example, Diana Hooper was told by a male colleague: '"You make me sick to have to look at you first thing in the morning."' The colleague went on to say that, should she be appointed to a full-time position, '"they had better send you to Penetang where you belong."'[18] Sometimes women have been taunted by groups of male correctional officers. Karla Preston's colleagues called her to look at what they were watching on television, namely, a gynaecologist conducting an internal examination. Karla Preston reported that she felt 'shocked and embarrassed, like they did it to see my reaction.'

Insulting and teasing of women has sometimes been indirect and anonymous, with ominous undertones. For example, women's property has been defaced. On one occasion, Kerry Beauchamp's shoes, which had been left in the kitchen, were filled with ketchup. The licence plates of Nora Diamond's vehicle were covered with ketchup, and, on another occasion, the mirrors on the side of her car were twisted backward. Melissa Jackson's car was subject to sadistic defacement; one night, when she came off duty at 11 PM, she found that a dead partridge had been placed on the windshield, and arranged so that the face of the bird was facing the interior.[19]

Offensive and Sexual Comments

Offensive and sexual comments appear to have been a routine characteristic of the culture at the Wakefield Jail. In general, the language was said to be 'vulgar.' Specific terms cited by the women as commonly being used include: 'fuck,' 'fucking,' 'fucking pigs,' 'goddamn fucking pigs,' 'cocksuckers,' 'pricks,' and 'shit.'

While this culture of vulgar language, and the prevalence of sexual and racist jokes, has been experienced by all correctional staff at the Wakefield Jail, it seems that female correctional officers have been particularly demeaned in being a primary target of objectionable comments.

The sexual harassment of Karla Preston by Superintendent Fred Ferguson demonstrates the lengths to which such offensive and sexual commentary have gone at the Wakefield Jail. In her case, sexist comments were initially interwoven with a perverse form of chivalry. Thus, on the day Karla Preston was hired as a casual cook, Ferguson commented on how beautiful she was. He also commented on the fact that she was single, and warned her that the inmates would have a hard time controlling themselves, and that, if she should have a problem with them, to go to him.

Karla Preston reported on how Ferguson started coming to the kitchen to visit her for non-professional, social reasons: 'He came twice a day, and timed his visits so that I was alone. He started asking about my kids. As time went on, the nature of the comments changed, and became extremely personal. He would notice if I gained or lost weight. He said that my ass looked good. He scrutinized me carefully and it felt like he was undressing me with his eyes. He said how good looking I was, how sexy I was ...'

As Karla Preston further reported, a combination of sexism, chivalry, and subjugation became routine characteristics of her encounters with Ferguson. For example, when she inquired about getting a ministry-issue coat:

> He said: 'We don't want you freezing your buns off. Of course, give my favourite girl a coat.' He asked if I wanted muffs and gloves. He told me about a stripper who wore a hat over her crotch, and gloves over her breasts, and did a strip dance like this. He said that I would look really good with the gloves and mitts. After watching me for a moment, he said: 'I had better get out of here quickly' ... because he could hardly control himself.

The offensive and sexist comments directed at the women have generally been more aggressive than those noted above. Thus, Karla Preston also reported that she would frequently hear sexual innuendos and remarks, for example: '"Once you fuck me, you'll never go back again."' Such remarks were made in the kitchen (where she worked). They also occurred in the sallyport, 'where they would not let me out until they said their thing.' One man, she said, 'described his vasectomy and his constipation to me.' Remarks also took explicitly derogatory forms. Thus, although Karla Preston was being subject to Ferguson repeatedly commenting on her beauty, and calling her '"my favourite little girl,"' other male colleagues were telling her 'how ugly [she] was.'

Accounts by other women further illustrate the predominantly aggressive and derogatory tone of comments. Nora Diamond reported: 'I've been called a fucking old bag,' and 'I've been directed to "open the door, you fucking old bag."' Nora Diamond was also told by a colleague passing her: '"If you didn't have such a big fucking ass, I might be able to get through,"' and '"You're so fucking ugly."'

In addition, Nora Diamond has been subject to offensive comments and unwanted information about her male colleagues' sexuality. For example, on one occasion her colleagues were reading a pornographic magazine and called her over to have a look. Nora Diamond replied that she did not want to. Her colleague ignored her, and held up the picture (of a woman) for her to see, and yelled: "I'd have to strap a two-by-four on my ass to get on this one."

On another occasion, on night shift, when Lt Laroche had been speaking on the phone to his wife, Nora Diamond reported that 'he grabbed his crotch and while he was rubbing it, he said: "I wish she wouldn't talk to me like that because I get so horny, and now I have to stay here all night."'

Nora Diamond also reported other offensive behaviour and comments on the part of Lt Laroche: 'Lt. Laroche found it humorous to walk up to someone and fart. And my reply to his ignorant attitude was: "Why don't you get a life?" He replied he was so constipated he had to stick his finger up his asshole and pick it out.'

Sharon West also reported being subject to unwanted information about a colleague's sex life. O'Reilly told her about how he had sex with a female ministry employee in the closet of a banquet hall during a ministry-sponsored seminar. Sharon West additionally reported:

> Laroche liked to grab his groin in front of female correctional officers. He would stand up against the wall and grab his groin – it was deliberate. He would see if we would look, and he would snigger – it was disgusting ... His language was terrible, he would refer to the genitals, etc. One night I was with him in the duty office, and he stated that he had just had his foreskin removed, and it had greatly improved his sex life ... I couldn't believe I was hearing this.

Other offensive comments experienced by the women include Francis Lalonde, who had just received flowers from her husband, being told by Fred Ferguson: '"He just wants to get into your pants."' Meanwhile, on another occasion, Lt Laroche telephoned Kathy Poirier at home about a shift, and addressed her with the question: '"Veut-tu travailler plut?"' ('"Do you want to work, old cunt?"').

Speculation and Rumours about Women's Sexuality

While women were sometimes provided with unwanted information about some of their colleagues' sexuality, they were simultaneously subject to unwanted probing into their own sex lives. For example, Diana Hooper – who, in 1984, was the first of the women who are the subject of this research to be hired – had a brief intimate friendship with a male correctional officer colleague. Pursuant to this, she was effectively put under surveillance while off-duty by the then superintendent, Mike Windsor. On one occasion, Superintendent Windsor himself followed Diana Hooper in his car while she was meeting her colleague away from the jail. The next day, the superintendent called her to his office, and said that he did not appreciate her behaviour. Such monitoring of off-duty conduct by the superintendent appears to go far beyond the bounds of any call of duty.

Diana Hooper's liaison with her colleague was subsequently used by other male colleagues as an opportunity to taunt her. One officer commented: '"if you wanted a good time, I could have showed you something better."' Some officers also subjected her to offensive and unwanted touching (which will be discussed below). Later, the prior existence of the liaison was allowed to become common knowledge among inmates. After this, Diana Hooper experienced problems, such as an inmate asking her for sexual favours. Rumours about her having sexual relationships with inmates were spread. According to Diana Hooper, one inmate said 'he had been told by a certain correctional officer that I was giving natives hand jobs.'

Overall, it appears that one brief liaison with a colleague left Diana Hooper particularly vulnerable to rumours concerning her sexuality and purported sexual improprieties with inmates.

Sharon West also was subjected to rumours about her sex life. In this case, following from O'Reilly frequently scheduling her to go on transfers with him, rumours started that they were having an affair. Although O'Reilly was making unwelcome sexual propositions to Sharon West (which will be discussed below), there was no truth to the rumours that an affair was taking place.

The spotlight on female correctional officers' sexuality sometimes took the form of direct and unappreciated queries by male colleagues. For example, Karla Preston was interrogated one day while going through the sallyport: 'they asked me if I owned a vibrator, if I knew how to use a vibrator.' On another occasion, she says, they 'asked me if I knew how to provide oral sex, and they went on to describe how I should be doing it.'

Unwelcome Intrusions and Sexual Propositions

As well as suffering anonymous attacks on their property, women at the Wakefield Jail received harassing telephone calls. According to Nora Diamond: 'At one point in time, numerous women were receiving harassing telephone calls ... [I]t seemed to go in cycles. If one of [us] started getting them, it would go full circle ... Sometimes the caller wouldn't say anything ... sometimes [they] would breathe heavily.'

According to Melissa Jackson, in her case, the calls went beyond silence and heavy breathing to involve 'physical threats.' At the time she received these threatening telephone calls: 'My number was unlisted except for people at the Jail. And I had a tracer put on my line, but it didn't help. I got my phone number changed and the calls stopped. I was angry. They came at all hours, but mainly in the night at 1–2–3 in the morning. I lived alone. I was missing out on overtime, so I eventually gave my number back to the Jail. The calls resumed.'

Receiving anonymous and threatening or sexual phone calls is an intimidating experience. Moreover, it is important to note that, although male correctional officers were the most likely source of the calls, the women – given their dependence on being telephoned to be called in for work – did not have the option of keeping their phone numbers from jail.

Several of the women reported being more directly sexually propositioned by their colleagues. For example, Sharon West reported that James Randell 'wanted to know about my personal life all the time. He wanted to be involved in my life.' Meanwhile, O'Reilly told her 'it would be OK to have an affair if his wife did not find out.' Sharon West was not interested. But O'Reilly persisted, for example by pestering her to give him a map to her place. O'Reilly offered to come over and help her study for examinations. She refused.

Karla Preston endured multiple intrusions and propositions by Fred Ferguson:

> He asked me if I had a boyfriend. When I said no, he said: 'What's wrong with the guys in the area? Don't they see how good looking you are?' He asked where I drank at nights. I don't drink ... He invited me to his house. He told me he would have a bottle of liquor waiting there for me. He said: 'I'm expecting you,' and [made it clear] that his wife would not be there.
>
> The next day, he asked: 'What happened you? I was waiting for you. You weren't there.' I felt the invitation was always open.
>
> Ferguson asked me if I wanted to go fishing. He asked me to go swimming. He asked me to go water skiing. I felt pressured by these invitations.

Fred Ferguson not only once, but repeatedly asked Karla Preston whether she had a boyfriend, if she wanted to go drinking, and if she wanted to come to his home. The provision of a uniform to Karla Preston was also marked by harassment by Ferguson, and additionally made her vulnerable to comments by other males. As she explained:

> There was no uniform for the cooks. And Fred Ferguson was looking at me one day, and didn't like what I had on. So he told Randell to get a new uniform ... When we got the new uniform, I was extremely shocked to see that they were transparent. When I told Fred Ferguson about it, he told me: 'that is the uniform. If you don't like it, you can go naked.'
>
> As I washed the uniform, it became thinner. The world could see my bra and panties when I wore it. Comments were made about the uniforms. The male population liked the uniform. I felt self-conscious, embarrassed, outraged. I would wear a large, long sweatshirt over top of it.

Unwanted and Sexual Touching

While much of the discrimination and harassment experienced by women at the Wakefield Jail has taken insidious, sometimes subtle, and verbal forms, some women have also experienced blatant sexual harassment. Specifically, they have been subject to unwanted and sexual touching. At least nine male colleagues – from a superintendent to lieutenants and correctional officers – were identified as engaging in such behaviours. Overall, as described below, these behaviours reveal that the culture at the Wakefield Jail reflected a poisoned environment where some of the offensive actions of men could well be defined as criminal.

Karla Preston reported that one day, when she was making cookies, James Randell 'grabbed my breast ... [He] also grabbed me one day in the stockroom, he grabbed me, forced me against the wall, and forced me to kiss him.'

Diana Hooper reported that correctional officer Maurice blew in her ear on at least six occasions. Other colleagues also intruded on her. For example, Lt Laroche 'would rub his leg against mine, and make a comment – "I wish you were not married."'

Of correctional officer Cooper, she said: 'He poked me in the behind with keys, and made a comment about my behind, and then [he] said – '"I guess you are going to charge me."'

Diana Hooper also reported that correctional officer George Gagnon harassed her in a similar way: 'I was walking upstairs and Gagnon poked [a] key in my backside. The second time it happened, I said "last warning."'

On another occasion, said Diana Hooper, correctional officer James Randell 'snapped my bra.'

Sharon West also experienced multiple sexual harassment. In her case, she said of James Randell that 'he grabbed my rear end in front of the kitchen door. He came from behind me. It wasn't a touch. It was [done] forcibly.' She also described how James Randell sexually propositioned her when they were doing transfers together: 'I did several transfers to Westbury with Mr. Randell. He would say he was looking for a mistress, and I would be his candidate. He had a plane, and he wanted to take me to his remote cottage ... These conversations took place on every trip we went on. I actually said to him that he was too old, and he didn't need a mistress.'

Even on her last day at work, Sharon West reported, she was not spared by James Randell: 'I dropped off my uniform on the last day at work, and [James Randell] was in charge of the [uniform] stores.

So I went in to drop it off, and he grabbed my hand, and he pulled me toward him, and tried to kiss me. And I pulled my hand away and left.'

Sharon West also felt physically intruded upon by O'Reilly. She reported: 'O'Reilly would brush up against me all the time in the hall and grab my waist. [He would] pinch me in the waist. He would kick me as he was walking by ... O'Reilly would put his arm around my shoulder. [This] happened once or twice. I felt uncomfortable ...'

On top of this sexual harassment, some women experienced aggressive attacks by men. For example, Micheline Pelletier reported that on one occasion Gerry Kennedy 'slammed the door in my face ... I asked aloud: "Is it something I said?" One individual said: "It's not what you said. It's who you are and the parts you carry."'

Nora Diamond reported an incident where Lt Laroche 'took his Bic lighter and attempted to set fire to the crotch of another female's pants. He said he was trying to start a "brush" or "bush" fire.'

Nora Diamond reported that she had been attacked on several occasions, in the confinement of the sallyport, by Joe Robert: 'I have been restrained by Joe Robert in the sallyport ... We were waiting in the sallyport. He was behind me, and he put his two arms around me, and lifted me off the floor. I was very surprised. You are in an environment where you are looking over your shoulder for inmates to do that. And I don't think it's fair to say that we should have to watch our co-workers for that.' On another occasion, she reported that 'Joe Robert came through the sallyport area and pinned me against the door.'

Such unwarranted and abusive assaults on the women can only be considered reprehensible and entirely unacceptable. It is disturbing, moreover, that so many different officers have been identified by the women as engaging in such behaviour. Not only discrimination and harassment, but also abusive behaviour must be recognized as generalized problems evidenced at the Wakefield Jail.

The Wakefield Jail as a Poisoned Environment

The research literature on women working in prisons for men commonly illustrates women's problems with respect to the male culture, micro-inequities, gender discrimination, and sexual harassment. But documented allegations of assault, and sexual assault, are comparatively rare. By contrast, the extent and pervasiveness of unwanted and sexual touching experienced by women at the Wakefield Jail – some of which crosses the border of legality – suggest that the culture of the jail in the early 1990s could be described as a poisoned environment.

That the Wakefield Jail embodied a poisoned environment is further revealed in the limited effectiveness of the ministry's responses in containing and ending problems of gender-based discrimination and harassment. Although some of the most blatant forms of sexual harassment, as well as the worst excesses of foul language, appear to have modified following Workplace Discrimination and Harassment Prevention training, and the transfer of Superintendent Ferguson (the most senior offender), many indicators of gender-based discrimination and harassment persisted in 1993 and 1994. For example, some women claimed that they continued to experience limitations on the hours of work available to them and differential assignments (for example, in the context of a situation being defined as an 'emergency'). In addition, women continued to be passed over in hiring and promotion. Derogatory comments, jokes, and cartoons were also a continuing feature of everyday life in the jail during this period.

Indeed, far from ending gender-based discrimination and harassment, it appears that Workplace Discrimination and Harassment Prevention training had – albeit often in subtle ways – exacerbated some of the very problems that were supposed to be addressed.[20]

Overall, the effectiveness of this exceptionally poisoned environment in excluding women from the male culture of the Wakefield Jail is mirrored in the fact that, by the summer of 1997, with only two female correctional officers – one of them casual – remaining, there were even fewer female correctional officers than there had been in the jail in the late 1980s and early 1990s. A review of women's feelings following discrimination and harassment helps to explain how the male culture of the Wakefield Jail facilitated the attrition, rather than the inclusion, of female workers.

Women's Feelings Following Discrimination and Harassment

> The adverse consequences of sexual harassment are not limited to the victim's job or work environment but may also extend to the victim's health and well-being. Victims of sexual harassment often suffer psychological and physical consequences in addition to economic consequences. Stress, fear and anxiety are frequently experienced by sexual harassment victims, both on and off the job, and they may eventually feel listless, powerless, and emotionally depressed. Victims may also experience decreased ambition, a dread of going to work, and a loss of self-confidence and self-esteem. Physically, victims may experience symptoms such as insomnia, headaches, neck and backaches, stomach problems, and hypertension. In some cases, victims are reduced to the point of psychological and physical breakdown, to such an extent that they require hospitalization. (Aggarwal 1992, 115)

Gender-based discrimination and harassment at the Wakefield Jail have had extremely debilitating consequences for the women concerned. Inquiries into the complaints have also been very stressful. Women have described feeling:

'worthless'	'scared'	'uneasy'
'belittled'	'mad'	'uncomfortable'
'very vulnerable'	'enraged'	'self-conscious'
'threatened'	'defensive'	'embarrassed'
'extremely threatened'	'unwelcome'	'outraged'
'worried'	'very hurt'	'shocked'
'insecure'	'surprised'	'unhappy'
'violated'	'an emotional wreck'	'intimidated'

These feelings had far-reaching consequences for some of the women. They affected the women's lives beyond the workplace. For example, Karla Preston continually worried about losing her job, and about being unable to provide for her children. Her concern was understandable, not least in light of the progressive reduction in hours which she experienced. After her experience of sexual harassment, Karla Preston had problems with her children, and also 'had a hard time with relationships, low self-esteem, low self-worth ... I tried to deny [the harassment], [I] felt I didn't want to get out of my bed. I tried to hide. [I] didn't want to deal with the children, and didn't cope very well.'

In trying to deal with the situation, Karla Preston sought medical help. This eventually became the stimulus to the first formal complaint. But the complaint processes, their repercussions, and aftermath, were also stressful. Karla Preston had to take several sick leaves, and was hospitalized. 'Now,' she reported to the Grievance Settlement Board in October of 1994, 'I feel physical symptoms. I feel like I would rather be anywhere else [than the Wakefield Jail]. And the only reason I continue is because of my children.'

Other women also experienced physical symptoms, and sought medical help. For example, Nora Diamond reported that, owing to O'Reilly's 'nitpicking' and discrimination, 'I didn't want to go to work. I would vomit before work. I had severe headaches. I developed a grind in my mouth, and had to purchase a bite-plate because I ground my teeth so badly at night. I developed an ulcer. [I am] still nursing an ulcer.'

For Nora Diamond, the processes and consequences of complaints were again extremely stressful. She needed medical attention. After the complaints were initiated, she said:

> I saw my family physician who instructed me to take 6 weeks off. At the time I was actually vomiting blood. In normal circumstances, a casual [correctional officer] doesn't have sick time benefits. I didn't see any alternative but to go to work. So I proceeded to enter the workplace with a lot of drugs ... A lot of this medication, especially Ativan, makes you very sleepy ... I also lost a substantial amount of weight – 25 lbs. My mouth would be ulcered. I had to go to the doctor to get that fixed up.

Diana Hooper similarly reported being 'mentally stressed and distressed. My job was the cause.' She was also medically ordered to take time off. Around the time of the complaints being laid, she reported: 'I felt this pressure in the abdomen. And I felt I could not breathe. And I was getting nausea. I was getting 3 hours of sleep a night. I kept going over in my mind what was happening ... I was having trouble doing daily things, such as washing [my] face, etc. I was lying in bed all day, I couldn't care for myself, kids, or husband.' Diana Hooper went on medical leave in November 1992, and was still on leave at the time of the hearings before the Grievance Settlement Board in 1994–95. Diana Hooper's doctor provided testimony to the Grievance Settlement Board. According to him, she was one of the most profoundly depressed persons he had ever treated and her depression was consequent to the sexual harassment and discrimination she experienced as a female correctional officer.

As noted not only in research on women working in prisons for men, but on women experiencing discrimination and harassment in the workplace more generally (see Aggarwal 1992, 115; Kadar 1983, 364), the stress victims experience has serious consequences, not only for the women's security and self-esteem, but also for their desire and ability to do their jobs. At the Wakefield Jail, women have not only constituted an even smaller proportion of the staff than is generally the case in Ontario institutions, but have also evidenced a high rate of turnover. Here, the feelings and response of Sharon West reflect the ultimate effectiveness of gender-based discrimination and harassment in undermining and excluding female workers: 'During the last of my days at the Wakefield Jail I was crying a lot. I didn't want to be around anybody. Nobody knew what I was going through. I sought medical advice. And she told me to quit my job. And I took her advice – I couldn't carry on ... I was very stressed and depressed ... I resigned from the Wakefield Jail.'

5 Impediments to Reporting Discrimination and Harassment

Research on Impediments to Reporting

> Although it is estimated that 50 to 90 percent of women have been harassed in the workplace, few incidents are reported because of the employer's failure to provide a safe environment for the lodging of complaints ... Other reasons for low rates of reporting include the fear of ridicule, embarrassment, reprisals, and of not being believed. (Canadian Panel 1993, 245)

As has been documented, research literature is consistent in identifying the discrimination and harassment experienced by women working in prisons for men. The literature is also consistent in identifying women's fear of, and impediments to, reporting their experiences. The fear of reporting appears to be almost as universal as the problem of harassment itself. The reluctance of women at the Wakefield Jail to come forward with complaints can, therefore, be seen as characteristic of a more general trend.

Why are women reluctant to complain? What are the obstacles they face? A review of the literature suggests, firstly, that the subtle nature of much harassment is an important explanatory factor. How, for example, does a female officer substantiate the claim that a male colleague '"undresses me with his eyes"'? (Zimmer 1986, 97). Such a form of harassment, while thoroughly demeaning in its consequences, is difficult to address through formal or legal procedures.

The second reason for not formally complaining is the perception on the part of female officers that they will not receive support from supervisors and administrators, especially when these positions are predominantly filled by men. As one female officer explained: 'When this male investigator tried to kiss me at work, I didn't tell anyone. It's not good to make waves that way. Your supervisors think you're just trying to cause trouble' (quoted in Jurik 1985, 386). That managers themselves may be sexist and not take women's complaints seriously is a major problem. It is difficult, for example, to imagine that any woman would bring a complaint to the administrator who commented – about a woman who had apparently quit after months of harassment – 'I can't believe anyone propositioned *her*. Have you ever seen her? She just wishes someone would make an advance at her and is angry because no one did' (quoted in Zimmer 1986, 97). As we shall see in the case of the Wakefield Jail, these general problems with reporting harassment to male supervisors are exacerbated when supervisors themselves are amongst those who discriminate against and harass women.

A third reason for not complaining, one related to the fear that they will not receive support, is women's fear that they will be further harassed, and perhaps even lose their jobs. This concern is especially strong for women who are in temporary, probationary, or otherwise insecure positions. In this context, it is important to note that, of those four women who experienced the worst forms of harassment at the Wakefield Jail, three of them were in casual – as opposed to full-time – positions. As indicated in the literature, as well as in the accounts of their situations by these individuals, women fear that if they complain, they run the risk that supervisors will give them a poor evaluation, and that this will impede their chances with respect to hiring and promotion.

Overall, the potential negative consequences of complaining are seen as greater than the potential benefits. Meanwhile, in the past, guard unions have often been of limited assistance. In part, this has been because the majority of union members have been male. Moreover, Zimmer (1986, 98) observes, as 'basically adversarial organizations, unions are best equipped to fight management, not solve conflicts between union members ... Unions typically defend members against all types of administrative disciplinary charges, and the implication of this general policy is that unions have had virtually no role in helping women solve the harassment problem.' Indeed, in those few cases in the United States, up until the mid-1980s where management did support women's claims, the unions 'backed the alleged harassers.'

Lack of union support has also been a problem in Canada. For example, in the early 1980s, Marlene Kadar (1983, 369) commented on the general resistance to unions addressing women's issues, and specifically observed that 'even when individual men and women wanted to support a campaign against sexual harassment within the union, others felt the pressure from peers not to break rank, not to diverge from the dominant view, or the needs, of the membership.' As of the early 1990s, the Canadian Panel on Violence Against Women (1993, 246) could similarly note that '[m]any unions, particularly those in a predominantly male work force, continue to reflect patriarchal assumptions and have not chosen to acknowledge harassment within their own membership.'

At the same time, although unions continue to be in an awkward situation with respect to issues of sexual harassment and conflict between members, the position of many of them on gender issues has improved.[1] No doubt this is due in part to the growing participation of women in the unions themselves, including at senior levels. For example, by the early 1990s, in the Public Service Alliance of Canada, women occupied 34 per cent of the chairs of union locals, and 48 per cent of the executive positions within locals (Canadian Panel 1993, 247). Also by that time, both the Canadian Labour Congress and the Canadian Auto Workers union were developing policy positions on issues of violence against women. Meanwhile, by the mid-1990s, the Ontario Public Service Employees Union had a woman (Leah Casselman) at the helm. The union had also demonstrated a growing awareness of, and concern about, gender-based discrimination and harassment. One tangible sign of this had been the negotiation of Articles A.1.1, 27.10.1, and 27.10.2, into the Collective Agreement. These articles are as follows:

ARTICLE A – NO DISCRIMINATION/EMPLOYMENT EQUITY

A.1.1 There shall be no discrimination practised by reason of race, ancestry, place of origin, colour, ethnic origin, citizenship, creed, sex, sexual orientation, age, marital status, family status, or handicap, as defined in section 10(1) of the Ontario Human Rights Code (OHRC).

SEXUAL HARASSMENT

27.10.1 All employees covered by this Agreement have a right to freedom from harassment in the workplace because of sex by his or her Employer or agent of the Employer or by another employee. Harassment means engaging in a course of vexatious comment or conduct that is known or ought reasonably to be known to be unwelcome.

27.10.2 Every employee covered by this Collective Agreement has a right to be free from,
   (a) a sexual solicitation or advance made by a person in a position to confer, grant or deny a benefit or advancement to the employee where the person making the solicitation or advance knows or ought reasonably to know that it is unwelcome; or
   (b) a reprisal or threat of reprisal for the rejection of a sexual solicitation or advance where the reprisal is made or threatened by a person in a position to confer, grant or deny a benefit or advancement to the employee.

In turn, the Ontario Public Services Employees Union has demonstrated its willingness in practice to carry such cases through to arbitration. The situation at the Wakefield Jail represents one instance of this.[2] Substantial amounts of time and money have been devoted by the Ontario Public Service Employees Union to assisting victims of harassment in this way.

The Ontario Public Service Employees Union's commitment to ending discrimination and harassment as they affect women (and other marginalized groups) was also indicated when the union's convention in May 1991 'passed an Employment Equity Policy and Plan, fully supporting employment equity principles, aims and objectives and "zero tolerance" for workplace discrimination and harassment' (Employment Systems Review 1994, 111). Within the

Ministry of Correctional Services, the Employment Systems Review Task Force and other joint management-union initiatives have given a practical expression to the union's willingness to confront and overcome real problems of discrimination and harassment. One of the major challenges such joint ventures face is how to translate this commitment into similar one at the local level, where such progressive stances are sometimes far less evident.

In general, research on women working in prisons for men reveals that it is not just the harassment, but the perceived lack of recourse, which subjects women to humiliating and alienating situations. In the absence of satisfactory means of redress, women adopt various coping mechanisms. For example, they may avoid male guards, and dress and behave in ways thought to minimize the possibility of harassment. Some women choose to terminate their employment, or seek work elsewhere. Others continue to work, and do the best they can to put up with the stress. In the words of one woman (quoted in Zimmer 1986, 100): 'Every day I wake up and ask myself if I can face another day. It's not the work, it's not the danger, it's not the inmates – it's the attitude of the male officers. One day I wanted to quit but took a sick day instead and decided to try it a bit longer. Right now I can't tell you if I'll make it [through the probationary period] or not ...'

Each of the factors discussed in the research is relevant in explaining women's reticence in reporting at the Wakefield Jail. In particular, the role of management in contributing to, and exacerbating, problems must be regarded as a key explanatory factor. This chapter will continue by looking again at the women's accounts, with a focus on the involvement of managers (including supervisors) in discriminatory and harassing behaviour. It will also present reasons given by the women for not complaining, and for not complaining sooner. The chapter will conclude with an examination of problems and reprisals following the initiation of complaints.

Management Staff's Contribution to, and Exacerbation of, Problems

How can a woman complain to her supervisor about sexual harassment by her peers when the supervisor is a participant? How can a

woman complain to management when the agency appears to condone such practices? (Breed 1981, 41)

One would hope – especially in light of the Ontario government's
policy on Workplace Discrimination and Harassment Prevention –
that management staff at the Wakefield Jail would have been at the
forefront of efforts to recognize and deal with harassment. Unfortunately, this was not the case, and managers contributed to problems both prior and subsequent to the implementation of the policy.
Specifically, some management staff[3] ignored, condoned, or affirmed
discriminatory and harassing behaviours towards women, and themselves harassed female workers.

With respect to blatant and persistent sexual harassment, former
superintendent Fred Ferguson was one of the worst offenders. In
addition to using foul language and making offensive and sexist
comments, he propositioned women, discriminated against them,
and made their work lives miserable.

Superintendent Fred Ferguson took advantage of his position of
power to provoke, taunt, and harass women. For example, Francis
Lalonde reported that Ferguson was 'very crude' and 'rude,' and
would walk through the office and refer to the female clerical staff
as '"fucking pigs"' or '"goddamn fucking pigs."' He would also call
people 'cocksuckers' and 'pricks.' As noted earlier, when Francis
Lalonde received flowers from her husband, Fred Ferguson said:
'"He just wants to get into your pants."' On another occasion, he
asked Francis Lalonde to come to his home, ostensibly to choose
colours. Nora Diamond also suffered from Ferguson's taunting, for
example, when he claimed that she would have to sleep in the same
room as her male colleague while on a training course.

The brunt of Fred Ferguson's harassment was felt by the casual
cook, Karla Preston. As has already been documented, she reported
that Fred Ferguson repeatedly propositioned and demeaned her.
In doing so, he took advantage of his position as superintendent in
trying to curry Karla Preston's favour by supplying her with institu-
tion-issue items, such as a coat. His harassment of her is arguably
reprehensible, not only in terms of the abuse of authority over a
female casual staff member which it involved, but also in its fluctua-

tion from sexist chivalry to denigration. Thus, on one occasion, Ferguson is said to have stated 'we don't want you freezing your buns off, of course give my favourite girl a coat,' and then, on another occasion, when Karla Preston had questioned having to wear a uniform that was transparent, he replied 'that is the uniform. If you don't like it, you can go naked.'

Meanwhile, the women's accounts indicate that Fred Ferguson was authoritarian or unresponsive when they raised concerns about gender issues. For example, when Nora Diamond questioned the mixed-gender composition of a transfer of four inmates, and her assignment to travel with them (discussed below), Superintendent Ferguson labelled this as 'insubordination.' When Diana Hooper raised questions with him concerning O'Reilly's instructions (to officer Fischer) – namely, that she be passed over as shift IC [supervisor/'in charge'] in favour of any male that might be available, even one with less seniority – he did not resolve the matter.[4]

Fred Ferguson's insensitivity to female colleagues' opinions and feelings was further revealed by his actions in connection with a going-away party for correctional officer Wallace. Apparently it was Ferguson's idea that the event be held in a strip club. Given this choice of venue (and that some women were not aware of its nature prior to the event), women who wished to pay their respects to their colleague were compelled to do so in an inappropriate environment. As if this was not discomfiting enough, Fred Ferguson clearly knew the stripper, and invited her to sit on his lap.

All of these alleged actions by Fred Ferguson are very disturbing. But they are even more so in light of the fact that there had previously been a human-rights complaint filed against him by a woman at another jail. It is understandable that women at the Wakefield Jail would feel offended, not only by Ferguson's behaviour, but also by the Ministry of Correctional Services' apparent betrayal of its responsibility to female staff. It seems irresponsible to place such an individual in a position of authority over women, and particularly in a relatively small institution where women often have had to work in isolation among males. In the case of Fred Ferguson, it is not only he, but also senior ministry management, who appear to be at fault.[5]

One of the ways in which management at the Wakefield Jail more generally contributed to a poisoned environment is through making offensive remarks. Karla Preston, for example, reported that 'both correctional officers and management were making offensive remarks.' In the case of Lieutenant Laroche, not only was he one of the offenders in this regard, but he also harassed women, physically intruded on them, and generally engaged in a wide range of objectionable and unprofessional behaviour. According to the women, his actions in front of female staff – most of which have already been mentioned – included the following. Lt Laroche:

- used abusive language to staff and inmates.
- called Kathy Poirier at home, and said: 'Veut-tu travailler plut?' ('Do you want to work, old cunt?').
- having talked with his wife on the phone, grabbed his crotch, and while rubbing it said: 'I wish she would not talk to me like that because I get so horny, and now I have to stay here all night.'
- rubbed his leg against Diana Hooper's, and said: 'I wish you were not married.' When she told him to stop, he did it again.
- said to Nora Diamond, while she was waiting in the sallyport to go home: 'Go on, get out of here. Go home and fuck your husband.'
- told Sharon West that he had his foreskin removed, and that it had greatly improved his sex life.
- grabbed his groin and snickered.
- used terrible language and referred to genitals, etc.
- would find it humorous to walk up to people and fart. He said he was so constipated that he had to stick his finger up his asshole to pick it out.
- very late at night, while on a transfer from Westbury with Sharon West, directed her to pull the van over, and went into the back of the van and changed his clothes. He snickered and said not to watch.
- harassed Patricia Murray, and called her 'irresponsible' and 'undependable.'
- took a Bic lighter and attempted to set fire to the crotch of a female correctional officer's pants, saying he was trying to set a 'brush' or 'bush' fire.

It is hard to imagine that a woman would feel comfortable in bringing concerns about gender issues to Lt. Laroche.

According to the grievors, harassing and discriminatory behaviour – albeit of a less blatantly sexual kind – was also evidenced by Lieutenant O'Reilly. One example of this is the Westbury transfer incident of August 1989. On that occasion, O'Reilly scheduled Nora Diamond to be the officer travelling with four inmates, three male and one female, locked with them in the back of the vehicle. Nora Diamond had questions about the safety of the transfer. She therefore got union representation and went to O'Reilly with her concerns. It is understandable that a correctional officer – male or female – might question this arrangement, especially given that two of the males had sexual offence charges. The transfer might also be seen as potentially volatile given that, in the words of Nora Diamond, the third male inmate 'was being removed from the Wakefield Jail because he was uncontrollable, bouncing off the walls in pain from advanced VD,' and the female inmate was charged with conspiracy to commit murder.

Whatever may have been the right decision about the safety of this planned transfer, O'Reilly's handling of the situation – and especially of Nora Diamond's concerns – was arguably insensitive, authoritarian, and paramilitaristic. Specifically, Nora Diamond reported that 'O'Reilly became very agitated about the situation.' According to her, O'Reilly said: '"She refused, she refused. I'm the boss. I call the shots. You do what you are told. Your input is of no value or consequence. You females are always crying for hours. I give you hours, and this is the thanks I get."'

According to Nora Diamond, O'Reilly then told her that the trip was off, and she was sent home. Diana Hooper was offered the same transfer, and refused it because it was unsafe. She was then counselled by O'Reilly for refusing an order. Later, the load was split, and the female inmate was taken separately. Nora Diamond was not offered an opportunity to do the transfer in the new configuration.

The next day, reported Nora Diamond, O'Reilly approached her with her contract and said: '"Do you realize this [contract] can be cancelled on one week's notice?"' O'Reilly filed an occurrence report. Nora Diamond filed a grievance.

Although O'Reilly later admitted that he was wrong about the transfer, and did not know the charges that the inmates had, this incident is just one example of a litany of objectionable behaviour on his part. Specifically, the women reported that O'Reilly:

- chastised Lt Page for scheduling females on O'Reilly's shift. O'Reilly said to Page that it made for a weak shift.
- commented, '[o]ne down and three to go,' after Sharon West quit her job.
- whited out Nora Diamond's hours, and gave them to another officer.
- told Diana Hooper that women make a weak shift. When Melissa Jackson and Diana Hooper were scheduled to work the same shift, O'Reilly called in sick. Later that day, O'Reilly arrived in street clothes and told James Randell he called in sick because he did not want to work with two females.
- was IC [supervisor/'in charge'] and instructed Fischer as shift IC that he did not care who was the next shift IC as long as it was not a female, and especially Diana Hooper. He later said he had been drinking that day and could not remember saying that.
- was IC when an inmate was being admitted. O'Reilly called for an officer to the front. Diana Hooper, as 'keys,' responded. When she arrived at the duty office, O'Reilly refused to let her into the sallyport and said he wanted a male correctional officer.
- ordered Diana Hooper to clean the male washrooms.
- made Diana Hooper's life (and those of people working with her) miserable. He dreamt up assignments, changed the assignments, and then changed them again.
- encouraged an inmate to file a sexual harassment complaint against Diana Hooper (Diana Hooper was escorting the inmate to the shower, and the inmate was concerned that she would watch him shower; but a female officer never watches a male inmate shower at the Wakefield Jail).
- while working with Diana Hooper, and when two Ontario Provincial Police officers (one male and one female) came to the Wakefield Jail to escort an inmate charged with murder, said to the male police officer: 'You would think they would send some-

one more capable.' O'Reilly also said that the female officers at the Wakefield Jail fell all over him.

- passed over Diana Hooper in assigning transfers, even when assigning her would have used less overtime, and a female inmate was being transferred.
- checked Diana Hooper's work much more closely than male officers' work, to the point of going down on his hands and knees to check for dust on the floor.

Sharon West also reported that O'Reilly took advantage of his supervisory position to romantically pursue her. Specifically, O'Reilly scheduled the transfers in such a way that they did many together. In the course of transfers, Sharon West said, it was clear he wanted to have an affair. Sharon West was not interested, but O'Reilly persisted. By spending so much transfer time with Sharon West, and by actions such a taking her on an alternate route via a former superintendent's apartment, the stage was set by O'Reilly whereby rumours could spread in the institution that he and Sharon West were having an affair. O'Reilly also told Sharon West about an occasion when he had sex with a woman in the closet of a banquet hall at a ministry training session. O'Reilly said it was okay to have affairs so long as his wife did not find out. Pursuant to all of this, O'Reilly's offer to use his pull in securing Sharon West a full-time position can be read as an effort by him to further his personal prospects with her.

Overall, Sharon West's experience with O'Reilly, similarly to Karla Preston's with Fred Ferguson, affirm Breed's (1981, 41) observation that much harassment 'is subtle and could be considered flirting, except that the elements become distorted when the flirter is your boss. No male correctional officer has ever been asked to meet his lieutenant at a nearby bar or apartment, nor has he been faced with the innuendo that rejection of advances will have an impact on future assignments and promotions. The repercussions for a female correctional officer ... are literally that she's damned if she does, and she's damned if she doesn't.'

In the case of O'Reilly, training under the Workplace Discrimination and Harassment Prevention policy appears not to have been successful in increasing his sensitivity to gender-related issues. Early in 1993 – after Workplace Discrimination and Harassment Prevention training had been provided for the jail staff – O'Reilly was accused of bringing a movie with sexually graphic content to work, and watching it while he was the shift supervisor.

Again, it is not difficult to imagine that women with potential complaints about issues of gender-based discrimination and harassment would be reticent in approaching such a supervisor.

Overall, it is clear that some managers at the Wakefield Jail have not only allowed a climate of discrimination and harassment to flourish, but have been primary contributors to gender-based discrimination and harassment. The existence of harassers among management has been a major impediment to reporting and dealing with gender-related problems at the Wakefield Jail.

Why Did Women Not Complain, or Not Complain Sooner?

A woman faced with unwanted and unsolicited sexual advances may feel confused, as well as frustrated and angry. She may not know how to react to the situation. She may think:

Should I confront the harasser? … Should I discuss it with fellow employees? Should I complain to the employer (the boss of the harasser, if any)? If I tell them, how will they react? Would they believe me? Would they not say I invited it on myself? Would I be labelled a troublemaker? Would they make my life hell on the job? What if I am fired? Where would I get another job? I have to have a job to make ends meet. (Aggarwal 1992, 127)

Questions are often asked about why women who are victims of discrimination, and especially of sexual harassment, do not complain. Such questions could also be raised concerning the women at the Wakefield Jail.[6] Specifically, various forms of objectionable behaviour have occurred at the Wakefield Jail since 1984, when Diana Hooper first started working there. Yet it was only in October 1992 that complaints were initiated under the Workplace Discrimination and Harassment Prevention policy by Karla Preston. Preliminary inquiries into her complaints facilitated two other women, Nora Diamond and Diana Hooper, in coming forward. Why, it has been asked, did it take so long for women to complain?

The first point to be made is that, prior to formally complaining, women *did* complain: they attempted to rebuff unwelcome behaviour in their own different ways. For example, Karla Preston repeatedly told Fred Ferguson that she had no interest in any of the activities – drinking, swimming, fishing, water skiing – that he was propositioning her to join him in. Sometimes women expressed their displeasure and asked for an apology (and occasionally received one).

Several of the women were more forthright and assertive in expressing their displeasure and discomfort. For example, Sharon West yelled at James Randell after he forcefully grabbed her rear end. When extremely provoked, Diana Hooper even physically retaliated against her colleagues' offensives. When correctional officer Maurice continually blew in her ear, she slapped him. When Lt Laroche rubbed his leg against her for the second time, she hit him. It is disturbing to learn that one colleague could be driven to striking another. Such behaviour is hardly the mark of a workplace with high professional standards. And it is also disturbing to learn that while Diana Hooper's physical rebuttals of correctional officer Maurice and Lt Laroche were successful in putting an end to the particular offensive behaviours, verbal efforts at rebuffing colleagues generally had less success.

Overall, it is notable that, despite severe duress, the women have not been vindictive toward their colleagues. Even in the course of telling the Grievance Settlement Board about the discrimination and harassment they encountered, women were generous in identifying their colleagues' positive characteristics. As is often the case with women's responses to abuse more generally, the long-term consequences of these victimizations have been felt more by the victims themselves than the perpetrators. As documented, some of the women became stressed and depressed, as well as physically and emotionally debilitated. Rather than lashing out at their colleagues, they tried to cope alone, and sometimes with the help of medical professionals.

In this context, it is important to again note that the first formal complaint took place largely as the result of the advice and intervention of Karla Preston's doctor. In turn, Karla Preston's initiative facilitated others in coming forward. Clearly, a degree of strength is required to make a complaint. This is evident in Karla Preston's response to a question about why she did not complain about incidents with correctional officer Randell, including his having grabbed her breast, and having grabbed her, forced her against a wall, and forced her to kiss him: 'I was an emotional wreck. I'm not that strong, I can only do so much. If it happened today, yes, I could now do it. At that time I couldn't – I'm sorry, I wish I did.'

On the one hand, women who have been discriminated against and harassed experience a decline in their emotional and personal strength. They often internalize their suffering, and are debilitated by it. On the other hand, the possibility of making a complaint appears to require having exceptional emotional strength. This combination reduces the probability of complaints being made.

The question arises: why do women feel that strength is needed in making complaints? The answer to this lies in their awareness of the many impediments to making complaints. Specifically, as identified by the women, and as elaborated on below, impediments to reporting at the Wakefield Jail have included fear of their colleagues' reactions, fear of their supervisors' reactions, a lack of knowledge about procedures available for complaining, the fear of reprisals, and a perceived lack of support from the union.

That women feared their colleagues' reactions is exemplified by Diana Hooper in her explanation of why she did not complain about being sent to clean an inmate's cell (a task not undertaken by male correctional officers): 'I did not report this to the Superintendent. You cannot cry every time someone says or does anything, or else it appears to your fellow officers that you are a rat. You have to deal with it. My way was to withdraw and try to deal with it.'

As this statement indicates, for a woman to complain is to risk violating the unwritten code of solidarity among correctional officer colleagues. In this context, research observations on policing are relevant. Specifically, it has been observed that a major attribute of the occupational subculture of police is a 'solidarity among officers that includes a "blue shield" of secrecy and in-group support' (Griffiths and Verdun-Jones 1994, 85). Such solidarity precludes drawing the attention of superiors to a colleague's failings. Violating the code is to invite the ultimate exclusionary label of 'rat.' In such a situation, the potential negative consequences of a complaint would appear to far outweigh any potential gain. As shall later be discussed (with respect to the threat of reprisals), Diana Hooper's fears in this instance were realistically grounded.

While women at the Wakefield Jail were fearful of their colleagues' potential reaction, their fear of their supervisors' reactions appears to have been even more significant. Thus Karla Preston reported that, although subject to serious sexual harassment by James Randell, one of the reasons she did not complain is because she would have had to go to Superintendent Ferguson. Given that Ferguson was himself harassing her, it is understandable that she did not want anything to do with him. Meanwhile, it was difficult for her to do anything about Ferguson himself, for, as she said: 'Fred Ferguson had power over me. He had the power to fire me, to give me shifts, and to take them away from me.'

Sharon West similarly explained why she did not complain about James Randell grabbing her rear end. In the first place, Superintendent Haines was there, and snickered and laughed with James Randell after this incident. More generally, Sharon West explained: 'I did not bring it up [make a complaint] because I was a casual officer. I wanted a promotion. I did not want to make waves. I did not want someone showing up at my door.'

Later, when O'Reilly, as her superior, constantly pestered and propositioned her, it was again difficult to complain given his position: 'He was my superior. I wanted a promotion. I did not want to be a troublemaker. I wanted my contract. I was the low man on the totem pole ... I thought that if I told O'Reilly to stop, he would have done something against me.'

Nora Diamond also described the condoning of abusive behaviour by superiors, which would make it difficult to complain: 'An individual [Joe Robert] put me in a headlock in front of the Lieutenant. The Lieutenant did not say anything ... It was as if it was accepted behaviour to be spoken to in a demeaning and hostile manner, and it was run of the mill to be rough-housed.'

In short, as exemplified in these comments, when confronted with problems of sexual harassment, it does not appear viable to go to individuals who are themselves a part, and sometimes the source, of a problem.

Women's lack of knowledge about procedures for dealing with complaints was alluded to by Nora Diamond (who only proceeded with her complaint after being contacted by the Workplace Discrimination and Harassment Prevention investigators): 'I was not familiar with the Workplace Discrimination and Harassment Prevention policy. I did not know the section in the collective agreement. At the onset, I thought is was behaviour I had to live with.'

Women's fear of reprisals is exemplified by Diana Hooper. Following the Westbury transfer incident, which she had refused (after Nora Diamond had already done so), O'Reilly talked to her about it. She said: 'He made a comment about [the] Ombudsman/Human Rights not taking complaints seriously if they receive too many. [He] suggested if I made a complaint to Human Rights they would call the Jail right away and it would be known. I took this as a threat.'

Later, once complaints had been initiated, the women's colleagues highlighted the ultimate reprisal that could be taken by the ministry, namely, that Wakefield Jail might be closed down. As Nora Diamond said: 'There was constant talk that because we had come forward, [it] would result in the Jail being closed, and it would all be our [the women's] fault.'

Finally, the perception that the union would not help, especially given her casual status, was expressed by Sharon West: 'Toward the end I complained to individuals in the union, and they wouldn't do anything for me. It was my last day, and I just wanted to get out as fast as I could.'

Overall, a variety of existing and perceived impediments, taken together with women's fears about the potential consequences that might follow from a complaint, help to explain women's reticence in complaining.

Problems and Reprisals Following the Initiation of Complaints

The atmosphere after complaints at the Jail was 40 below zero. (Nora Diamond)

Women's fears about the problems that might follow should complaints be initiated have been borne out in a variety of ways. Those few women working at the jail between late 1992, when complaints were initiated, and the conclusion of arbitration hearings in 1995, reported that the atmosphere at the jail was extremely strained and uncomfortable. Moreover, while the period following the complaints appears to have seen a decline in blatant sexual harassment (for example, in the form of unwanted touching and sexual propositions), women continued to be subject to insidious, and sometimes anonymous, forms of harassment.

A major focus in this ongoing harassment was the issue of complaints themselves, and the actions that were taken pursuant to the complaints. Overall, some women were not only targeted for making complaints, but were also effectively held responsible for problems in the ministry's handling of complaints. Here, some of these problems and reprisals with respect, firstly, to male correctional officers, and, secondly, supervisors and management at the jail, will be discussed.

Where correctional officers are concerned, according to Karla Preston, following the initiation of complaints: 'I have been ostracized ... [and] a few officers refuse to speak to me.'

As these comments indicate, colleagues' hostility largely took an exclusionary form. It also, said Karla Preston, took an 'underground' form: 'They were very, very angry with me. This is when the "underground" started happening; the doodles, memos, little messages.' As elaborated by Karla Preston, one of the 'doodles' was put on a chartboard: 'There was a female saying: "I have a complaint," and then a cartoon of a male (which said Mr. Laroche). And the male was saying: "Fuck off, you're fired." The chart had been used for a management Workplace Discrimination and Harassment Prevention meeting.'

That Karla Preston has been ostracized was confirmed by another cook, Kerry Beauchamp: 'After the Workplace Discrimination and Harassment Prevention complaint, there was a cold shoulder. Karla was being cooling [sic] accepted ... not treated the same way as before ... People did not spend time with her. People did not talk with her ...'

Nora Diamond similarly reported occasions of being ostracized. Specifically, she stated of the correctional officers following the complaints:

They were furious that we had sought outside help, [and] assistance. The group became very divisive. There was a freeze-out atmosphere.

On one occasion I entered a common spot during shift change. When I arrived there were 8 male officers in the room talking. And the second I walked through the door, there wasn't a word, and everybody hung their heads and looked at the floor. 30 seconds was like 30 minutes ... It was shocking, just like someone [had] cut with a knife.

When I got to my post that day, there was a cartoon left for me ...

On another occasion, reported Nora Diamond: 'There was a poster put up in the staff room downstairs (a Workplace Discrimination and Harassment Prevention poster). And someone had written on the poster: "stop unfair complaints."'

That the Workplace Discrimination and Harassment Prevention training that took place after the complaints was not successful in eliminating insensitive behaviour is further evident in Nora Diamond's account of what happened during the lunch break of a training session in the town of South Ridge. Male correctional officers (who had the keys to the ministry vehicle) said to her: '"you can come with us, we're going to Fanny's [a strip joint] ..." At the Workplace Discrimination and Harassment Prevention [training] they offered to take me to a strip joint. I said: "This training is really helping."'

Observations by Micheline Pelletier also reaffirmed that problems continued. Indeed, Micheline Pelletier's observations are of particular note, given that she commenced working at the Jail in July 1993, *after* many of the incidents and events that initially gave rise to formal complaints, and after various responses to the complaints had been undertaken (including the completion of some investigations, the imposition of penalties, and the initiation of training for jail staff). Micheline Pelletier's observations are also noteworthy because during the period following the complaints, as Diana Hooper was on leave, she was the only full-time female correctional officer at the Wakefield Jail, and was therefore more secure in her job than her female colleagues. As well, Micheline Pelletier's observations are notable given that she was not a formal complainant.

Relevant to correctional officers, Micheline Pelletier reported that:

- The language used was abusive with a lot of swearing. 'It made me upset, it made me cringe.'
- Gerry Kennedy refers to women as '"dames."' '[H]is attitude is that he does not want to see women correctional officers in the Jail, I believe.'
- Gerry Kennedy slammed a door in her face. And an individual said: '"It's not what you said, it's the parts you carry."'
- She was told that two women make a weak shift.
- The reaction of males to Workplace Discrimination and Harassment Prevention Training was 'negative – they didn't like outsiders coming in to settle their problems. During a human rights session, Mr. George Gagnon spoke up and said that female officers don't belong in the institution ... [his comment] made me feel defensive and unwelcome, and I surely had my work cut out to prove myself.'
- While working for [a Community College] in 1991, she became a Workplace Discrimination and Harassment Prevention advisor. In her time as advisor, she had never seen the kind of environment that she has seen at the Wakefield Jail.
- Jokes of a sexual and racial type were told in the workplace (to which she objected).

On the positive side, Micheline Pelletier has observed that, following training, sexual jokes decreased. Also, staff swearing decreased in her presence, and in some individuals was gone completely. Overall, however, it can be seen that basic problems persisted at the Wakefield Jail.

Where supervisors and management are concerned, ongoing problems were again evident. Some examples of this are also provided by Micheline Pelletier, in her observations that:

- A military hierarchy was evident at the Wakefield Jail.
- She was passed over two days in a row for medical escorts/transfers.
- Being passed over for escorts bothered her. But she did not go to the superintendent about it: 'I am not going to the Superintendent and squeal or rat out on them.'

- There were constant games being played. People were given jobs which it is known they do not like to do, as 'a way of getting back [at them].'

This final observation again suggests that, while some of the most blatant and sexual forms of harassment among management may have subsided, discrimination continued in its more subtle forms.

Ongoing problems with management must be considered as particularly serious. As discussed earlier, an institution's ability to succeed with respect to equity issues is strongly dependent on management. In this context, employees' ability to complain about a supervisor to another member of management is crucial. It is therefore disturbing to learn that, when Nora Diamond complained about O'Reilly, who, while in charge of the institution on night shift, watched a sexually graphic movie, Superintendent Smith said to her in response: '"next time I'll bring cheese."' Nora Diamond stated: 'I took that to mean he thought I was a rat.' This interpretation seems reasonable.

Such a statement by the superintendent undermines any trust women at the Wakefield Jail might have in the management's commitment to the cessation of discrimination and harassment. In addition, the fact that O'Reilly was censured for watching television while on duty, but apparently not for the *content* of what he was watching, must have further undermined faith in managerial commitment to the cessation of behaviour objectionable to women. At the Wakefield Jail, as in the case of Bell Cairn, the gendered nature of the behaviour and problem was often overlooked by management. Where in the case of Bell Cairn some credence might be given to an argument that in the early months of the offensive behaviour that took place, the gendered basis was not immediately apparent, it is difficult to see how any such argument could be made during the period following complaints at the Wakefield Jail. On the contrary, the ongoing failure of management to acknowledge the gender-based elements of offensive behaviour – such as a senior staff member watching a sexually graphic movie while in charge – must surely itself be read as a powerful and active contribution to gender-based discrimination and harassment.

Overall, the commitments expressed by the senior management of the Ministry of Correctional Services and the Ontario Public Services Employees Union to engaging in joint ventures toward improving the situation of women have stood in sharp contrast to the reality of the everyday culture at the Wakefield Jail: rather than working toward more satisfactorily including women, management and correctional officers at the Wakefield Jail appear to have worked in the direction of excluding them. Moreover, the increasingly subtle nature of some of these exclusionary tactics did not bode well for women who wished to challenge their exclusion. Given this environment, it is not surprising to learn that, although she only commenced work at the Wakefield Jail in 1993, by early 1995 Micheline Pelletier was considering looking elsewhere for a job. 'With a little luck,' she said, 'I'll be out of this ministry.'

In a situation where all but one of the female correctional officers and cooks at the Wakefield Jail continued to work on a casual or part-time basis; where the women generally could identify many problems that occurred following the laying of complaints and ministry responses, and where the *only* full-time female correctional officer was expressing a desire to get away from this job and ministry, a negative conclusion about the situation at the Wakefield Jail after gender-based problems there were brought to light seems unavoidable. The problems and reprisals that followed the initiation of complaints undermined and worked against the positive intentions of such remedies as were undertaken. Again, the fact that there were even fewer women among correctional officers at the jail in 1995 than was the case in the late 1980s and early 1990s, can be read as a tangible result of impediments to not only reporting, but successfully dealing with discrimination and harassment.

6 Responding to, and Ending, Discrimination and Harassment

Strategies toward Dealing with Discrimination and Harassment

Gender-based discrimination and harassment at the Wakefield Jail were an ongoing problem until at least the mid-1990s. Ministry attempts to deal with the problem were unsatisfactory. Although one of the worst offenders with respect to blatant sexual harassment – former superintendent Fred Ferguson – was transferred to another workplace, others who have engaged in objectionable behaviour remained. Overall, it is noticeable that more female victims than male perpetrators left the Wakefield Jail.[1] Meanwhile, for those women who remained, and for new women who came in, problems persisted. The fact that some of these problems became more subtle than ever makes it all the more imperative that serious consideration be given to how such problems might be addressed.

Although the case study presented here has focused on the Wakefield Jail, it is important to recall that the problems of gender-based discrimination and harassment that have been documented are by no means unique. Information available about other provincial prisons in Ontario testifies to problems experienced by women there, too (Symes 1995, 47–9). And surveys conducted in the federal Correctional Service of Canada have indicated many problems of discrimination and harassment in institutions across the country. For example, in a survey of 760 female employees in the Ontario region of the Correctional Service of Canada, 428 – or 56.3 per cent – stated that they had experienced discrimination or harassment (Henriksen 1993, 21).

Internationally, the available research suggests that problems of gender-based discrimination and harassment have often been experienced by women working in prisons for men in the United States. Also, while there has been less research conducted elsewhere, it appears that gender-based discrimination and harassment are a problem in prisons in Australia, New Zealand, and other countries.[2] In short, while much further research is needed to document the scope and nature of problems of discrimination and harassment experienced by women working in prisons for men, the existence of the problem is indisputable.

Given the apparent pervasiveness of problems of discrimination and harassment, it would be a pleasure to conclude this book with a set of recommendations that, if implemented, would guarantee progressive change, not only in Canada, but also internationally. But it is unrealistic to provide simplistic solutions to complex problems. As has already been documented, a plethora of procedures, processes, educational programs, inquiries, investigations, admonishments, and rhetorical flourishes do not of themselves guarantee progress. Indeed, they can sometimes impede fundamental change – especially when men who do not think that they have engaged in objectionable behaviour feel that they are being unfairly targeted. Heavy-handed and unduly high-profile approaches run the risk of alienating those who are among the major facilitators of women's satisfactory occupational integration – namely male correctional officers and managers.

The only guarantee of change lies in the most amorphous aspect of change, that is, in the occupational culture as it is constituted, and reconstituted, by correctional management and staff. In light of this, what *should not* be done is considered here to be as important as what *should*. A proliferation of new procedures for preventing problems, ensuring accountability, and imposing penalties is not enough in isolation. Any new procedures must be meaningful for those subject to them. They must be meaningful in that they must work not only on paper, and not only from the top down. They must also work from the bottom up, and radiate from the middle out. Procedures must offer not only women, but also men, more than a modicum of dignity and respect. It must be recognized that there are systemic problems, and it is not, therefore, helpful to engage in the equivalent of witch hunts of a few, while ignoring the transgressions of many.

In short, it is the male culture of the prison system as a whole that must be challenged and transcended. Moreover, this needs to be undertaken in a manner that is predominantly supportive rather than punitive, and predominantly cooperative rather than coercive. The only way that such a transformation can be accomplished is through the management and unions working in tandem, and with the cooperation of staff at individual prisons. Ultimately, however, although the cooperation of unions and staff is essential, the onus for initiating meaningful strategies toward change rests with management.

While the most appropriate solutions to problems of gender-based discrimination and harassment can only be developed within individual institutions and jurisdictions, this chapter identifies, and briefly discusses, issues and principles which generally need to be addressed. Although events in Ontario are the immediate stimulus to this discussion, it is hoped that the basic points are pertinent for all those working toward progressive change, both in Canada and internationally. The specific strategies discussed below include: recognizing operational matters as policy issues; implementing meaningful responses and penalties; providing effective training for staff; and improving hiring, promotion, and support systems for women.

Recognizing Operational Matters as Policy Issues

As was noted earlier – particularly with respect to events at Bell Cairn – whether an issue is defined as being operational, or a matter of policy, can have major implications for how it is seen and dealt with. Specifically, at Bell Cairn, initial problems with rowdiness were defined largely in terms of the operational concern of security. Subsequent attention was devoted to examining and enhancing various aspects of security (e.g., lighting at the rear of the building, the installation of a speaker system at the front entrance, and devising a security system that would monitor if private security guards were doing rounds regularly). In the course of this operational focus, the fact that the key issue was a policy one – namely that of gender relations – was slow in being recognized.

The phenomenon whereby defining issues as operational obscures their policy components is a problem in corrections more generally. In turn, defining issues as operational, rather than policy, can shield them from the attention of at least some senior levels of the ministry. To give one example of this, when I was policy advisor, and later chief-of-staff, to ministers of Correctional Services in Ontario, the general tendency among senior civil servants and management in the ministry was to exclude the minister, and the minister's staff, from consideration of issues defined as 'operational.' One had the sense that the minister's job was to deal with policy, while the operational issues, involving everyday administrative tasks necessary to running the ministry's institutions and programs, were not the proper domain of the minister's attention.

The perspective that the minister should deal with policy rather than operations is understandable. No one would suggest that government ministers should spend inordinate amounts of time dealing with routine administrative items and tasks, which – although essential to the everyday functioning of a ministry – are not of immediate policy or political import. But the questions need to be posed: when does an operational matter become a policy one? On what basis is an issue defined as operational or policy? Are too many matters defined as operational, with their policy significance thereby being likely to be overlooked?

It is suggested here that the policy significance of operational issues *has* been too often glossed over, or overlooked. When the Bell Cairn scandal broke in the Ontario Legislature, this was the first that the minister and his staff had heard about any problems at Bell Cairn. Yet problems had occurred there continually for over nine months.

Where the running of prisons for men is concerned, there are many relevant operational matters that could be examined for the potential obstacles they pose to the occupational advancement of women. In this context, the report of the Employment Systems Review makes an important observation (1994, 89, emphasis added): 'It would appear that the strategies used to date to increase the representation of women in the [correctional officer] occupational category have been of minimal success. There is no single barrier, but *several operational issues may have served as barriers.*'

The joint management/union task force goes on to discuss the operational matter of modesty barriers for inmates. It is clear that this operational item has major consequences for what might be described at the 'mobility' of female officers within an institution (89–90): 'While many modifications have been made to our facilities in the interests of inmate privacy (e.g. privacy/modesty panels in small jails) an audit of all institutional facilities should be undertaken to determine what modifications would be necessary to ensure that female C.O. staff would not breach inmate privacy if a female was posted to that area.'

The task force continues with the more general suggestion (90):

> Following or coinciding with this audit, institutions should be required to audit all posts in the institution and identify those, if any, which cannot be filled by female staff. The focus of the post audit should be the identification of reasons, if any, for excluding female staff, instead of specifying how many female staff can be accommodated. The assumption should be that staff of both genders can rotate through all areas of the institution unless there are specific and legitimate modesty grounds for exclusion.

It is suggested here that there is a widespread need in corrections to do an even more general analysis of how operational matters impact on women's occupational equity. For example, if one considers the basic administrative matter of telephoning a correctional officer at home in order to speak with them about overtime hours, the process through which this is done could differentially affect women. To describe an hypothetical scenario, women may be more likely than men to be single-parents with custody of children, and thereby routinely, and periodically, absent from the home while bringing children to, or collecting them from, school. If an institution's timing of making calls about overtime should be regularly done at the time of school opening or closing, some women could be at a serious disadvantage. Yet such a disadvantage would never show up in the records of calls to correctional officers at home made by the institution.[3] Equity in this case would require women being able to inform the institution about the optimal times when they will be able to speak on the phone, and the institution's calling at those times.

In short, operational matters such as procedures for contacting staff about work schedules, and for allocating shifts and overtime, must be recognized as having a significant policy component. The same applies with respect to decisions about who will get training or sit on interview boards. Beyond this, there are numerous other areas where the same point applies. Those best able to identify them and to suggest ways of dealing with them are the staff working within prisons, and especially women employees themselves.

Implementing Meaningful Responses and Penalties

In countering problems of gender-based discrimination and harassment, it is also crucial that the responses taken to problems once they arise are carefully scrutinized. To respond per se is not sufficient. Rather, responses and penalties must be meaningful.

If events in Ontario can be considered in any way typical, there appear to be numerous problems with both investigations and penalties following complaints. Where investigators are concerned, from the information available, it appears that some of them have lacked a holistic or contextual approach to issues of discrimination and harassment. Their reports have given little indication of the systemic and systematic nature of these problems. Because of this, incidents at the Wakefield Jail, such as placing a dead partridge on the windshield of a female officer's car, the twisting of a female officer's car mirrors, and the filling of a cook's shoes with ketchup, appear to have been trivialized, and not sufficiently recognized as problems that have a gendered basis. While such problems can be considered less serious than physical assaults on female officers, in practice – and as the previous chapters have demonstrated – they still have extremely ominous undertones when viewed within a systemic pattern of harassment. It is further disturbing when the authorities also trivialize physical intrusions on women by viewing them as unimportant. This occurred, for example, when the final submission of the Ministry of Correctional Services to the Grievance Settlement Board described situations where male officers blew in a woman's ear, rubbed a leg against a woman, and poked keys in a woman's behind, as 'small incidents' (Marvy 1995, 18).

From the information available, it also appears that investigators have devoted a disproportionate amount of attention to, and emphasis on, rumours about women's sexuality and sex lives. Such rumours need to be recognized for what they are – an integral component of gender-based harassment and discrimination.

Moreover, when investigators have received a specific item of information about a woman's sex life, this also appears to be given an inordinate amount of attention. One specific example of this is the attention given to Diana Hooper's brief liaison with a colleague in 1985. This event was the opening information given in ministry investigations of complaints made by her. The accompanying statement – 'This information is in no way provided to make any type of moral judgement on Ms Howe but is important in order to understand a number of incidents which succeeded these events' – directs attention to the very possibility of making such a moral judgment. Here a traditional problem in trials involving sexual assault and rape is apparent: the victim is effectively put on trial, and their credibility is thereby undermined. This is not to suggest that Diana Hooper's liaison (albeit off-duty) was not relevant, as it is relevant to her ensuing problems with rumours about her sexuality being circulated among staff and inmates. The problem is the placing of this information at the outset of the reports, and implying that it is centrally relevant to the multifarious experiences and events subsequently discussed.

A further problem with investigations that have been undertaken is that individual investigators sometimes appear to be familiar only with the specifics of the immediate case with which they are dealing (even when several investigations are overlapping as in the case of the Wakefield Jail). Again, awareness of the broader and potentially systemic nature, of problems appears to be lacking.

It is important, therefore, that care be taken in selecting the personnel who investigate allegations of gender-based discrimination and harassment. Investigators should have an awareness of the contextual, structural, and systemic aspects of problems experienced by women working in prisons for men (including the male culture, micro-inequities, gender discrimination, and sexual harassment). Moreover, when investigations are undertaken at institutions, such as the Wakefield Jail, which have had a history of gender-based discrimination and harassment, it is imperative that investigators be fully briefed on the historical and generalized nature of problems at the jail.

Where penalties are concerned, their purpose is to affirm the boundaries of acceptable attitudes and behaviour with respect to gender issues, and to respond when these boundaries have been violated. As such, they should, firstly, validate the experience of victims; secondly, send a clear, and critical, message to the perpetrator(s) involved; thirdly, clarify norms and expectations of the ministry for other staff; and, fourthly, demonstrate the consequences that will follow when these norms and boundaries are not upheld.

At the Wakefield Jail, where penalties are concerned, there have been numerous problems. One of these is that penalties often did not seem to be sufficient. For example, the loss of a few days work, especially when the person being penalized was subsequently given opportunities to do overtime, seems token. One might even question whether a temporary suspension from work is an appropriate penalty for gender-based discrimination and harassment.

It seems that some creative thinking is needed in order to create a more diverse and appropriate range of remedies.[4] This need not always mean that a more punitive approach should be taken. In some cases, both the victim and the harasser may prefer to take a 'dispute resolution' approach and try to resolve a situation informally. In such cases, if the victim is amenable, and if the harasser is willing to publicly acknowledge and express regret for wrongdoing, an apology might be sufficient and appropriate. In allowing this remedy, however, it is essential that the victim not be cajoled or coerced into pursuing such a course. This is particularly important when the harasser occupies a supervisory position. For, as has been described, women's wishes not to 'make waves' – especially with management – can come into conflict with their desire to have the wrongdoing meaningfully addressed and remedied.

Another problem with penalties – as evidenced at the Wakefield Jail – is that victims, and other staff, often did not know exactly what they consisted of. Specifically, at the Wakefield Jail, formal complaints were first made in October 1992, and some men were sanctioned in February and March of 1993. But it was not until over a year later that women learned the details of actions taken subsequent to their complaints and the investigations. This lack of knowledge on the part of victims has been identified as a more general problem in corrections. For example, Sheila Henriksen has remarked – following from her survey of female officers in the Ontario region of the Correctional Service of Canada (1993, 104): 'Often the complainant did not know what action was taken on a found allegation ... [V]erbal sanctions were frequently used and this tended to support the perception that harassers get off lightly.'

To remedy women's lack of knowledge about penalties imposed, it is suggested that women should promptly be provided with full details of responses to alleged harassers, including penalties administered. The complainant should be sent copies of the correspondence at the same time as it is sent to the alleged harasser. The word 'alleged' with respect to the harasser is used here to indicate that complainants should receive copies of correspondence, not only when a complaint is founded, but also when it has not been substantiated. Complainants should also be fully informed about any verbal warnings administered to, and discipline imposed on, harassers.

In some cases of harassment involving supervisors that are recognized as particularly serious, the ministry has transferred the harasser. As a penalty, this can be extremely problematic. One reason for this is because harassers are sometimes transferred to other institutions where they immediately, or later, assume supervisory positions.[5] Clearly, although a transfer may be experienced as punitive by the perpetrators, such a response is not beneficial for the women at the institutions to which they have been transferred.

A lack of communication within the ministry appears to have exacerbated related problems. For example, it appears that there has been little, and sometimes no, communication among regional directors in the Ministry of Correctional Services (who make important decisions about the assignment of superintendents to prisons) concerning managers who have been disciplined for sexual harassment. Thus, once senior supervisors who have harassed have been transferred out of one region, decisions about their reassignment – often to senior levels of management in the institutions – have been made in the absence of detailed knowledge about what took place in their former positions. In turn, such a lack of knowledge must inhibit regional directors in adequately monitoring the performance of transferees in their new workplaces.

Meanwhile, the non-circulation of precise information about the outcome of complaints, especially with respect to penalties applied to harassers, fuels the circulation of rumours about alleged harassers. Particularly in the institution where the alleged harassment took place, such transfers can feed the impression that some individuals are profiting from, rather than being penalized for, harassing women.

In general, there seems to be much to recommend improved circulation of information with respect to complaints of discrimination and harassment when allegations have been upheld. This is particularly the case if it is agreed that the purpose of penalties includes sharing a more general message with correctional staff about what is and is not acceptable behaviour. It is therefore suggested that full information should be provided to complainants and staff at institutions where upheld complaints originate. It is also suggested that when perpetrators are transferred, information about their transgressions and the penalties imposed should be provided to colleagues in their new workplaces. Such information is very important in assisting women should any new instances of harassment arise on the part of the individual involved.

In addition, questions need to be raised about practices of transferring known perpetrators. Most fundamentally, the question must be raised: if someone is found to be have been abusive to the point that a judgment is made that they cannot retain their previous position, what position – if any – should they be allowed to retain?

As they stand, remedies under the Workplace Discrimination and Harassment Prevention policy in Ontario allow for dismissal as a penalty. Arguably, individuals who persistently harass should be dismissed. In this context, persistent harassment includes not only those who continue to engage in unwanted and sexual touching, but also those who persist in the use of vulgar language, in the making of sexist, sexual, and lewd comments, and who continue to exclude women from the everyday culture, activities, and worklife of the institution.

Overall, towards more generally improving responses to, and remedies for, harassment, the recommendation by Sheila Henriksen (103) is pertinent: 'Oral or written complaints of harassment must be given a sensitive, impartial, timely, fair, confidential and thorough investigation, swift resolution and feedback to the alleged victim and alleged harasser, and an appropriate remedy including meaningful and effective sanctions for proven harassers.'

Providing Effective Training for Staff

In responding to complaints of gender-based discrimination and harassment, it is not only penalties that are important. The provision of education and training for staff is arguably equally, or even more, so. In Ontario corrections, the 1990s have seen intensive efforts at providing Workplace Discrimination and Harassment Prevention training across the ministry (Dowrich Management Services 1995). The intensity of the training process received added impetus following the scandal at the Bell Cairn Staff Training School. For staff of the Wakefield Jail, attempts at training received additional impetus pursuant to complaints being laid about discrimination and harassment.

Despite the good intentions of the training process, many problems have been evident. This has been particularly apparent in the reaction of staff at the Wakefield Jail. Some women appeared to be disappointed with the training. They were frustrated by some of their male colleagues' comments during training, and by the anger and resentment expressed by men about the training process in general.

Overall, from women's accounts to the Grievance Settlement Board, it appears that the training following complaints did not work. This was reflected, for example, in the ongoing nature of problematic behaviours on the part of male colleagues that have been discussed earlier (ranging from women being sent off the floor during emergencies, to the male in charge of the Wakefield Jail during night shift watching a sexually explicit movie while on duty).

Why was the training less than successful? Fully answering this question is beyond the scope of this research. It is, however, significant that the handling of opinions expressed by some men in training workshops was sometimes problematic. For example, at training sessions, men expressed opinions that women have no place in correctional institutions for men. One colleague also expressed concern about the possibility of being falsely accused of rape by a woman while working on a night shift. Women were very disturbed by these comments, especially as they were made by colleagues who had not generally been perceived as harassers.

It is suggested here that the making of these comments in themselves is not necessarily a problem. Effective training workshops should be able to create a climate where staff can express their fears – even if those fears happen to be only occasional, and even if the fears expressed happen to be unreasonable, irrational, or downright sexist. Indeed, one important function of workshops should be to evoke unjustified or irrational fears believed to exist, and then seek to refute them in a reasoned and informative way.

Part of the problem seemed to lie in that some of the comments were made immediately prior to the end of the training session, and the session ended without the comments being addressed. Staff then returned to the Wakefield Jail without the content of the comments having been adequately confronted or worked through.

Again, if experiences at the Wakefield Jail are in any way typical, there may be a need to generally review both the structure and content of training workshops. In this context, it is disappointing that the evaluation of the Workplace Discrimination and Harassment Prevention policy training within the ministry – *Building a Partnership for Change* – appears not to have included actual participation in, or observation of, workshops. The 'Executive Summary' states (Dowrich Management Services 1995, 4):

> Several evaluation approaches were used to address and fulfil ... project objectives. These included an analysis of the workshop evaluations; follow-up to the training, using a mailed self-administered survey; direct face-to-face interviews and focus groups with designated and other special interest groups; an examination of complaints data available

through the WDHP Coordinator of the Ministry; and interviews with key informants/participants associated with the three-partner organizations.

Given the signs of trouble in the handling of comments made in workshops, and the omission of a participant-observational analysis of the dynamics occurring in workshops, there may be a need to conduct such an analysis, and to review the actual content of workshops themselves. With the omission of this methodology, the evaluation of the ministry's Workplace Discrimination and Harassment Prevention training was restricted to noting that 'anecdotal comments' were made by some staff on their course evaluation sheets that the training workshops 'accommodated too much resentment by disgruntled staff' (35).

Problems experienced during training sessions run by female leaders for staff at the Wakefield Jail also indicate that there may also be a need to make personnel changes in the facilitators of workshops. Specifically, the hostility of male correctional officers to education and training on issues of harassment and discrimination may make them particularly unresponsive to sessions led by women. By the same token, they may be more appreciative of sessions delivered by men. Following from this, workshops and training sessions might benefit from the inclusion of male-only sessions, as well as female-only sessions. If facilitators could sometimes include former perpetrators, their impact could also be enhanced.

The hostility of some male staff at the Wakefield Jail to this training following complaints may have also been fuelled by the fact that these training sessions were exclusively a function of management (in contrast to other Workplace Discrimination and Harassment Prevention training sessions in the province, where, more generally, both management and union were involved in the planning and delivery). Indeed, the Ontario Public Service Employees Union had expressed concern to the ministry about the timing and content of these particular sessions for the Wakefield Jail staff. The then superintendent had also expressed concern about the open-ended format of sessions. But the ministry did not heed these concerns. Arguably, the effectiveness of training is enhanced when it is clearly a joint venture of the management and union, and tailored to the situation within the institution where it is taking place.

The hostility of staff at the Wakefield Jail to training was yet further increased by the ministry's decision to close the Wakefield Jail for two weeks to facilitate the staff's attendance at workshops. While this closure may have been well-intentioned, it reinforced some staff's perception that training was a punishment, rather than a helpful tool. The closure was also interpreted as a threat that the ministry might close down the Wakefield Jail completely. Pursuant to this, women were effectively blamed for the jail's temporary closure. They were also burdened with responsibility for the possible closure of jail in the future – especially if further complaints are made.

It is understandable that the threat of a permanent closure of the Wakefield Jail might have contributed to a negative climate in the training workshops. It is also questionable as to whether the decision to close the jail in order to facilitate training was a good one. In addition, during the recent period of fiscal difficulty being experienced by government, staff fears that problems among colleagues might be used as an excuse for closing the Wakefield Jail completely seem reasonable.[6]

Overall, problems experienced in the training process subsequent to complaints at the Wakefield Jail suggest a number of lessons with respect to educating correctional staff more generally about problems of gender-based discrimination and harassment. Most importantly, education should ideally and clearly be a joint initiative of management and union, and one directed toward enhancement of the work environment; men as well as women should be involved in the delivery of education and training; discussions should be frank, with thorny issues being engaged rather than side-stepped or dismissed; and evaluation of sessions should involve the gathering of primary (i.e., observational), as well as secondary (e.g., survey) data, and should be directly drawn upon in ongoing efforts to improve the content of educational and training courses. Finally, it is also to be hoped that social scientists will conduct further scholarly research on this important, but neglected topic of the content and effectiveness of training programs addressing problems of discrimination and harassment.[7]

Improving Hiring, Promotion, and Support Systems for Women

Improving hiring, promotion, and support systems for women is crucial, not only in advancing the occupational equity of women, but also in countering problems of gender-based discrimination and harassment that they may confront. Examination of these issues in the particular context of the Wakefield Jail serves to illustrate their importance in the correctional field more generally.

As discussed earlier, while women have been under-represented among correctional officers in the Ministry of Correctional Services as a whole, the proportion of women hired at the Wakefield Jail – specifically in the role of correctional officers – has been even lower than the ministry average. As of the mid 1990s, *no* women were in management at the jail. Of the three female correctional officers at the jail, two were in casual – and thereby insecure – positions (and in early 1997, Nora Diamond's contract was not renewed, leaving only two female correctional officers working at the jail). Meanwhile, all three of the female cooks at the jail were in casual or part-time positions, while the only male cook was full-time and senior to the female cooks. Overall, the employment situation of females at the Wakefield Jail – with the exception of those in specifically administrative positions – was even worse than it was in the late 1980s and early 1990s. Such a situation can be considered as flying in the face of the Ministry of Correctional Services' stated commitment to gender equity.

In light of this dearth of women employees, it is not surprising that women at the Wakefield Jail commented on their isolation among male colleagues. The degree of isolation they have experienced is further reflected in the fact that, for a long time, prior to the laying of complaints in the fall of 1992, individual women did not know that other women were having similar problems with male colleagues. Arguably, the accomplishment of satisfactory and meaningful change at the jail would require not only that women already there be treated fairly, but also that top priority should be given to females in future hirings at the Wakefield Jail.

It is important to note that, of those women who were hired at the jail, their concentration among casual staff and lack of representation among full-time staff has apparently not arisen on the basis of lack of effort on their parts toward being hired full-time, and/or promoted. On the contrary, women often applied for better positions, but were unsuccessful. Their impression that women who have been hired in casual positions have been held back at the jail appears to be well founded.

Thus, for example, although correctional officer Nora Diamond repeatedly applied for a full-time position, and had positive evaluations of her job performance, she was not successful. At the same time, the other males who started working at the same time as her (except one who quit) were successful in becoming full-time.

One factor cited by the authorities as impeding Nora Diamond's occupational advancement was her lack of French-language training. Yet she had repeatedly applied for such training, but had not been accepted. Moreover, the reasons why she was not accepted were not made sufficiently clear. While not every employee can expect to be successful in every competition for additional training – and especially when the ministry was experiencing fiscal constraints – it seems only fair that applicants should have information about the criteria for selection, and thereby some understanding of why they were or were not selected in any given instance.[8]

Meanwhile, although former correctional officer Sharon West does speak French, she was passed over in several competitions that would have enabled her to move from a casual to a full-time position. Casual cook Karla Preston was also repeatedly passed over. The reasons for these women's lack of success were again by no means clear to them. It is understandable that they would feel discriminated against in light of other forms of discrimination and harassment to which they were subject. The tendency for women to be passed over with respect to supervisory positions, including acting ones, further reinforces the impression of discrimination.

Such vagaries in hiring and promotion have by no means been unique to the Wakefield Jail. The have also occurred in the ministry more generally. There, as in the specific case of the Wakefield Jail, documenting the precise source and nature of discrimination involved is not possible, owing to the lack of precise information. Indeed, this lack of information itself can be considered a key characteristic of the hiring process, which facilitates discrimination both in taking place, and in having low visibility. As a consulting firm noted of the screening component of the ministry's hiring process (Avebury Research 1992, quoted in Employment Systems Review 1994, 65): 'Documentation of screening varied from competition to competition and from region to region, [and] Ministry files were generally weak in this regard ... In many cases, it was difficult to determine which applicants were screened in, which were screened out, who was making these decisions, and upon what basis these decisions were being made.'

The consulting firm went on to provide specific examples of inconsistencies and anomalies in the hiring process. Unfortunately, the impact of these on women as a specific category of applicants is not identified. Nonetheless, the scenarios documented vividly illustrate the arbitrariness of the hiring process, within which, as we have seen, women are vulnerable (66–7):

- Two applicants (both members of racial minorities) were informed by letter that they were screened out of a competition because their applications were late. However, the Ministry date stamp on both resumes indicated that they had been received prior to the closing date.

- In a few competitions, the scores awarded to applicants based on criteria on the formal screening sheet were ignored. For example, applicants who were awarded only 4 out of 25 points on the screening criterion were invited for an interview, while others who scored considerably higher were not interviewed.

- Although a competition was restricted to applicants within [a] 40 kms radius, one applicant who was from a city at the opposite end of the province was screened in and invited to attend an interview. In this same competition, an applicant from the same city as the other applicant, was screened out because the person was outside the 40kms radius.

- An applicant who had no experience or training as a probation officer but who was a 'volunteer worship leader in a security (*sic*) facility' was given full marks for experience in a probation/parole setting. Other applicants who had volunteer or work placement experience in a corrections facility were not awarded points for their experience.

- Some applicants were screened out simply because they were 'overqualified.'
- A number of the files reviewed were incomplete. In some cases, only the resumes of the candidates invited to attend the interview were on file. In another case, where 11 people were interviewed, only the interview notes of the top three candidates were on file.

Clearly, in face of such arbitrariness, and the low visibility of decision-making with respect to hiring and promotion, both of which appear to adversely affect women – there is a strong need for reform in this area. Many of the key issues to be considered in undertaking the reform have already been identified by the Employment Systems Review (1994). In general, what is required is greater involvement of previously marginalized groups such as women in designing and conducting the hiring process, and more precision and accountability in hiring. It is also imperative that correctional authorities' stated commitment to equity in hiring and promotion move beyond the level of rhetoric to that of action and implementation. This is particularly important in an era when politicians – who are exposed to a barrage of rhetoric about strategies being undertaken to enhance the position of women, yet are simultaneously unaware of, or sometimes unconcerned by, the subtleties and complexities of discrimination that continue to undermine women's advancement – take steps to reduce what is perceived to be too forceful a government commitment to equity issues.[9] Overall, problems in hiring and promotion are systemic ones, which require committed, systemic responses.

Where providing support systems for women is concerned, acting on some of the suggestions already made here would do much to create a more supportive environment for women in corrections. For example, making the hiring and promotion of women, as well as sensitivity to issues of gender-based discrimination, priorities would contribute to improving the occupational culture.

Additional supports are also needed, and are particularly important in, institutions where gender-based discrimination and harassment have become generalized problems. This is because once investigations have been initiated, their aftermath can pose new problems for all women at an institution, whether or not they individually have previously been targets of harassment. One such problem that arose at the Wakefield Jail in the aftermath of complaints is that some male colleagues appear to have adopted a strategy of 'divide and rule.' Women who had made complaints were effectively labelled as outsiders. In such a situation, those women who did not make formal complaints may find themselves torn. They may empathize with their female colleagues but be reluctant to express this because they do not wish themselves to be shunned by their male colleagues. Here, female empathy and the desire for occupational acceptance come into conflict. It is likely that male colleagues recognize this dilemma, and that some of them may take advantage of whatever opportunities present themselves to create divisions among the women.

Such 'divide and rule' tactics may be evidenced not only by correctional officer colleagues, but also by management. For example, where Karla Preston is concerned, questions can be raised as to why a decision was made to hire another casual cook when she was already available, and keen to get more hours. Moreover, not only was another cook hired, but Karla Preston's hours were further reduced following a decision to split hours between her and the new cook. A critical reading of Karla Preston's experience would note that her hours were progressively reduced as she became more effective in identifying and trying to do something about discrimination and harassment. In her case, the decision to hire another female cook, and (following the initiation of complaints) to transfer some of her hours to the new cook, could be read as an excellent way of setting the stage for dividing and ruling. Ironically moreover, the decision to split the hours could be persuasively rationalized on the grounds of equity. Once again, what may appear equitable from a solely operational point of view might actually be the result of a very different – including discriminatory – agenda.

In terms of support systems that should be made available to women, priority should be given to those which women themselves identify as desirable and necessary. At the very least, female employees should be encouraged to periodically meet and discuss matters of mutual interest.

The development of wider support systems should also be considered a priority. For example, in the federal Correctional Service of Canada, conferences have periodically been held for female staff. Such conferences can facilitate women in coming together to focus on issues of particular interest. More frequent holding of such conferences and the participation of female staff from provincial prisons in Canada could do much to enhance networking and mutual support among women, and thereby counter the isolation experienced by many of them.

7 Conclusion

Harassment and Discrimination as 1990s Issues

> [T]he civil law, as well as nature herself, has always recognized a wide difference in the respective spheres and destinies of man and woman. Man is or should be, woman's protector and defender. The natural and proper timidity and delicacy which belongs to the female sex evidently unfit it for many of the occupations of civil life ... The paramount destiny and mission of woman are to fulfill the noble and benign offices of wife and mother. (Justice Bradley 1873,[1] quoted in Nallin 1981, 17)

Women's occupational advancement in North America has come a long way since Justice Bradley of the U.S. Supreme Court made the above statement in *Bradwell vs. Illinois,* where he, 'concurring with the court, upheld the refusal of Illinois to grant Myra Bradwell admission to practice law' (18). By the 1970s, a century later, women had entered many occupations from which they were previously barred and excluded. Meanwhile, the legacy of the civil rights movement, along with women's and feminist movements, ensured that legal and policy barriers would continue to be removed. In accordance with this, the last two decades have seen further advancement of women in the workplace, to the point that their participation in virtually all spheres of working life – albeit sometimes disproportionately low – is now often taken-for-granted.

At the same time, the transition whereby women have become increasingly present throughout the workplace has not been an easy one. Nor has progress always been steady. Indeed, in the 'nasty 1990s,' underlying conflicts concerning women's involvement continue to be apparent. Such conflicts are obvious not only between the sexes, but also among women themselves.[2] Thus, while the 1970s and 1980s saw the gradual opening of traditionally male occupations to women, the 1990s are seeing many heated disputes around related issues. Some of these disputes are best described in terms of a 'backlash' against the various legislative supports to women's advancement, with attendant calls that any perceived privileging of women's advancement be restricted. Debaters argue about whether affirmative action, employment equity, equal opportunity, and other such programs actually do more harm than good for women – particularly when those individual women who do 'make it' are perceived as having done so primarily by virtue of their sex, rather than because of any innate abilities or talents they may have. Such debates seem to become particularly acute when women are perceived as having benefitted from – and men as concurrently having suffered from – 'quota' systems in various occupations and positions.[3]

Moreover, while in the 1970s the women's movement was relatively united around the goal of advancing women's position generally, in the 1990s the various fissions, divisions, and disagreements among women of different perspectives are now so obvious that it sometimes seems difficult to speak of a women's movement at all. The salient points of related debates are far too numerous and complex to recount here. But, for example, where workplace issues are concerned, it is by no means unusual for the media and other interested parties to pit women who favour further occupational advancement for women against those who favour policies that facilitate women's return to hearth, family, and home (as if most women can be neatly slotted into one of these two categories when, in fact, they cannot). Meanwhile, those who wish to take a step back from such often oversimplified debates in order to seek a unified theoretical approach on feminist issues are doomed to disappointment as they confront seemingly incompatible epistemologies reflected in liberal, radical, equity, socialist, standpoint, postmodern, and other feminist perspectives.

However one might chart the course of women's and feminist

movements over the past few decades, it is clear that sex, sexual harassment, abuse, and rape are flashpoint issues during the 1990s. This applies not only in the theoretical realm, but also in the public culture generally. Adele Stan's (1995, xix) observation of the United States resonates in Canada: 'If, up to this point, the 1990s bear any singular theme, that theme is sex and its place in American life.' As she reminds the reader in the American context, by the mid-1990s the decade had seen major media and public preoccupations with related events including Anita Hill's allegations of sexual harassment against Supreme Court nominee Clarence Smith, the date-rape trial of William Kennedy Smith, the Tailhook sexual harassment scandal in the American navy, Lorena Bobbitt's severing of her husband's penis, and the rape trial of boxer Mike Tyson.

In Canada, issues of sex, harassment, and abuse have similarly been to the fore, with the focus extended to male (specifically young male) as well as female victims, and with an emphasis as much on organizations and institutions involving multiple offenders and victims as on individuals. Indeed, this preoccupation dates back to the 1980s, when there was a dramatic growth in attention to the abuse and rape of women in Canadian society, with reactions to the horrific killing of fourteen women by Marc Lepine at the University of Montreal in 1989 helping to stimulate attention not only to stranger-initiated crimes, but also to the dangers posed to women by male family members, friends, and acquaintances. During the 1990s the 'Montreal massacre' has been commemorated yearly, and a steady flow of news accounts has helped to confirm the pervasiveness of sexual harassment, abuse, and rape as major social problems. Thus there has been extensive documentation of offences that took place decades ago, including the abuse of boys in Mount Cashel Orphanage in Newfoundland, and at the St. Joseph's and St. John's Training Schools in Ontario, as well as of allegations of abuse of girls at the Grandview Training School in Ontario. There has also been a major focus on contemporary allegations of sexual harassment, including – to name but a few – within the Canadian military, at the Department of Political Science at the University of British Columbia, by a Speaker of the House at the Ontario Legislature, and within Canada's hockey world. Indeed, hardly a day goes by without the media reporting on new allegations by individuals in diverse social contexts.[4]

Yet despite, and perhaps because of, this relentless focus on issues of sex, sexual harassment, and abuse, many of the heated discussions that ensue seem more effective at confusing rather than clarifying related issues. In particular, the details of what actually happened in specific cases are often obscure, especially in cases where the 'facts' boil down to one person's word against another's, and any third-party conclusions about the matter remain, of necessity, based on assumptions, ideology, and speculation.

Why are discussions of harassment often so inconclusive? In part, as alluded to above, this is because of the nature of the object itself. Changing mores and norms on what constitutes appropriate behaviour, coupled with individuals' differing perceptions of situations, inhibit agreement as to what actually took place in any given incident, and perhaps especially in those considered less serious. In turn, the picture can become even more murky when viewed through the lenses of those discourses and frameworks that currently predominate in the public culture. In the first place, a rigid 'politically correct' world-view and advocacy of 'zero tolerance' for sexual harassment can overlook the nuances of any given situation, and allow the difference between trivial and more serious forms to be obscured. Such rigid views can also contribute to moral panics around issues of sexual harassment and abuse to the point that people adjust otherwise reasonable behaviours for fear of leaving themselves open to spurious allegations.[5]

Other discourses, approaches, and frameworks bring their own limitations – some of which have been alluded to in this research. Thus, criminal approaches are often ineffective where no physical abuse has taken place, and, even in serious cases involving physical harm, are thwarted by victims' reluctance to come forward. Political discourses and politicians, by definition, are more concerned with that which is immediately expedient than with inquiring into the complexities of any given case. Bureaucratic and managerial approaches – as advanced by government officials – tend to put an emphasis on procedures, and important components of any given case can be missed. Finally, legal approaches can often be constrained by their individualistic focus, and the systemic aspects of some of the problems being addressed can be excluded.

The confusion to which these competing and ultimately unsatisfying approaches give rise has acted as a major stimulus to this research. My aim has been to present a case study of corrections in Ontario, which, while sometimes drawing from these different approaches, transcends their limitations and provides a more comprehensive picture. Thus, for example, while management and legal inquiries into incidents at the Wakefield Jail understandably centre on those that actually resulted in complaints, the social scientific approach taken here has been able to be equally attentive to incidents and events not resulting in formal procedures. With this more holistic approach, it has been possible to make the systemic aspects of problems of gender-based discrimination and harassment more apparent.

Overall, I hope that my approach has served to illustrate that, while incidents vary in their severity, and while the content of any individual incident may remain in dispute, gender-based discrimination and harassment *are* real problems. Moreover, while it is individual women who suffer, and suffer disproportionately from their effects, the problems must be recognized as systemic ones within corrections, and ones where incidents that may appear trivial, or even irrelevant, at first glance, are in practice interwoven with, and part of a continuum of, more serious forms of harassment, the overall consequences of which are very detrimental for women. By documenting this in the specific case of corrections, it is my hope that readers – empathetic and sceptical alike – will be stimulated to raise and address more complex questions about the nature, context, and consequences of discrimination and harassment, not only in corrections, but also in other social spheres.

The Need for Systemic Solutions

In conclusion, one might ask: what is the most basic lesson learned from this study of gender-based discrimination and harassment in corrections? While I have suggested some specific reform strategies, perhaps the major point to be reiterated is that the problem in corrections is primarily an *organizational* one. As noted earlier, one of the reasons that gender-based discrimination and harassment have continued to flourish in corrections, and specifically in prisons for men, rests in the hidden nature of prisons themselves. Moreover, this hidden nature of the prison world has arguably brought adverse consequences not only for women working in prison for men, but also for inmates, male staff, and even management. Documenting these broader problems is beyond the scope of this book. But, if problems of gender-based discrimination and harassment are to be seriously addressed, then correctional authorities must be open and accountable. As Stenning (1995, 58) has observed, 'Secrecy is the very antithesis of accountability.' In sum, within corrections it must be acknowledged that it is not only individuals, but the penal system as a whole, that is culpable for the problems experienced by women that have been documented here. Merely tinkering with individual policies, therefore, is not of itself a sufficient response. Rather, what is required is a deeper, broader, and holistic approach to this general problem.

Epilogue: The Arbitration Decision about the Wakefield Grievances

This chapter was co-authored by Maeve McMahon and Beth Symes. Beth Symes is a lawyer with Eberts Symes Street and Corbett in Toronto, and was the lawyer retained by the union in pursuing the grievances of the women at the Wakefield Jail.

A Decision at Last

On 5 November 1997 (about three months after the text of this book had been completed), the Ontario Grievance Settlement Board's decision with respect to the three grievors at the Wakefield Jail was finally released.[1] This was five years after Nora Diamond, Diana Hooper, and Karla Preston first made their complaints under the Workplace Discrimination and Harassment Prevention policy in 1992, over three years after the Grievance Settlement Board began hearings on their grievances, and two years after the Grievance Settlement Board had completed their hearings.

One might think that with the decision of the Grievance Settlement Board having been made at last, a sense of closure might have been experienced by the three grievors, as well as by the staff, past and present, at the jail. Indeed, as of the summer of 1997, the grievors were very tired of waiting for the decision, and anticipated that its release would restore some semblance of order to their lives and those of their families. But, for several reasons, even when the decision did come down, there was little sense of closure. Although from a strictly legal perspective binding decisions had been made about their complaints – with the Board finding in the grievors' favour, affirming that sexual harassment and discrimination on the basis of sex had taken place, and identifying the Wakefield Jail as a poisoned work environment – the grievors still had to live with outstanding matters that remained unresolved, and with new issues arising from the decision and the remedies which it entailed. Staff at the jail, as well as the Union and managers of the Ministry of Correctional Services, were also confronted by new challenges arising from the decision. In this epilogue, therefore, we wish to comment both on the content of the Grievance Settlement Board decision in this case, and on issues outstanding, unresolved, and new.

Legal Foundation of the Grievance Settlement Board's Decision

The Grievance Settlement Board's decision was lengthy, totalling 92 pages. Having identified the specific grievances made by each of the grievors, and having described the relevant evidence gathered at the hearings, the Board outlined the legal principles on which it based its decision (Dissanayake et al. 1997, 52 et seq.). In doing so, the Board noted that sexual harassment is 'a form of discrimination on the basis of sex,' that it can take many forms, that it includes a variety of gender-based comments and conduct that can have a demeaning effect on victims, and that a victim's reticence in complaining (for example, for fear of losing one's job) does not obviate the fact that unwelcome comments or conduct did occur.

The Board also emphasized the remedial emphasis of Canadian human-rights legislation with respect to discrimination and harassment. This concern with the effects, as opposed to the causes, of discrimination reaffirms the employer's responsibility for remedying the effects of discrimination by providing a healthy work environment. In making these important points, the Board quoted La Forest J. of the Supreme Court of Canada in *Robichaud v. The Queen*:[2]

> [Human rights legislation] is not aimed at determining fault or punishing conduct. It is remedial. Its aim is to identify and eliminate discrimination. If this is to be done, then the remedies must be effective, consistent with the 'almost constitutional' nature of the rights protected ...
>
> Indeed if the [*Canadian Human Rights Code*] is concerned with the *effects* of discrimination rather than its *causes* (or motivations), it must

be admitted that only an employer can remedy undesirable effects; only an employer can provide the most important remedy – a healthy work environment.

The Board then considered the extent to which an employer is liable when discrimination and harassment has occurred in the workplace. Rejecting the argument that 'strict liability' applies – whereby the employer would be considered responsible in every case where sexual harassment occurred – the Board took the position that the employer's liability should be determined by its knowledge of the offensive conduct, and by its response to it. The Board also noted, however, that employers have a more immediate responsibility for the conduct of managers compared to other employees, as 'the acts of management are the acts of the employer itself.'

'Therefore,' continued the Board, 'it makes very good sense to hold the employer liable for the sexual harassment committed by members of management in all cases.'[3]

In further delineating the basis of its response to discrimination on the basis of sex, the Board pointed to Articles A.1 and 27 of the collective agreement. As documented earlier in this book (see Chapter 5), these provisions state that there shall be 'no discrimination' on the basis of sex or other attributes, and that employees 'have a right to freedom from [sexual] harassment in the workplace' by colleagues, supervisors, or employers. Article 27 also affirms an employee's right to be free from reprisals or threats of reprisal following from the rejection of a sexual solicitation or advance by a person in a position to confer, grant or deny a benefit to an employee.

The Board also referred to the phenomenon of a 'poisoned work environment' as defined by the government of Ontario under the Workplace Discrimination and Harassment Prevention policy[4], and quoted Judge Inger Hansen's (1993, 26) observation that: 'A "poisoned environment" includes an environment where an employee is subjected to sexually oriented remarks, behaviour or surroundings that can create an intimidating, hostile or offensive work environment, or behaviour or surroundings which are conducive to sexual harassment.'

Finally, the Board adopted the definition of sexual harassment from the Workplace Discrimination and Harassment Prevention policy as existing in situations where:

> An employee receives unwelcome sexual attention from any employee and such comment or conduct is known or should reasonably be known to be offensive, inappropriate, intimidating and/or hostile behaviour;
>   An employee receives unwelcome sexual attention and is threatened or penalized by a loss of job, denial of advancement, raise or other employment benefit for noncompliance with sexual demands by a person in a position of authority who knows or should reasonably know that the sexual attention is unwelcome.

Having outlined this legal framework,[5] the Board then examined the experiences of each of the grievors within it.

Findings of the Board about Individual Grievances

With respect to the casual cook, Karla Preston, the Grievance Settlement Board found that 'there can be absolutely no doubt' that she had been sexually harassed by Superintendent Ferguson. Moreover, given that he was the top manager at the jail, the Board found that the ministry was responsible for his actions, and that article 27 of the collective agreement had been breached.

The Board also found that Karla Preston had been sexually assaulted by James Randell, the maintenance worker, by his 'sexually touching and kissing her.' Here, too, the Board found the ministry bore some responsibility. In the Board's words (Dissanayake et al. 1997, 60–1):

> The employer must take responsibility for this behaviour [by James Randell] because it knowingly allowed the creation and continuance of a poisoned environment at the Jail. There is abundant evidence ... that some lieutenants, who are part of management, routinely condoned, and on many occasions participated in, sexual harassment of women employees at the [Wakefield] Jail. Moreover, the person in charge of the jail, the Superintendent, was sexually harassing [Ms. Preston]. The Board is convinced that this behaviour on the part of members of man-

agement would have encouraged subordinates to engage in similar offensive behaviour. In other words, the employer, through the actions and omissions of its management staff, created and fostered a poisoned work environment, where male employees felt secure that no adverse employment consequences would flow from their offensive conduct and women employees were made to feel that they had no choice but to endure such conduct if they continued to be employed at the [Wakefield] Jail. By creating and allowing such a poisoned work environment to continue, the employer was in violation of article 27.10.1 which imposes a positive duty on it to ensure that its employees are free from harassment in the workplace because of sex.

Karla Preston's grievances also included her belief that one of the reprisals she experienced after complaining was management's refusal in 1995 to interview her for a casual correctional-officer position for which she was qualified. Having examined the evidence presented, and having noted that the Superintendent Smith 'conceded that he was angry about Ms. [Preston's] WDHP complaint,' a sentiment still reflected in his demeanour while testifying before the Board, the Board concluded that 'the only reasonable inference is that Mr. [Smith] was motivated by a desire to retaliate against Ms. [Preston] ...' (76, 77). In short, the Board agreed that Karla Preston had the qualifications necessary for the position, and that she had suffered a reprisal arising from her complaint. In the Board's opinion this reprisal also violated the collective agreement.[6]

With respect to Nora Diamond's sexual harassment grievance, the Board found that she had been harassed, as, '[t]here is abundant evidence that, like other women employees at [Wakefield] Jail, Ms. [Diamond] was exposed to comments and conduct degrading to her as a woman ... [C]omments degrading women were commonplace.' In addition, said the Board, she had been subjected to 'unwanted and unwelcome physical contact,' and '[s]ome of the most reprehensible actions were by a lieutenant, Mr. [Laroche]' (61).

As in the case of Karla Preston, the Board found that the ministry was responsible for the existence of a poisoned work environment, which allowed this harassment of Nora Diamond to happen. Given that the ministry had not taken steps to stop the offensive behaviour, the Board determined that it thereby must take responsibility not only for the actions of managers, but also for the harassment by other employees.

The Board further commented that although Mr. O'Reilly did not intend to sexually harass Nora Diamond by watching a '"porno-graphic"' video at work, he should have been more sensitive, and his 'reckless disregard' in watching the video constituted sexual har-assment of her (61). Similarly, the Board found that sexual harass-ment of Nora Diamond and Diana Hooper had occurred when the retirement party for a colleague was held at a '"strip joint"' and that Mr. Ferguson as superintendent 'ought to have reasonably known' that having the function there, and that his having physical and personal contact with the stripper, 'would be offensive to some em-ployees, particularly females' (62).

Turning to Diana Hooper, the Board found that she too had been 'required to work in an environment hostile and demeaning to women.' (62). Moreover, she appeared to have been particularly resented because she was a classified (i.e., full-time) correctional officer, a position that some of her male colleagues, including man-agement, felt that she – as a woman – should not be in.

The Board determined that Diana Hooper had been harassed as a result of the unwanted physical contact to which she had been subjected, including having her bra snapped, her ear blown in, her back and buttocks poked, and her legs rubbed. Once again, the Board saw this conduct as indicative of a poisoned work environ-ment, and held the ministry to be in violation of the collective agree-ment.[7]

In addition, the Board found that Diana Hooper had suffered discrimination on the basis of sex, for example when she was as-signed by Mr. O'Reilly to do laundry and cleaning (in contrast to her male colleagues, who were assigned to supervise inmates in do-ing this work). This, too, said the Board, contributed to a poisoned work environment. The Board also found that the practice (exem-plified by Lieutenant O'Reilly)[8] of scheduling only one woman per shift adversely impacted on Diana Hooper, and denied her experi-ence that would have been useful for promotion. Although it could not specify the actual extent of discrimination suffered by Diana Hooper, the Board was undeterred from finding that she had been discriminated against on the basis of her sex, and that the collective agreement had again been contravened.

The Board's Innovative Imposition of Systemic Remedies

The range of incidents and events at the Wakefield Jail discussed by the Grievance Settlement Board in its decision is somewhat narrower than those that have been addressed in this book. The reason for this is that while testimony at the hearings, and evidence in exhibits given to the Board, provided a broad array of information about sexual harassment and discrimination experienced by all of the three grievors, as well as by other female colleagues, only items relevant to the three grievors' individual grievances fell within the Board's mandate. To be specific, Karla Preston had grieved sexual harassment and reprisals, Diana Hooper had grieved sexual harassment and discrimination, and Nora Diamond had grieved sexual harassment. So, for example, while the Board also heard evidence of discrimination and reprisals against Nora Diamond, it did not directly address these events in the decision. Nor did the Board comment individually on other women at the jail who testified and had clearly been sexually harassed and discriminated against, but who were not formal grievors.

Despite this legal constraint, and the fact that the women's grievances were pursued as 'individual' rather than 'union' ones (which directly address policy issues),[9] the Board determined that '[i]f remedying an individual grievance requires a systemic remedy it is within the Board's jurisdiction to order such remedy' (82). In taking this stance, the Board reasoned that '[i]n each case, whether policy or individual grievance, the Board must ask itself, what is required to remedy the particular grievance before it. Whatever is so required, the Board has jurisdiction to grant. If the Board determines that a systemic type of remedy is required to remedy a grievance filed by an individual employee, it ought to grant that remedy' (82).

In short, the Board deemed that not only did it have the power to instruct the ministry as the employer to individually compensate each of the women, it also interpreted its jurisdiction as allowing for the imposition of systemic remedies that would address the environment within the jail more generally. Thus the Board stated (86):

The Board has determined that in order to fully remedy the violations found with regard to these three grievors, merely compensating each of them for the losses suffered would not be adequate. In order to eradicate the poisoned environment which led to the violations, some systemic remedies are required. Without such remedies, there is a probability that the grievors would continue to be exposed to the same environment and culture that existed at [Wakefield] Jail, which resulted in the violations.

The decision of the Grievance Settlement Board to order systemic remedies represents an important step towards the broad and holistic approaches to dealing with sexual harassment and discrimination which were advocated in Chapter 7 of this book. Moreover, viewed in the context of previous arbitration decisions with respect to sexual harassment and discrimination, the Grievance Settlement Board decision can be described as truly dramatic and ground-breaking. Specifically, the more general tendency of arbitrators' decisions dealing with sexual harassment has been a reluctance to address broader gender and social relations in the workplace concerned (Fudge 1991). Nor have there been attempts to change the structure of the workplace through arbitration decisions on individual grievances. Thus, while individuals may have secured redress, and while arbitrators have occasionally 'gone so far as to impose an affirmative duty on the employer to issue a sexual harassment policy' (Fudge 1991, 128),[10] systemic remedies directly confronting and seeking to change gender relations within a specific workplace have been absent.[11] In this case, however, the Board was extremely innovative in moving beyond the traditional focus of unions, employers, and arbitrators on issues of fault (or the identification of 'bad apples' in the workplace), and in recognizing and addressing the larger picture of the poisoned work environment that had so negatively affected the grievors.

As the systemic remedies directed by the Board are unique, they are quoted here in full. Recognizing the need for systemic remedies, and 'the particular evidence in this case,' the board directed as follows (Dissanayake et al. 1997, 86–8):

(a) The employer is directed to create a Joint Management-Union As-

Assessment Team, ('The Team') including in it local management and staff from the jail itself, with a mandate to review and determine the needs in order to eliminate sexual harassment and discrimination on the basis of sex at [Wakefield] Jail.

(b) Upon completion of the review, the team shall create an action plan, including goals and timetables for the steps to be taken with a view to the elimination of sexual harassment and discrimination on the basis of sex. ('The Plan'). This action plan must be completed within 6 months of the release of this decision, unless agreed to in writing by the employer and the union for an extension. This Board remains seized in the event that there are any problems with respect to implementation of the plan.

(c) Upon request, the employer shall make available to any management or bargaining unit member, counselling with regard to WDHP or stress management. This counselling shall be made available in [Wakefield] at the employer's expense.

(d) The employer shall provide training to its management staff at the [Wakefield] Jail, on the legal obligations with regard to sexual harassment and discrimination on the basis of sex, both substantive and procedural. This training should be made mandatory for every member of the management at the jail and should be completed within six months of the date of release of this decision. Every individual who joins the management of the jail in the period of 2 years from the date of this decision must be provided with this training within the first 3 months of his [sic] assuming management responsibilities.

(e) The employer is directed to develop an affirmative action program for the hiring of women as correctional officers and as shift supervisors, when vacancies occur in these positions. The goal of this program should be to make the proportion of women at [Wakefield] Jail in these positions, equal to the proportion of women in the same positions in the Ministry, as soon as possible. The affirmative action plan should be prepared and filed with this Board within six months of the date of release of this decision. The Board remains seized if there are any problems implementing the plan.

Most striking among these systemic remedies is the Board's order that the ministry develop and implement an affirmative action plan to hire women as correctional officers and supervisors at the jail. Such an order – which will involve the proportion of female correctional officers at the jail increasing to over 20 per cent of the total – is unprecedented in labour arbitration.[12] Later in this epilogue we will discuss how the Board's decisions on systemic remedies were received at the jail, and by the union and management more generally.

Individual Remedies for the Grievors

The remedies for the individual grievors were as follows.

The Board directed that Karla Preston, the casual cook, be appointed to a casual correctional-officer position at Wakefield or at another institution in the province. The appointment was to be on a secondment basis for a period of not less than a year, and was to guarantee no less than twenty-five hours of employment weekly. If the appointment involved her moving, the ministry was also to assume all of her reasonable relocation costs. The Board additionally directed that (Dissanayake et al. 1997, 90):

(a) [Ms. Preston] shall be reimbursed for all earnings lost due to absence from work due to stress related illness during the period of her employment to the date of this decision.
(b) Interest shall be paid on the above amounts based on the average annual prime rate for each applicable year.
(c) [Ms. Preston] shall be paid the sum of five thousand dollars ($5,000) as compensation for pain and suffering.

With respect to Nora Diamond, the Board instructed that (90):

(a) [Ms. Diamond] shall be compensated for any loss of earnings resulting from stress related illness, to the date of this decision.
(b) Interest shall be paid on the above, calculated on the basis of the average annual prime rate for each applicable year.
(c) [Ms. Diamond] shall be paid the sum of five hundred ($500) dollars as compensation for pain and suffering as a result of the sexual harassment and the poisoned work environment she was made to endure.

With respect to Diana Hooper, the Board determined that the

triggering event which had caused her to go on disability leave in 1992 was the poisoned work environment at the Wakefield jail. The Board found that she was not able to return to work in a correctional capacity. It then directed that, if and when she was medically fit to return to work, the ministry must place her in a full-time position in a different government department in the area in which she lives. Should she be appointed in another area, the ministry should pay reasonable relocation costs. The Board additionally directed that (91–2):

(a) [Ms. Hooper] shall be paid the difference between LTD [long-term disability] payments received and [which she] will receive, and the wages she would have received had she been able to continue working at [Wakefield] jail, for the period beginning in November 1992 to the time she is provided work in a position pursuant to this decision.

(b) Interest shall be paid on the above amounts past due, calculated on the basis of the average annual prime rate for each applicable year.

(c) She shall be paid the sum of two thousand dollars ($2,000) as compensation for pain and suffering.

The Grievors' Reactions to the Decision

At first glance the decision seems reasonable. Yet in the months following the decision, the women were less than content. In particular, the three grievors were very disappointed at the lack of penalties imposed on their harassers. In addition, they were each concerned about how the gains now made in the decision would translate into practice.

Where the lack of penalties imposed on the men is concerned, the Board's failure to penalize them is not unusual. As Fudge (1991, 128) has observed, 'arbitrators have refused to order apologies, transfers, fines, or discipline with respect to the harasser.' While there have been exceptions to this, Cornish and Lopez (1994: 121) confirm that, similarly to human-rights adjudicators, arbitrators have 'generally refused to order apologies' and 'have also been reluctant to order the transfer or discipline of a sexual harasser.'[13] In the case of the Wakefield jail, although the Grievance Settlement Board had deemed during the hearings that it did have the power to impose discipline, it found the union's call for Fred Ferguson and Pat O'Reilly to be dismissed 'unwarranted and inappropriate' (Dissanayake et al. 1997, 88). The Board, while calling Superintendent Ferguson's behaviour – especially with respect to Karla Preston – 'very serious,' and while observing that 'he has not given any indication of remorse either,' highlighted the fact that he had been removed from the jail, and that it was unlikely that he would ever 'be in a position of authority over any of the three grievors at [Wakefield] jail' (98). While the Board may be correct in this observation, it also seems to demonstrate the limits of its willingness to step into the shoes of the employer and terminate managers who sexually harass. For its part, the ministry has arguably been less reluctant in disciplining bargaining-unit employees who sexually harass than in disciplining managers.

From the women's perspective, Fred Ferguson had hardly suffered at all for his transgressions, and had merely been transferred to a secure management position at one of the ministry's head offices. While from Ferguson's and the ministry's perspectives a substantial consequence had ensued in that his career was stalled, the women's frustration that he had escaped unscathed is, we think, understandable.

The women were also disappointed with the Board's limited criticism of Pat O'Reilly. In his case, the Board said that his conduct was 'less serious but still cannot be trivialized' (88). The source of all of his problems, the Board thought, was his belief at the time of the problems 'that women were unsuited to correctional work.' When he appeared before the Board[14], its members found him to be a 'generally credible and honest person.' The Board was satisfied with his explanation that he had not received Workplace Discrimination and Harassment Prevention training at the time of the alleged actions, and that he had since changed his attitudes. The Board also said that it 'observed a sense of sincere remorse on his part.' Finally, the Board declared itself 'satisfied that Mr. O'Reilly is fully aware that he would be jeopardizing his career, if not his employment itself, should he fail to mend his attitudes towards females in corrections' (88). The Board concluded that no further reaction to Lieutenant O'Reilly beyond the earlier three-day suspension imposed on him by the ministry was necessary in remedying any of the grievances under consideration.

Consequent to this, O'Reilly remained as a manager at the Wakefield jail. While dismissal might have been an excessively severe penalty, it is disappointing that there did not seem to be any intermediate way in which O'Reilly's culpability could have been given more concrete expression. In the absence of such a strategy, the women's perception that O'Reilly has not really paid the price for his bad conduct is understandable.

Following the decision, both the grievors and at least one other woman still working at the jail were of the opinion that, however O'Reilly might have presented himself at the hearings, he did not evidence remorse in his everyday life. Rather, in their view, he was confident and asserted that he and his behaviour were 'untouchable.' Whether O'Reilly has changed his attitude to women in corrections remains an open question.

In sum, the grievors were very disappointed by the fact that the Grievance Settlement Board did not order the ministry to impose additional penalties on either Fred Ferguson or Pat O'Reilly.[15]

The women's feelings of a lack of closure with respect to the imposition of penalties on the harassers was exacerbated by the realization that fully activating each of their compensation packages would take time, and much negotiation on the part of the union's lawyer. For example, dollar amounts had to be figured out and agreed by the ministry and the union with respect to the loss of earnings experienced as a result of stress-related illness by Karla Preston and Nora Diamond. The difference between the wages she would have made and the monies she did receive from long-term disability payments had to be similarly calculated for Diana Hooper.

Each of these calculations brought its own quirks and points of dispute. Meanwhile, at the time of the decision, Karla Preston and Nora Diamond still had over twenty outstanding grievances between them, concerning discrimination and reprisals after the period addressed by the Board. For example, Nora Diamond was grieving the termination of her contract earlier in 1997. The months following the decision saw efforts to resolve these grievances in conjunction with figuring out the details of their compensation packages.

Media attention to events at the Wakefield jail in the period following the Grievance Settlement Board decision also contributed to the women's sense of a lack of closure. With accounts of what had happened being published from one end of the province to the other, and with particularly extensive coverage in towns close to the jail, each of the women's experiences were exposed to the public. This was stressful.[16] No doubt this stress was intensified given the fact that the communities the women live in are small, and the women see staff of the Wakefield jail, and their families and friends, on a daily basis.

Throughout the time of the Grievance Settlement Board's deliberations, the women had already suffered rejection by some members of the community, who felt that the men of the Wakefield jail were being unjustly vilified, and even routine activities such as shopping could bring them face-to-face with these distressing sentiments. Karla Preston, for example, had been asked on the street: '"What did you do to those poor guys? How could you do that to them? How could you be so mean to them?"' (Interview with McMahon, June 1997.) Meanwhile, when she went to the hockey rink with her son, other people there would avoid her company.

During the hearings and before the decision, Nora Diamond particularly dreaded meeting staff from the jail in the course of her daily activities, and experienced periods of agoraphobia. She explained 'I wouldn't leave the house. And if I did leave the house, that's when I would have a panic attack. I went to the mall one day and I thought: "I'm going to run into somebody from that Jail." And do you know what? Boom! I had a panic attack. I sat in the car and waited until it passed and I drove back home. I couldn't go for groceries. You're bound to run into somebody.' (Interview with McMahon, June 1997).

The media coverage following the decision certainly did not ameliorate the women's public discomfort. Even Karla Preston, who had been eager to 'go public,' identify herself, and tell her story,[17] and who initially welcomed press attention, was less than enthusiastic about its results. Although she had thought that media coverage would help her feel 'vindicated,' in practice her experience went the other way. She was still snubbed by people and perceived by them as thinking 'it's my fault' (Personal communication with McMahon, January 1998).

For Nora Diamond and Diana Hooper, the media coverage was in some ways even more onerous, as, in contrast to Karla Preston's willingness to communicate her experiences publicly, they did not wish any media publicity at all, and were reluctant to discuss the past with people they did not know well.[18] The media documentation of their experiences, and the naming of their names, was very distressing as even more people in the area became aware of what had happened. They, too, experienced at least some of the public as unsympathetic. For example, Diana Hooper was told by one local person: "'You didn't accomplish anything other than embarrassment to yourself'" (Personal communication with McMahon, January 1998). For her part, immediately after the decision, Nora Diamond was disconcerted by the feeling that 'all eyes are on me' and wished that she was in a large city where 'you could just mix in with the crowd.' She again avoided public places for a while. Meanwhile, even when people did seem sympathetic, they appeared to have difficulty communicating their feelings. At Nora Diamond's new place of employment, for example, she felt that 'people were apprehensive about discussion with me' (Personal communications with McMahon, November 1997 and January 1998).

As of late January 1998, each of the grievors was experiencing emotional upheaval. Karla Preston, with the assistance of lawyer Beth Symes, was trying to work out the details of her settlement and her outstanding grievances. For reasons which will be discussed below, she was on leave from her position as cook at the jail and completing the placement requirement of a social-work course she had been taking at a local community college. She had chosen an institution for young offenders in another area of Ontario, where she hoped that the ministry would give her a position as a correctional officer. Although the logistics of moving herself and her four children were daunting, and although she was frustrated because it seemed that 'we have to fight tooth and nail [with the ministry] on every issue,' she was upbeat in facing the future.

Diana Hooper was struggling to cope with the fallout from the decision, and finding the negotiations about what salary compensation she would actually receive rather frustrating. Having been on long-term disability for over five years, she was nervous about the possibility of re-entering public service in the local area. She worried about whether she would be fit to return to work, about what job options would be open to her, and about whether – in view of the current downsizing of the public service – her new job would last. Diana Hooper was also anxious about how new colleagues would relate to her. Would they resent her getting a job through a Grievance Settlement Board decision? Would she be shunned because she had complained about sexual discrimination and harassment?

Nora Diamond was also having difficulties. For her, as for the other women, the decision had brought a 'whole new wave of emotions.' Her grievance that the non-renewal of her contract was a reprisal for her complaints remained unresolved, as was the amount of the dollar settlement that she would actually receive from the ministry.

Overall, the Grievance Settlement Board decision is a major legal victory for the three grievors, for women working in prisons for men, and for the union. But the brunt of the human cost of this victory has been borne by Karla Preston, Diana Hooper, and Nora Diamond, who had the courage to come forward, and, with the union's strong encouragement, to pursue their complaints through the arbitration process. In particular, the length of time[19] that the overall process took inflicted further psychic pain on top of that already inflicted through the sexual harassment and discrimination. As Nora Diamond expressed it in June 1997, the process arising from their complaints 'was like going down a road that had no end to it' (Interview with McMahon). Several months after the decision this statement continued to be apt. By the end of February 1998, however, the three cases had finally been settled to the satisfaction of all parties. The contents of the agreements are confidential.

Reactions at the Jail

Reactions at the Wakefield Jail to the Grievance Settlement Board decisions indicate that those working on the systemic remedies directed by the Grievance Settlement Board would have their work cut out for them. By all accounts,[20] the staff at the jail were furious with the decision. Karla Preston, who was still working at the jail on the day the decision was released, again felt that she was being ostracized.

A major source of the correctional officers' fury was their perception that they were all, as the saying goes, 'being tarred with the same brush.' The male officers were further infuriated by the media coverage, and especially by some comments made by their local Member of the Provincial Parliament, who was also the opposition critic for corrections in Ontario, and who was formerly the minister of correctional services (in the early 1980s). Apparently, the MPP stated that, during his time as minister, those working in jails caused him more trouble than those behind bars. The former minister was also quoted as saying that: 'In management, there is an old boys' network and the attitude is that boys will be boys ... instead of taking the attitude that the person should be fired' (Brennan 1997a, A5).[21] In response to this, and to the community scrutiny they were experiencing as a result of the media coverage, staff members asked the superintendent to sue the MPP. Not surprisingly, no such action was taken.

The superintendent (a recent newcomer to the jail) did write a memorandum attempting to calm the staff. His memorandum acknowledged that dealing with the media coverage was difficult as the jail had taken a 'pounding' where all employees were painted with the same brush. He said that there was not sufficient emphasis on the fact that the events in question had taken place some time ago. The superintendent also encouraged the staff to pull together with the support of their families and friends, to recognize that the Grievance Settlement Board decision was closure to an issue that had been outstanding for a long time, to overcome self-pity, and to work together in putting the matter behind them and moving into the future. In response to this, a correctional officer defaced the memo with lengthy quotations from Proverbs and Revelations. These quotations were very distressing for the grievors, as they felt that they were being characterized as Satan, and as deserving of God's retribution.

In short, as described by one union official, the Grievance Settlement Board decision was marked by 'a lot of backlash in the workplace' (Personal communication with McMahon, January 1998). Indeed, the anger at the Wakefield Jail was so intense that the Ontario Public Service Employees Union determined that it was not safe for Karla Preston to stay in that workplace. Ministry officials agreed that they could not ensure her safety at the jail, and she was removed.

Challenges Facing the Union and the Ministry

The immediate challenges facing the union and the ministry included responding to the backlash at the jail. The longer-term challenges facing them included implementing the systemic remedies ordered by the Grievance Settlement Board. A step in both of these directions was taken when a joint union-management delegation visited the jail to speak with staff. The group included Leah Casselman, president of the Ontario Public Service Employees Union, and an assistant deputy minister responsible for correctional services. The meeting gave the jail staff an opportunity to have their feelings and concerns heard. It also allowed the union and the ministry to directly communicate their shared commitment to eradicating sexual harassment in corrections, and to encourage the support of staff in doing so. By mid-January, the 'Joint Management-Union Assessment Team' had been established, as directed by the Grievance Settlement Board, and had met. Thus, while the Grievance Settlement Board decision did not bring instant closure, it did, as one union official expressed it, take the important step of '[allowing] closure to begin.'

We hope that this book will not label the Ontario correctional system as a particular den of problems of discrimination and sexual harassment. We believe this behaviour occurs in many male-dominated correctional settings. Ontario corrections are by no means unique in this regard. What has been unique in this case, rather, has been the opportunity to document this culture, and do research on the systemic aspects of gender-based discrimination and harassment, with rich qualitative data. Hopefully, arising from the process of systemic remedies set in motion by the Grievance Settlement board, as well as from both the Ontario Public Service Employees Union and the Ministry of Correctional Services' more general willingness to work together on gender-related issues, Ontario might also become known for acknowledging these problems and for its innovative responses to problems of gender-based discrimination and harassment. Time will tell.

Postscript

Time will indeed tell how successful Ontario can become in address-ing discrimination and harassment – but not in the case of the Wakefield Jail. On 9 July 1998, as this book was going to press, the Ministry of the Solicitor General and Correctional Services quietly made a dramatic announcement: the Wakefield Jail was to be closed by the end of the month.

The ministry also announced the closure of two other small jails in the province, and stated that the closures were part of a 'massive capital restructuring of Ontario's adult correctional system aimed at replacing less efficient institutions with large ultra-efficient insti-tutions' (Correctional Services, communications release, 9 July 1998).

Earlier in this book (104, 123, 191 n.6), the possibility of the jail's closure was identified. It was noted that women who had made com-plaints about discrimination and harassment were blamed when the Wakefield Jail was closed for two weeks for related training. They were also burdened with responsibility for the complete closure of the jail in the future, and particularly if complaints continued.

The ministry rationale for its current direction of privatization, 'superjails,' downsizing of the workforce, and adoption of more tech-nological forms of control (e.g., surveillance cameras) is resolutely fiscal and pragmatic. Humanistic concerns about both inmates and staff do not seem to be a priority.

Did the gender-related troubles at the Wakefield Jail contribute to its being sent to the top portion of the list of those fourteen insti-tutions slated for closure? Certainly there is a perception among staff that this is the case. And this in turn does not bode well for victims at other correctional institutions in pursuing their complains – especially where complaints are warranted en masse.

APPENDIX: Workplace Discrimination and Harassment Prevention:

Policy Directive and Guideline, Ontario Government, 1992

Objective

- To provide the principles and mandatory requirements essential to creating a work environment that is free from discrimination and harassment.
- To maintain, through proactive measures and enforcement, such a work environment.
- To identify corporate, ministry and agency responsibilities for the maintenance of such a work environment.

Application and Scope

This directive applies to:

- all ministries and schedule agencies subject to Management Board of Cabinet directives;
- all employees, both classified and unclassified, including interns, summer students and co-op students, appointed under the *Public Service Act*;
- employment-related discrimination and harassment, except systemic discrimination (see guideline, *Exceptions*), regardless of whether it occurs at the workplace or not;
- discrimination against a person because of his or her relationship, association or dealings with a person who belongs or is presumed to belong to a group designated under this directive;
- reprisal or threat of reprisal against employees who claim or pursue their rights under this directive including complainants, their representatives

and witnesses. Employees who believe that a reprisal has occurred have the right to file a complaint under this directive;
• employment-related discrimination or harassment of OPS employees by people who are not OPS employees.

This directive does not apply to discrimination or harassment against external applicants for positions with the OPS, consultants or government clients [see guideline, *Problems Outside the Directive*].

See guideline for definition of discrimination and harassment.

Principles

• The Ontario government as an employer is responsible for providing a workplace that is free from harassment and discrimination.
• All management and supervisory staff have an obligation to act quickly upon information concerning incidents of discrimination and harassment.
• A work environment that is free from harassment, as defined in this directive, does not tolerate an abusive atmosphere where an employee is subject to offensive remarks, behavior or surroundings that create intimidating, hostile or humiliating working conditions.
• Employees have the right to fair and equitable conditions of employment without discrimination or harassment because of race/color, ancestry, place of origin, ethnic origin, language or dialect spoken, citizenship, religion, sex (including pregnancy), sexual orientation, age (16–64), marital status, criminal charges or criminal record.
• Discrimination and harassment inhibit the achievement of employment equity in the Ontario Public Service.
• The complainant and alleged offender are to be treated fairly, while preserving the dignity, privacy and self-respect of all persons involved.
• Complaints must be filed within a reasonable time after the alleged discrimination occurred. A reasonable delay may be caused by factors such as an illness or vacation, unsuccessful effort to resolve the matter by other means, or lack of awareness at the time of the incident that the alleged conduct was in breach of the directive.
• All complaints must be forwarded within two days of filing to the Discrimination/Harassment Prevention Unit. Following consultation, Management Board Secretariat must decide within three days whether the complaint will be investigated centrally or by the ministry.
• An impartial investigation of the complaint must be conducted through the redress procedures established under this directive.

- The alleged offender must be notified as soon as possible, provided with a copy of the complaint, and given the opportunity to respond to the allegations.
- There must be no interference with an investigation or attempt to coach or intimidate a witness.
- Each party must be given the opportunity to be represented and accompanied by someone – union steward, lawyer (at own expense) or co-worker – during any meetings related to the complaint which they are required or entitled to attend. If a co-worker seeks his/her manager's approval to attend, the manager must make every reasonable effort to comply.
- The parties to a complaint and all witnesses must be advised about the application of the *Freedom of Information and Protection of Privacy Act* to any evidence gathered, and about potential disclosure of such evidence required according to law.
- The parties must be kept informed throughout the process, subject to *FOI*.
- Where possible, the investigator must send a report of the investigation findings within 60 working days from the date the complaint was filed to the relevant deputy minister and discrimination/harassment prevention co-ordinator.
- Complaints against uniformed members of the Ontario Provincial Police must be referred to the Deputy Solicitor General for action. [*Police Services Act*]

Remedies

- Each case must be assessed on its individual merits. If discipline is warranted, human resources and employment equity staff must be consulted, where appropriate.
- Any remedy must attempt, to the extent possible, to put the complainant into the situation that he or she would have been in had the discrimination not occurred.
- Discrimination and harassment are serious offences and appropriate disciplinary action must be taken where the complaint is substantiated. Discipline must also be imposed against managers who condone discrimination or harassment.
- Employees who have been disciplined for a violation of this directive must be advised of their right to lodge a grievance against such actions under the *Collective Agreement* or the *PSA*, whichever is applicable.
- Complainants who are not satisfied with the outcome of their complaints

must be told they can lodge a grievance under the *Collective Agreement* or file a complaint under the Ontario *Human Rights Code*.

Confidentiality and Data Collection

- Throughout the complaint and investigation process all information must remain confidential, subject to the *Freedom of Information and Protection of Privacy Act* and the requirement to disclose information or give evidence as required by law, such as grievance arbitrations, Ontario Human Rights Commission proceedings and judicial proceedings [see *FOI and the Discrimination/Harassment Complaint Process* booklet, Workplace Discrimination/Harassment Prevention Unit, MBS for more information]
- Any institution has the authority to collect personal information indirectly in response to complaints or requests for advice made under this directive.
- This directive requires the disclosure of personal information from one institution to another in the following circumstances:

  - for the purposes of complaint investigation, reporting and resolution, where the investigator is employed by a ministry other than the ministry in which the complaint originated, or where the complaint involves employees of more than one ministry;
  - in order to allow a ministry and Management Board Secretariat to confer about the application of the directive to a complaint;
  - in order to allow Management Board Secretariat to monitor the effective implementation of the directive.

- All records must be kept in a secure filing system, in accordance with Management Board of Cabinet's *Information Technology Security Directive*, with access restricted to those persons who need the record to perform the necessary and proper functions of the institution.
- Where an investigation results in a formal warning or disciplinary action this information must be placed in the offender's personal file. Where the complaint has not been substantiated, no reference must be placed on the personnel file of either party.
- Evidence that an employee has lodged a complaint maliciously or in bad faith must be placed on his/her personnel file with a report of any discipline imposed for such conduct.
- Statistical information on the number, nature and type of formal and informal complaints resolved must be kept and reports filed quarterly

with the deputy head and the Discrimination/Harassment Prevention Unit, Management Board Secretariat.

Responsibilities

Deputy Heads

Deputy Heads are responsible for:

- adhering to the requirements contained in this directive and upholding its principles;
- ensuring that all employees are informed of their rights under this directive and their responsibilities in preventing discrimination and harassment in the workplace;
- ensuring that all managers and supervisors have the knowledge and skills to create and maintain a work environment that is free from discrimination and harassment, and are held responsible for doing so;
- appointing discrimination/harassment prevention co-ordinators, advisors and investigators, where the size of the ministry warrants internal investigative capacity, and ensuring they are trained;
- providing employees with full access to the ministry advisor;
- where ministry advisors are assigned, ensuring that the investigation of complaints is completed, where possible, within 60 working days;
- ensuring complainants are remedied when the complaint has been substantiated;
- imposing upon offenders penalties that reflect the seriousness of the misconduct and are consistent with good disciplinary practices;
- imposing penalties upon members of line management who condone discrimination and harassment;
- sending to the parties, within 15 working days of receiving the investigator's report, a written summary of the investigation findings, and, if the complaint is upheld, notification that discipline has been imposed;
- monitoring the situation until satisfied that any settlement has been complied with by the parties.

Discrimination/Harassment Prevention Co-ordinator

The Discrimination/Harassment Prevention co-ordinator is responsible for:

- acting as a point of contact for all persons responsible for implementing this directive;
- referring complaints to the Discrimination/Harassment Prevention Unit, Management Board Secretariat within two working days of receipt;
- co-ordinating educational programs;
- collection on prescribed forms and maintaining statistical information on the number, nature and type of formal and informal complaints resolved, recording the number and type of inquiries, consultations and referrals handled by the advisors and forwarding a report of these findings on a quarterly basis to the Discrimination/Harassment Prevention Unit, Management Board Secretariat.

Advisors

Advisors are responsible for providing confidential advice about this directive to all employees who request it.

Investigators

Investigators are responsible for:

- investigating complaints filed under this directive;
- sending written reports of the investigation findings to the co-ordinator and deputy head.

Managers and Supervisors

Managers and supervisors are responsible for:

- establishing and maintaining a work environment that is free from harassment and discrimination;
- refusing to participate in or condone harassment or discrimination;
- ensuring that no employee is instructed to discriminate against another employee, or to participate in such discrimination;
- ensuring compliance with this directive;
- ensuring that employees are aware of their rights and responsibilities under this directive and the mechanism in place to resolve discrimination or harassment complaints.
- initiating, in consultation with appropriate individuals, remedial proce-

dures with respect to discrimination, harassment or reprisal as quickly as possible upon becoming aware of it, whether or not a complaint has been filed;

- addressing and resolving informal complaints;
- protecting the confidentiality of all parties and witnesses to the complaint to the greatest degree possible; [see *Confidentiality and Data Collection*]
- co-operating with persons who investigate complaints;
- imposing penalties upon offenders in accordance with the directive and guideline and with ministry guidelines for delegation of disciplinary authority.

Management Board Secretariat

Management Board Secretariat is responsible for:

- establishing and administering the Discrimination/Harassment Prevention Unit;
- advising and supporting the ministries on the application of this directive;
- investigating certain complaints following consultation with the ministry involved;
- establishing or approving training courses for advisors and investigators;
- preparing or consulting with ministries regarding communications materials on the directive and its implementation to ensure consistency of approach;
- monitoring enforcement of this directive and compiling statistics on complaints and their resolution;
- monitoring corporate trends relating to the enforcement of this directive and recommending improvements when necessary;
- publishing an annual report with statistical information on the types and dispositions of complaints resolved and the nature of settlements obtained, ensuring confidentiality of the parties.

GUIDELINE

The Ontario government has a commitment to all employees within the Ontario Public Service to ensure that a work environment free from discrimination and harassment is established and maintained.

Application

The *Workplace Discrimination and Harassment Prevention* directive applies to discrimination in any aspect of employment, including recruitment, promotion, training, transfer, receipt of benefits, dismissal, lay-off, discipline, performance appraisal and working conditions such as overtime, hours of work and shift work.

It applies to all discrimination with workplace repercussions, regardless of where it occurs, for example, physical work sites, cafeterias, washrooms, elevators, conferences, business travel, office parties.

If OPS employees are being discriminated against by non-OPS employees – such as parliamentary staff, Order-in-Council appointees, clients, members of the public, contractors, consultants and delivery people – the employer is obligated to respond (see *Complaints against persons outside the OPS section*).

The directive also applies to employees with disabilities who are refused the accommodation required to enable them to perform their job duties. See the directive and guideline on *Accommodation in Employment for Persons with Disabilities* in the *Workforce Planning* section of this manual for more information, or contact the Workforce Planning and Employment Equity Branch, Management Board Secretariat.

The Right to Equal Treatment

Unequal treatment means treating a person differently, usually less favorably, because of membership in a specific group. Discrimination may be practised openly, for example, where an employer candidly refuses to hire women for certain jobs. Or it may be concealed and denied; if women enquire about job openings, the employer may tell them there are no positions when this is not true.

A person need not intend to discriminate for discrimination to occur. The *Workplace Discrimination and Harassment Prevention* directive is concerned with the inequality resulting from differential treatment regardless of the motives of the person who committed the discriminatory act. For example, a manager reassigns a pregnant employee to other less responsible duties out of a concern for her health, with no intention of excluding or demoting her.

Also prohibited is discrimination because of the employee's actual or presumed relationship, association or dealings with other individuals who belong to a group designated by any of the grounds set out above. For example, a manager may not exclude from work-related social functions a white employee because she is married to a South Asian.

Exceptions

Systemic Discrimination

The directive does not cover systemic discrimination. Systemic discrimination occurs when policies and practices are applied to all employees, but have an adverse impact on disadvantaged groups. While systemic discrimination is against the law, ministries are addressing this problem by means of Employment Systems Reviews and other ongoing reviews of employment practices [see *Employment Systems Review Directive*].

This does not relieve ministries of the responsibility to eliminate systemic discrimination wherever it is identified.

Ministries and agencies are encouraged to refer complaints of systemic discrimination to their employment systems review task force for investigation, and to consult with Management Board Secretariat regarding their resolution.

Exceptions under Code

The *Ontario Human Rights Code*, ss. 16, 17, 24 and 25, permits exceptions to certain provisions in this directive. For example the need for public decency or sex-role identification can warrant a designation of males or females only. Nurses' aides providing intimate care for chronically ill persons who request same-sex care and female counsellors for battered women are two examples.

Or safety concerns may allow an employer to exclude individuals with a serious criminal record of sexual assault of developmentally disabled children from positions involving the care of such children. Managers and supervisors should consult the *Code* regarding the exact wording of these provisions.

Employment Equity

This directive cannot be used to undermine a genuine employment equity program such as the government's policy requiring positive measures to increase the employment of minorities and women. Section 14 of the *Code* permits special programs designed to assist disadvantaged persons or groups to achieve equality.

Examples of Discrimination

Following are examples of situations involving discrimination that fall within the directive.

Race/color – A black food services worker is assigned to kitchen duties because his manager believes the residents of the facility will object to black workers in the public areas of the cafeteria.

Ethnic origin/language spoken – A secretary originally from Greece, is not allowed to talk with a co-worker in her native language in the office, even during meal breaks.

Sex, marital/family status – A woman is passed over for promotion by a less qualified male because the job requires travel and the director believes she will be less available for out-of-town assignment.

Sexual orientation – A lawyer is refused a transfer to another branch because the director believes the staff will exclude her from meetings and office activities because she is a lesbian.

Age – A 62–year-old systems analyst is refused approval for a training program because of the manager's policy to provide training only to employees who are under 60 years of age.

Disability – A childcare worker with limited use of one arm is refused a promotion because the employer believes she will be unable to lift the children in her care.

Criminal charges/criminal record – A lab technician facing charges of auto theft, a charge which is not related to his job duties, is suspended until the case is decided by the courts.

The Right to Freedom from Harassment

Harassment is a form of discrimination. In this directive, harassment is defined as any comment or conduct that is:

- based on race/color, ancestry, place of origin, ethnic origin, language or dialect spoken, citizenship, religion, sex, sexual orientation, age, marital status, family status, physical or mental disability, criminal charges or criminal record; and
- offensive to any employee, and is known, or should reasonably be known, to be unwelcome.

The comments or conduct need not make reference to a specific group for a violation to take place. For example, a member of a racial minority could be subjected to racially motivated slurs or gestures that do not expressly refer to his race or color.

Unfair and improper terms and conditions of employment and forms of discipline may constitute both discrimination and harassment as defined here.

Harassment can include such conduct as demands or threats, gestures, innuendo, remarks, jokes or slurs, display of offensive material, physical or sexual assault or taunting about a person's body, attire, habits, customs, or mannerisms where they are related to any of the above grounds. It can also include inappropriate or unwelcome focus or comments on a person's physical characteristics or appearance.

Poisoned Work Environment

Harassment may also result from comments or conduct that tend to ridicule or disparage a protected group even if not directed at a specific employee. This type of harassment, because of its harmful effects, is often referred to as a poisoned work environment and is prohibited under the directive. A single remark or action could be in violation of the directive if it is serious enough to poison the environment for the person subjected to it.

Excluding minorities and women from important activities within a workplace can also create a poisoned environment by generating a climate where such groups believe their contributions are not valued.

Harassment can be practised by co-workers, by supervisors toward their employees or by employees towards supervisors. For example racial minority, female, gay or lesbian managers may be subjected to harassment by those who report to them.

Efforts of a co-worker to undermine the well-being or job performance of an employee or failure to provide appropriate support and encouragement because of the grounds set out above can also constitute harassment. Such conduct undermines self-esteem and contributes to stereotyping and discrimination.

Sexual Harassment

Sexual harassment is further defined as a situation where:

• an employee receives unwelcome sexual attention from any employee and such comment or conduct is known or should reasonably be known to be offensive, inappropriate, intimidating and/or hostile behavior;

- an employee receives unwelcome sexual attention and is threatened or penalized by a loss of job, denial of advancement, raise or other employment benefit for noncompliance with sexual demands by a person in a position of authority who knows or should reasonably know that sexual attention is unwelcome.

Examples of Harassment

Following are examples of situations that fall within the harassment provisions of the directive.

Sex – The supervisor of a female purchasing officer makes belittling comments about her and other women in the branch. He criticizes their work and ignores their suggestions at meetings. In general, female staff are not treated as well as male staff.

Race/color – A South-east Asian information officers finds cartoons in his in-tray depicting derogatory references to members of his group.

Religion – Several office workers are persistent in their efforts to persuade a co-worker, who is not of their faith, to read their religious literature and attend services despite her response that these efforts are unwelcome.

Disability – A developmentally disabled clerk is called names such as 'dummy' by two of her co-workers. She has raised the problem with her supervisor who tells her that the co-workers don't mean any harm. Management takes no steps to educate the co-workers and forbid the behavior.

Sexual orientation – A gay male reports finding graffiti referring to gays as being carriers of AIDS.

Against the Law

Discrimination and harassment are illegal behaviors that will not be tolerated within the OPS.

A Management Issue

The Ontario *Human Rights Code* and case law indicate that persons with the authority to penalize or prevent discrimination and harassment may be held responsible for failing to exercise their authority to do so. Supreme Court of Canada decisions have established a trend towards greater employer liability. An employer cannot afford to handle problems of discrimination and harassment ineffectively.

Failure to take action against discrimination or harassment can result in:

- violation of the *Code, Collective Agreement* and the *PSA* by both the manager and employer;
- lack of trust and confidence in management or supervisory staff among employees;
- harm to the complainant, for example severe stress that can induce physical or mental illness requiring lost work time, declining quality of work and productivity, loss of self-worth;
- harm to the complainant's co-workers, for example discrimination or harassment against other persons in the same group, resentment of management inaction, poor morale and staff relations;
- a continuing pattern of increasingly serious discrimination or harassment against the initial victim and other employees;
- costly financial liability for both the employer and the manager or supervisor could result if a complaint were filed under the *Code* or *Collective Agreement*;
- disciplinary action against a manager or supervisor who condones or fails to address discrimination or harassment;
- accusations of prior knowledge or condoning of harassment or discrimination by the ministry;
- significant public embarrassment to the employer and the manager or supervisor;
- a poisoned work environment, characterized by low morale, poor staff relations, tension and friction among staff, greater number of transfers and resignations.

Non-Discriminatory Work Environment

Communication and education are effective methods of raising awareness and preventing discrimination or harassment. Combined, they will contribute to a respectful work environment that discourages workplace discrimination.

The aim of the discrimination/harassment prevention directive, like that of the *Code*, is to create in the workplace a climate of understanding and mutual respect, in which all employees will be made to feel that all are equal in dignity and rights.

Examples of proactive measures include:

- surveying ministry employees to determine their experiences with discrimination and awareness of the OPS directive;
- producing articles on the directive in the ministry newsletter;
- inviting a ministry workplace discrimination/harassment prevention advisor to discuss the program at a staff meeting;
- designing and displaying posters about discrimination and harassment.

Redress Mechanisms

Employees may consult an advisor about alternative mechanisms for resolving problems relating to harassment or discrimination.

Employees are encouraged:

- to inform alleged harassers that the harassment is unwelcome;
- to seek assistance from an advisor, manager, or supervisor if the harasser's behavior does not change or if circumstances make it difficult to approach that person;
- to speak to a manager, supervisor or advisor if they think that a co-worker is being discriminated against or harassed.

Informal Resolutions

Informal resolution options include:

- confronting the alleged offender personally or in writing and informing him or her that the discrimination or harassment is unwelcome and must stop;
- requesting an educational session on discrimination and harassment for the work unit in question;
- asking a supervisor, manager or other employee, such as employment equity human resources staff, to help resolve the matter.

Manager's or supervisor's involvement

A manager responding to an informal complaint should consult others, such as advisors, investigators, human resources staff, or the Discrimination/Harassment Prevention Unit before handling an issue, and particularly under the following circumstances:

- the allegations indicate a relatively serious form of harassment which merits formal, not informal, intervention;
- if proven, the allegations warrant either disciplinary action that is more serious than a warning or a formal response from management;
- there is more than one aggrieved person, according to the complainant's allegations;
- the alleged offender is disputing to a significant extent the complainant's version of what happened.

Although a full investigation is normally conducted only for formal complaints, a manager or supervisor may request that an informal complaint be referred to an investigator.

Formal resolutions

Formal resolution options include:

- filing a complaint under the *Workplace Discrimination and Harassment Prevention* directive;
- filing a grievance under the *Collective Agreement* (bargaining unit members);
- filing a complaint with the Ontario Human Rights Commission;
- where the situation allows, pursuing a remedy through the courts (for example, where harassment also involves assault);
- remedies provided under such employee protection legislation as the *Occupational Health and Safety Act*, which requires employers to provide safe workplaces, and the *Workers' Compensation Act*, where the discrimination results in compensable injury or stress.

Complaints should be lodged with one of the following: the complainant's supervisor, any manager within the ministry, an advisor, the Discrimination/Harassment Prevention Unit, Management Board Secretariat or with the deputy minister, agency head or discrimination/harassment prevention co-ordinator.

Advice/Counselling

In addition to choosing one or more of the above options, the employee may seek:

- personal counselling from the Ministry of Government Services Employee

Counselling Service, outside community services, advocacy groups, the clergy, family doctor, therapist or specialist.

- legal advice (at employee's own expense);

The ministry advisor can provide further information on the above options.

Advisory Services/Complaint Resolution

Prevention Co-ordinator

The deputy minister appoints a member of the Senior Management Group or the employment equity manager as the discrimination/harassment prevention co-ordinator and main contact for the directive and its implementation. The co-ordinator:

- receives information from the Discrimination/Harassment Prevention Unit, Management Board Secretariat regarding the directive and conveys it to ministry advisors and investigators.
- collates data regarding complaints and prepares statistical reports for the deputy and the Discrimination/Harassment Prevention Unit.
- assists the Discrimination/Harassment Prevention Unit in co-ordinating training programs that include sensitivity to discrimination and harassment issues and the means for resolving problems and complaints.
- stocks and distributes written material describing the directive and complaint procedures.

Advisory Services

The advisor:

- provides confidential consultation services and information to all employees upon request, including managers, supervisors and union stewards, on the application and scope of the *Workplace Discrimination and Harassment Prevention* directive [see directive for parameters of confidentiality];
- clarifies options (internal and external) available to employees seeking to resolve discrimination or harassment;

- consults with the complainant about the drafting of the complaint;
- is a neutral source of information and advice and cannot act as an advocate for any particular individual;
- may not initiate complaint procedures.

Processing the Complaint

The unit will notify the ministry co-ordinator when it receives a complaint directly. If the complaint is submitted to someone in the ministry other than the deputy minister, the recipient will forward it to the ministry co-ordinator.

The complainant may stipulate that the complaint be investigated by the Discrimination/Harassment Prevention Unit. Where no preference is indicated, they will decide, in consultation with the ministry, whether the complaint should be investigated centrally, by the ministry or by another ministry.

Unit Investigations

Complaints should normally be investigated by the unit where they involve:

- complex application of human rights jurisprudence;
- issues that warrant handling by an outside investigator, for example where the alleged offender is a senior ministry official;
- a conflict of interest, for example if the ministry investigator is related to one of the parties, or the complaint is in the investigator's branch or involves someone to whom the investigator reports directly or indirectly.

Other circumstances under which complaints should be handled by the unit include situations where:

- concern has been expressed about the quality of the ministry's investigation or the ministry's ability to handle the complaint impartially and confidentially;
- there is no ministry investigator in place or sufficiently trained;
- it would be more efficient for the unit to investigate the complaint in terms of workload;
- a ministry is too small to warrant its own investigator.

The unit bears the cost of all investigations it conducts.

Investigation of Complaints

Once a complaint has been filed and it has been determined whether the Discrimination/Harassment Prevention Unit or the ministry will investigate, the unit, the deputy minister or the co-ordinator assigns an investigator, who:

- informs the alleged offender as soon as possible and provides him or her with the copy of the complaint;
- advises both parties the complaint is under investigation and informs them about the complaints resolution process;
- plans and conducts the investigation, in accordance with the guidelines established by Management Board Secretariat as set out in the investigators' training program.

To ensure confidence of both parties in the neutrality of investigators, person who have an advocacy or adversarial role in the staff relations area or who have a direct influence on the career of either party should not be appointed as investigators.

The Report

The report of the investigation and conclusions regarding resolution should, wherever possible, be submitted within 60 working days of the complaint being filed, unless extenuating circumstances occur, such as unusually complex investigations or lengthy absences on the part of witnesses. It is sent to the discrimination/harassment prevention co-ordinator and to the deputy head for decision on remedies.

If there is no single aggrieved party – for example, where the offence involved graffiti or offensive posters in a public area of the workplace – the investigator's report is sent to the deputy head, the ministry discrimination/harassment prevention co-ordinator or the manager of the unit in question.

Remedies

Burden/Standard of Proof

Before discipline can be imposed or a remedy provided, management needs to prove on the balance of probabilities that the alleged offender practised discrimination or harassment.

In cases of dismissal where severe discipline is at issue, the proof formula should be based on clear and convincing evidence.

It is not necessary for the ministry to prove the offence 'beyond a reasonable doubt,' which is the standard of proof used in criminal courts.

Examples of Remedies

Investigators do not recommend specific remedies; their conclusions should be limited to an analysis of the evidence and information such as the nature and amount of losses the complainant has suffered.

Some examples of remedies are: reinstatement of a complainant who was dismissed for discriminatory reasons, removal of offensive posters or cartoon from a work area and a human rights seminar for a person found in violation of the directive.

Management can only discipline once for inappropriate behavior – that is, it can decide either not to act or to impose a specific penalty. The deputy or manager should, therefore, seek advice from human resources staff, the Discrimination/Harassment Prevention Unit and employment equity staff before imposing discipline or deciding that a penalty is unwarranted. Employment equity staff can provide useful information on the impact of discrimination and harassment on employees and the types of remedies considered appropriate from a human rights perspective.

Disciplinary measures should be consistent with those outlined in the *PSA* and the *Human Resources Directives and Guidelines.* They may include transfer, subject to *Collective Agreement* provisions where applicable, verbal reprimands or warnings, suspension without pay, or dismissal. Removal of discriminatory policies and practices and other systemic remedies may also be appropriate.

Complainants and respondents should be informed when the decision is rendered of their right to appeal the results of an investigation. [see directive, *Remedies*]

Factors to Consider

The following factors should be considered when deciding on appropriate disciplinary action:

- how serious the offence was that precipitated the discipline;
- the severity of the consequences to the complainant of the harassment or discriminatory act, for example denial of a promotion, exclusion from

a training program, lost work time as a result of physical or emotional trauma suffered;

- whether the offender has previously committed any other violations of the directive;
- the ongoing nature of the discrimination or harassment, that is, the period of time over which it occurred;
- whether or not the complainant was subjected to coercion, assaults, threats, or reprisals;
- whether the offender's conduct was premeditated or repetitive, or was a momentary and emotional incident, perhaps provoked by someone else;
- if harassment, the nature of the harassment: was it verbal, physical or both;
- the degree of offensiveness, aggressiveness or physical contact in the harassment;
- the frequency of the harassment;
- an abuse of power, authority, or assigned responsibilities where a prohibited ground is involved.
- public embarrassment or wilful or reckless damage to the complainant's status in the workplace or in the community;
- taking advantage of vulnerability on the part of the complainant, for example due to personal situation, personality, or isolated location;
- wilful or reckless damage to victim's self-esteem, emotional health, or ability to function effectively at work;
- length of service;
- disciplinary record.

Complaints against Persons outside the OPS

Alleged discriminatory acts or harassment committed against an OPS employee by a client, recipient of a service, consultant or delivery person, should be handled in the following manner:

- the allegations should be investigated in accordance with the procedure set out in this guideline;
- where the alleged offender is in a business or contractual relationship with the government, he or she should be advised that discriminatory conduct or harassment may result in termination of the relationship and deletion from inventories of services;
- where a relationship with a client or resident of a government or broader public sector facility is involved, and termination of the relationship is

not possible or feasible, the alleged offender should be informed that discrimination and harassment are contrary to government policy and will not be tolerated;

- where harassment is practised by a person who may not understand or accept the government's policy against such conduct, that person should be transferred away from the OPS employee in question, if possible. An employee who has been subjected to discrimination or harassment should not be forced to transfer out of the work area;
- in all substantiated complaints, managers or supervisors should acknowledge to complainants that discrimination or harassment has occurred and assure them that steps are being taken to remedy the situation. In serious cases, the manager, supervisor or director should write a letter to the complainant, stating that discrimination and harassment are in violation of government policy and setting out the action that has been taken.
- any penalty that is imposed should be decided by the relevant deputy minister in consultation with appropriate ministry staff. Where the offence involves a person or business that offers goods or services throughout government, the deputy should consult the ministry's legal services staff with respect to a government-wide remedy;
- the complainant should be included in any resolution of the problem and consulted regarding remedy where the complaint has been substantiated;
- the complainant should be advised of the right to file a complaint with the Ontario Human Rights Commission if not satisfied with the outcome.

Problems outside the Directive

External applicants for positions within the OPS, consultants, or clients of government programs or services cannot file complaints under the *Workplace Discrimination and Harassment Prevention* directive. However, ministries and agencies are encouraged to resolve problems involving such persons informally, where feasible, and may wish to consult an advisor or the Discrimination/Harassment Prevention Unit. Such conduct comes under the *Code* and could become the subject of a complaint to the Ontario Human Rights Commission.

Notes

CHAPTER 1. Women Working in Corrections and in Prisons for Men

1 For example, in Ontario until the late 1800s, there was no penal institution specifically for female offenders. Women served their time in prisons with men, and sometimes even in the same cells as men (see Strange 1985, 80). In 1874, the Andrew Mercer Ontario Reformatory for women was opened, and was staffed almost exclusively by women (Strange, 1985). Yet it appears that many women in Ontario continued to be imprisoned in male institutions. A similar situation has applied in the USA. As observed by Zupan (1992, 297; see also Freedman 1981):

> The supervision of female inmates by male officers is neither a recent nor a novel innovation. In the earliest penal institutions, male and female prisoners lived communally and were watched over by male staff. Even after women inmates were segregated in separate wings of male prisons in the late eighteenth century, they were still guarded by men ... Since many penal institutions for women were simply adjuncts to male prisons, they were also administered by male wardens. More often than not, women prisoners suffered at the hands of their male keepers.

In recent decades in Ontario, the only provincial prison dedicated solely to women has been the Vanier Centre in Brampton. At the end of 1992, out of the total of 67 correctional officers employed there, 23 were male – a little over one-third of correctional staff. This proportion is higher than that which will be documented for female correctional staff in prisons for men. The ratio of staffing at the female unit in the Metropolitan Toronto West Detention Centre is more comparable to that of women across the province in prisons for men: of 68 correctional officers, 11 were male (Employment Systems Review 1994, 91, 93).

2. Szockyj (1989), and Sakowski (1985) are among the few research sources available that address the Canadian situation. Publications from provincial and federal correctional agencies also provide some useful information (Caron 1981; Correctional Service of Canada 1992; Employment Systems Task Force 1994; Henriksen 1993).

3. It might be noted that the inception of the prison as a major form of punishment signified a shift from punishing in the public sphere, to punishing in a more private and hidden way. Specifically, prior to the inception of prisons, punishment was often directed at the body (e.g., whipping, flogging, stocks and pillories, and hanging), and was carried out in public places (e.g., the market square). The widespread use of prisons from the early 1800s had the effect of removing the process of punishment from public view (for a theoretical account of the shift from the public to the private sphere in punishment, see Foucault 1977; for accounts of the early history of prisons in Canada, see Beattie 1977, and Griffiths and Verdun-Jones 1994, Chapter 10).

4. For discussions and debates about the occupational culture of correctional officers, see Griffiths and Verdun-Jones 1994; Klofas and Toch 1982; Philliber 1987.

5. The focus of the media in 1994, 1995, and 1996, on problematic events at the Kingston Prison for Women – and specifically on the involvement of male members of the Emergency Response Team in stripping and searching female inmates – is a case in point.

6. The follow-up to the strip-searching incidents at the Prison for Women (mentioned in the previous note) illustrates the tendency of prison administrators to withhold information. The incidents (which took place in late April 1994) were recorded on videotape, and were subsequently internally reviewed by the Correctional Service of Canada's Board of Investigation.

   In February 1995, R.L. Stewart, the federal Correctional Investigator who is more independent of the correctional service, issued a special report concerning the incidents and subsequent inquiry. Mr. Stewart's criticisms of the Correctional Service's inquiry included the following (1995, 2, 6):

   > The Correctional Service of Canada failed to ensure that its investigative process into these incidents was and was seen to be open, independent and objective. The characterization of the Board of Investigation Report as a 'white wash' by the offenders involved and the Elizabeth Fry Society is no surprise given the make-up of the Board ... The Board of Investigation Report is at best incomplete, inconclusive, and self-serving.

   In addition, Mr. Stewart noted that although he had requested the videotape of the incidents in late June 1994, and several times the following November, he did not receive access to the videotape until 27 January 1995 (1995, 4). During the period between the incidents, and the publication of his special report, he also expressed concerns about the segregation of some of the female inmates who had been stripped. His description of the Correctional Service of Canada's response is as follows (1995, 8; emphases in original):

> The Correctional Service of Canada, in responding to these concerns, has taken no action which can be seen as timely, adequate or appropriate. The Service's responses to this entire matter can be characterized as **'admit no wrong, give as little as possible and time will eventually resolve the matter.'** *Hardly consistent with the Service's motto of Accountability, Integrity, Openness.*

While the correctional authorities' responses were typical in their tendency to withhold information, this case is also atypical in the amount of public attention that the strip-searching incidents did eventually receive. Here, the existence of the videotape of the events is significant. In February 1995, sections of the tape were broadcast on national television, and soon afterwards a royal commission was established to examine related events. The report of the commission was thorough, frank, and critical, in its discussion of related events (Arbour 1996). One suspects that if the videotape had not existed, or had not been made public, the incidents and their context would have, as is more generally the case, escaped systematic scrutiny.

7. These opportunities arose following the election of the New Democratic Party in the province of Ontario in the fall of 1990. It was this social democratic party's first time being elected in the province, and, for many of the members of caucus, including some cabinet members, their first time holding seats. While the party had well-articulated policies in many areas – for example with respect to labour, the environment, and women's issues – their policies in other areas, including justice, were less developed. To help deal with this, the new government sought to involve supporters with relevant policy and research knowledge, and this is how I was able to successfully apply for positions within the minister's office.

8. Prior to my personal involvement in the ministry, my research interests were primarily in issues of imprisonment and alternatives (McMahon 1990; 1992), privatization and criminal justice (Ericson et al. 1987), and police accountability (McMahon and Ericson 1984; McMahon 1988). Subsequent publications that document some of my observations on criminal justice from the 'inside' include McMahon 1996a, 1996b).

9. I was in Paris doing research in the summer of 1992, and received word of the scandal from friends and former colleagues, who called me and sent newspaper clippings.

10. This point applies of course not only to scandals and controversies involving correctional and justice ministries, but to all government ministries.

11. I spent the 1993–4 academic year in Lithuania as a visiting lecturer at Vilnius University, and was unable to pursue the topic of Canadian women working in corrections during this period.

12. The Wakefield Jail is a pseudonym, and pseudonyms are also used for all individuals associated with the jail, including the three grievors. Pseudonyms are also used for several other ministry institutions – specifically Montcalm, South Ridge, and Westbury – which are mentioned later in this book. Other institutions discussed in this book (i.e., the Bell Cairn Training Centre, and the Windsor Jail, and other prisons) are identified by their real names.

13. From the Second World War until the mid-1990s, prisons in Ontario had their own government department or ministry (first the Department of Reform Institutions, later the Department of Correctional Services, and lastly the Ministry of Correctional Services). As of the mid-1990s, the Ministry of Correctional Services was amalgamated with the Ministry of the Solicitor General (whose responsibilities include police, coroners, and firefighters in the province). The full title of the ministry now responsible for the Wakefield Jail is therefore, the Ministry of the Solicitor General and Correctional Services.

    As most of the incidents at the Wakefield Jail to be considered here took place before this amalgamation, and as the same applies with respect to the Bell Cairn Staff Training Centre, this book will refer to the Ministry of Correctional Services. The reason for this is not only because during most of the period being considered these institutions were under the sole jurisdiction of the Ministry of Correctional Services, but also to avoid potential confusion about policies in other areas of the reconstituted ministry.

    The Ontario Ministry of Correctional Services is responsible for adult inmates serving sentences of less than two years, as well as for inmates on remand. The ministry also administers provincial probation and parole services.

14. The vast majority of the documents were presented as exhibits before the Grievance Settlement Board. They included ministry memos, investigation reports, and other documentation concerning incidents and complaints of harassment and discrimination at the Wakefield Jail. They also included government, ministry, and union statements concerning relevant policies (for example, concerning cross-gender supervision, and concerning equal-opportunity, affirmative-action, and employment-equity programs). Docu-

ments presented to the Board further included details of past and current ministry initiatives with respect to staffing and gender issues.

Beth Symes also provided me with notes on the hearings prepared by her legal assistants of testimony at the hearings by the participants. In addition to drawing from these documents, my report, and this book, also draw from publications concerning corrections in Ontario, from other research materials concerning the ministry that I have gathered over the years (most notably those while preparing *The Persistent Prison?*), and from discussions and interviews with various people.

15. It is not possible to document the experiences of all of the women affected at either Bell Cairn or the Wakefield Jail. As will be discussed, women are typically reluctant to complain about gender-based discrimination and harassment. This reluctance applies not only in cases of what might be described as more trivial forms of harassment (as experienced by women at both Bell Cairn and the Wakefield Jail), but also in particularly serious cases (as exemplified in relation to the alleged 'gang-rapes' at Bell Cairn). Again, what is unusual about many of the situations to be discussed in this book is not that they occurred, but that at least some women were willing to make official complaints about them, and to pursue their complaints in the face of adversity.

CHAPTER 2. A History of Women Working in Corrections and in Prisons for Men

1. As noted, the provincial prison system is responsible for prisoners on remand, and those serving sentences of under two years, as well as for administering provincial probation and parole services. This chapter also provides some comparative observations concerning the federal Correctional Service of Canada, which is responsible for prisoners serving sentences of two years and over.

2. See Caron (1985) for some observations on nursing staff at the Guelph Reformatory.

3. This reference to incarceration pursuant to 'alcoholism' most likely refers to imprisonment following from an inability to pay, or from defaulting on, a fine for public drunkenness. It has been estimated that close to 50 per cent of all sentenced admissions to prison in Ontario between 1951 and 1960 arose 'from an inability to pay fines in court following conviction for intoxication' (McMahon 1992, 137). Meanwhile, a study of the Correctional Centre for Women in Ontario in the 1960s indicates that, during the first half of the decade, at least a third of the women's admissions followed from liquor offences (Benson, 1971).

4. Data presented in a report by Bronskill (1980) suggests that female 'correctional officers' were hired prior to the 1970s in several Ontario institutions. From the way in which the data is presented, it is not clear if these women were hired solely to work with female inmates in the institutions, or if Bronskill is using the term 'correctional officer' for the 'matrons' in the institutions. The fact that matrons were present at the Don Jail prior to the 1970s, and that Bronskill identifies 1977 as the year in which that jail began hiring female 'correctional officers' would suggest that she is not conflating the terms. On the other hand, one would think that the Ministry of Correctional Services' (1983) historical retrospective, given its focus on women as matrons in the jails, would also have identified if some women did more specifically fulfil the role of correctional officer prior to the 1970s. Clearly, more research is needed to clarify the precise dates, locations, and other details concerning the introduction of female correctional officers into prisons for men in Ontario.

Overall, Bronskill's data should be treated with caution. For example, on page 2, she states: 'In 1975, there were sixteen classified female correctional officers working with male inmates in various provincial institutions. By April 1980, that number had increased to a total of 312.' This statement suggests that in 1980 there were 312 female correctional officers working with male inmates. But another Ministry source (Employment Equity Program, 1990) reveals that in 1980, there was a total of 313 female correctional staff, of whom 154 were working in male institutions.

5. Data is not available for all years. Data for 1998 was supplied by Ross Virgo, Communications, Ministry of the Solicitor General and Correctional Services.

It should be noted that, with the apparent exception of the data for 1975, some of the women in the category 'Female Correctional Officers in Male Institutions' were working in the sections for female inmates within those prisons. Unfortunately, reliable data on the size of this sub-category is lacking.

The topic of the incarceration of women in prisons for men in Canada during this century is yet another correctional issue crying out for attention.

6. It must be emphasized that the data presented here is *rudimentary*. Different sources provide conflicting information. A more specific and complete account of the situation of women working in prisons for men would include:

- relevant statistics for all years.
- data on the percentage of correctional officer positions in prisons for men held by women (as opposed to the percentage of female correctional officers among total correctional officers).

- data on female and male correctional officers in prisons for men who are unclassified.
- data concerning women and men who hold positions as assistant super-intendent, deputy superintendent, and superintendent in prisons for men.

7. Title VII of the 1964 Civil Rights Act in the United States 'provided for no employment discrimination on the bases of race, color, religion, sex or national origin. Employers could no longer fail or refuse to hire or to discharge individuals on discriminatory bases, nor could they limit, segregate or classify employees or applicants on these bases' (Graham 1981, 28). The potential impact of this legislation was limited, however, by the fact that the Equal Employment Opportunity Commission administering it had no enforcement powers (28). Meanwhile, the businesses to which it was supposed to apply could also avail themselves of various exemptions and exceptions, most notably the BFOQ – that is, the Bona Fide Occupational Qualification. Under the BFOQ, women could be excluded from jobs on the grounds of height and weight requirements, and even due to 'the fact that a job was traditionally only occupied by men because of their strength or because of the "dangerousness of the job"' (29).

8. Similarly, the growth of women working in federal prisons for men in Canada from 1978 (Caron 1981, 11) also appears to have coincided with a philosophical shift within the Correctional Service of Canada. In particular, their hiring appears to have been associated with the therapeutic and reintegrative approach of the 'living units' established within federal institutions at that time. Consider, for example, the following observations in a 1980 pamphlet of the Service (Correctional Service of Canada 1980):

> But will women be able to control male inmates? The answer seems to be 'yes' because a radical change in the philosophy of corrections has occurred over the last ten years. With the introduction of the living unit concept, a greater emphasis has been placed on the development of positive interpersonal relationships with inmates. In other words, our institutions are no longer warehouses where those convicted of criminal offences are stored. Working to change attitudes, encouraging positive behaviour in inmates and dealing with the causes of negative acts are as necessary as maintaining security. A correctional officer's job is twofold – to help as well as to hold. ... If we believe that our institutions are more than just row upon row of cells and that our goals are protection *and* resocialization then the introduction of women into the Service can only be viewed as a positive step.

9. The hiring and exit data in the report includes both classified and unclassified positions (exceeding 3 months duration).
10. A similar situation applied in federal corrections in the early 1990s, where women represented 'almost a third' of the Correctional Service overall, and 15 per cent of correctional officers. Meanwhile, '[m]ost CSC women remain clustered in the "pink ghetto" of clerical and secretarial jobs and only 14.7% of senior managers are women' (Stanley 1992).

CHAPTER 3. Gender-Based Discrimination and Harassment: From Policy Initiatives to Problems at Bell Cairn

1. The Workplace Discrimination and Harassment Prevention policy of the Ontario government is included as Appendix I.
2. *Conway v. The Queen*, [1993] 2 S.C.C. 872.
3. Information about the ministry's activities in this subsection is drawn from the memoranda released in the ministry's *Chronology of Events* (Ministry of Correctional Services 1992).
4. Suggested responses included informal ones, such as challenging the harasser, approaching other colleagues for support, and talking to ministry advisors on harassment and/or union stewards. More formal responses were also suggested. These included filing a formal complaint, filing a complaint with the Ontario Human Rights Commission, pressing criminal charges, and filing a civil suit.
5. Remedies included reinstating employees fired for discriminatory reasons, removal of offensive cartoons and posters from work areas, and making harassers attend human-rights seminars. The remedies also included disciplinary responses, such as transfers, verbal reprimands and warnings, suspension without pay, and dismissal.
6. When the Progressive Conservative Party came to power in 1995, Bob Runciman was appointed solicitor general and minister of correctional services.
7. For example, Patricia (Patti) Starr, a political lobbyist who had spent several months at the Vanier Detention Centre for Women after pleading guilty to charges of fraud and breach of trust, alleged that correctional officers had sexually assaulted female inmates, had verbally abused them, and had offered inmates preferential treatment in return for sexual favours (*Globe and Mail*, 17 July 1992).
8. The Bell Cairn Staff Training Centre actually started operating in August 1990. At that time, only classrooms were used. Course participants had

accommodation elsewhere. By the spring of 1991, the cafeteria at the centre had started operating. With the opening of the residence in August 1991, the centre became fully operational (Hansen 1993, 15).

9. From the limited information available, however, it appears that the 2 victims of the alleged 'gang-rapes' were female correctional (i.e., prison) officers.

10. A memo from the deputy minister to the secretary of cabinet nine months later in July of 1992 states that, in this case, 'Participants were cautioned by their trainers about inappropriate behaviour and told that they would be asked to leave the centre if there were further incidents.' No information is given about whether correctional officers' supervisors – the superintendents of their prisons – were informed about the incidents or asked to take any action. The fact that no statement is made about this could be interpreted as suggesting that the information was *not* passed on.

11. The ministry decided that they would not shut off the phones, because it could be a disservice to individuals needing assistance (e.g., in the case of illness). Instead, they opted not to give out participants' room numbers, which corresponded to phone numbers. As discussed later, female residents continued to receive obscene phone calls at night after this action had been taken.

12. The woman was advised that she could complain. After thinking it over, she decided not to proceed (Ministry of Correctional Services 1992, 12). The more general reticence of women in making complaints will discussed in relation to incidents at the Wakefield Jail (see Chapter 5).

13. To 'counsel' is a form of discipline, akin to a warning.

14. The minister and the minister's staff regularly receive 'Incident Reports' from the ministry's prisons, and probation and parole offices. These 'Incident Reports' provide details of problematic and potentially contentious events. Such events include, for example, escapes, hunger-strikes, use of mace by prison staff, deaths in custody, and assaults. It appears that, while procedures were in place to keep the minister continually informed about incidents involving inmates and probationers, and problematic events involving them and ministry staff, no procedure was in place to routinely report to the highest level in cases where *only* staff were involved, and/or were away from their home institution.

15. The officers were returned to their home institutions without completing the course, and were given letters of counsel (Ministry of Correctional Services 1992, 9).

16. A later memo additionally states that these incidents 'were described as starting with excessive alcohol abuse by all involved, and then escalating into "sexual harassment." There was also racial harassment of one victim.'

This allegation of racial harassment appears to have not been a focus of attention in the ensuing political scandal and inquiries. Dealing with the issue of racial harassment is beyond the present scope, primarily due to the lack of further information about the incidents concerned. It must be said, however, that issues of racial discrimination – as they concern both staff and inmates – are in need of attention with respect to the ministry of Correctional Services (cf. Lewis 1992). Important steps toward examining related issues have been taken by the Employment Systems Review (1994), and the Commission on Systemic Racism (1994, 1995).

17. This particular sentence was censored in the ministry's *Chronology of Events* under section 21 of the Freedom of Information Act. It was, however, published in several media sources on 17 and 18 July 1992.

18. Issues of the significance of defining issues as operational, as opposed to policy, will be discussed in more detail in Chapter 6.

19. The women concerned had received counselling from a social worker who was in private practice. It was he who advised a staff member at Bell Cairn that they had been sexually assaulted while on a course. According to the *Chronology of Events* 1992, (11), '[t]he women had indicated to the social worker that they did not want to report the incident because they feared retaliation from their peers.'

    The subsequent police investigation did not result in any charges, apparently due to a lack of evidence.

20. The Inquiry Team interviewed a total of 162 people, including training-course participants, security staff, Bell Cairn centre staff, other ministry of Correctional Services staff, and various other individuals. Altogether, approximately 1,300 people who had attended residential courses at Bell Cairn were contacted by a letter that offered them an opportunity for an interview. Only 50 of those interviewed were Bell Cairn participants, however. Other sources of information included visits by Judge Hansen to 19 institutions, and meetings with groups of staff.

21. For example, Henriksen (1993, 17) documents that a survey within the Canadian Forces in the early 1990s of over 4,000 members found that 26 per cent of females reported that they had been sexually harassed, while only 2 per cent of males so reported. For some comments on sexual discrimination and harassment in the Canadian military, see Harrison and Laliberté (1994, 38–43).

22. Judge Hansen's recommendations included enhanced security at the centre; 24-hour management presence; attention to the after-hours needs of participants for food, study, and recreation; a new policy and procedures manual including attention to the Workplace Discrimination and Harass-

ment Prevention policy; and the provision of information about medical services, counselling, and other resources. Judge Hansen had also recommended a reconsideration of policies on alcohol at the centre, and the ministry banned its possession and consumption on the premises.

23. The size of the random samples ranged between 3 per cent and 8 per cent of the 8,000-plus course participants. Specifically, 600 (i.e., 7.5 per cent) of the participants' reaction sheets were analyzed. A follow-up survey was sent to 500 participants, and 270 (3.4 per cent) were returned. Face-to-face interviews – with a questionnaire guiding discussions of up to two hours in length – were conducted with 287 (3.6 per cent) participants.

CHAPTER 4. Discrimination and Harassment at the Wakefield Jail: A Research Perspective

1. My initial work in exploring this literature was undertaken together with Kelly Hannah Moffat, then of the University of Toronto, and now with Brock University.

2. For examples of literature in these genres, see Alpert 1984; Alpert and Crouch 1991; Bennett 1995; Bowersox 1981; Petersen 1982; Kissel and Katsampes 1980; Maschke 1996; Lovrich and Stohr 1993; Walters 1992, 1993; Wright and Saylor 1991.

3. For overviews on research and debates concerning these topics in the Canadian context, see Griffiths and Verdun-Jones 1994.

4. This staff/inmate ratio may appear rather high, with more staff than inmates. But it must be remembered that some of the staff have been part-time. Moreover, with staff generally working shifts, the staff/inmate ratio at any given moment would be lower than these aggregate figures suggest.

5. Two other women were hired as correctional officers on a casual basis following the formal end point of this study (December 1995). Both left their employment at the jail by the summer of 1997. As these women were not present at the jail during the period of events that were the subject of arbitration hearings before the Grievance Settlement Board of Ontario (held in 1994 and 1995), their experiences are not discussed here.

6. Subsequent to the complaints and grievances at the Wakefield Jail, and the transfer of the superintendent out of the jail, the jail had four temporary superintendents. One of these was a woman. My point is to highlight the lack of success experienced by women working at the jail in moving into more secure, and senior, positions.

7. Notes on the hearings before the Grievance Settlement Board were taken by assistants to Beth Symes, the lawyer retained by OPSEU.

8. As will be seen, some women were subject to anonymous phone calls. Unidentified persons also hung offensive cartoons and played pranks on women at the jail.

9. Such a portrayal is at odds with the actuality of most male inmates in Ontario provincial prisons (which contain inmates serving fewer than two years, and people waiting for trial). For decades in the Ontario provincial system, over 70 per cent of sentenced admissions were for less than 90 days duration, and over 20 per cent of sentenced admissions were fine-defaulters serving very short sentences. Overall, the average stay in Ontario prisons was less than two months in length (McMahon 1992). Data presented in annual reports of the Ontario Ministry of Correctional Services suggest that these trends continued in the early 1990s. The vast majority of those admitted to Ontario prisons, therefore, are there for less, rather than more, serious offences.

10. For a discussion of the various stereotypes to which female correctional officers are subject by their male colleagues, and the women's strategies in responding to them, see Jurik 1988.

11. For a discussion of female officers' relations with staff and inmates in one Canadian prison, see Szockyj 1989.

12. Some of Britton's (1995, 122) comments, however, are pertinent here. From her interviews with female correctional officers in a prison for men, she observes that 'female CO's were somewhat more likely than male officers to compare inmates to children. Several officers likened the management of inmates to the care of children as did this woman: "What did you do before?" "I was a teacher in a day-care center. And it's basically the same except for the kids are a lot bigger [in prison]."'

13. The women's accounts, and quotes, are derived from the hearing notes.

14. Nora Diamond confronted officer Harding about his statement, and he apologized.

15. The course in question took place in the spring of 1991 – that is, before the Bell Cairn Staff Training Centre became fully residential in the fall of that year. At the time, only lunch was provided at Bell Cairn. Course participants stayed at a hotel, and paid for their own breakfasts and dinners (for which they were reimbursed).

16. This incident took place several days before the Westbury transfer incident, which will be discussed in the next chapter (p. 97).

17. Melissa Jackson raised concerns to Lieutenant Page about this, and received an apology.

18. Penetang is an Ontario institution for the criminally insane.

19. The grievors' lawyer, Beth Symes, has also heard of 'pranks' at other ministry

institutions. One particularly chilling incident occurred during a going-away party for the superintendent. All correctional officers who were not on duty were at the party. One of the few female correctional officers, a brand-new recruit, was at work during the party. She was required to do perimeter checks of the institution. One of the party-goers snuck up on her and confronted her with a starter's pistol during one of her perimeter checks. Apparently, the woman has never fully recovered from the shock.

20. Some specific examples of this will be discussed in the next two chapters.

CHAPTER 5. Impediments to Reporting Discrimination and Harassment

1. For a discussion of the legal dilemmas and obligations faced by unions in face of sexual harassment issues, see Aggarwal 1992, especially Chapter 8.

2. During the 1990s, the union also assisted a female correctional officer from the Windsor Jail in bringing her grievances of gender-based discrimination and harassment for arbitration. The ministry of Correctional Services and the union came to a settlement on the issue in July 1995, with the ministry acknowledging, amongst other things, the existence of 'poisoned working environment' at the Windsor Jail. Overall, the experiences of the female grievor from the Windsor Jail have many similarities to those reported by the grievors at the Wakefield Jail. Unfortunately, however, the terms of the settlement agreed to by the parties concerning confidentiality preclude documentation of the precise details of these similarities.

3. Not all management staff, at all times, have contributed to, or exacerbated harassment. But the primary concern here is to discuss actions by management personnel that women experienced as problematic.

4. In this case, as noted earlier, O'Reilly told Ferguson that he had been drinking that day, and he did not remember instructing that Diana Hooper be passed over. Ferguson said that it was officer Fischer's word against O'Reilly's and the matter seems to have ended there. It seems remarkable firstly, that O'Reilly could be in a position to give instructions when he had been drinking; and secondly, that his account (which did not even amount to a denial) would be accepted over that of officer Fischer.

5. Prior to placing Fred Ferguson as acting superintendent at the Wakefield Jail in August 1989, the regional director checked his personnel file, and saw that a human-rights complaint had previously been filed against him by a female correctional officer. The regional director called the former superintendent and deputy superintendent of the institution concerned. She learned that the complaint had been withdrawn, and the Human Rights Commission had been unable to substantiate it. The regional director also

learned that the union had previously approached management with concerns about what it considered to be inappropriate behaviour on the part of Ferguson.

Despite these signs of potential trouble, the regional director supported the appointment of Ferguson as acting superintendent. Moreover, in early 1990 – impressed by factors such as the cleaner appearance of the jail, the reduction in overtime hours, and what she perceived as good relations with staff – the regional director recommended to the assistant deputy minister that the competition for superintendent of the Wakefield Jail be waived, and Fred Ferguson appointed.

Viewed in retrospect, the ministry's lack of initiative in assessing Fred Ferguson's suitability for a supervisory position involving female staff is noticeable. No effort seems to have been made to gain a fuller picture at the institution where a sexual harassment complaint previously arose against him. Nor were the views solicited of women working at the Wakefield Jail during his period as acting superintendent. Overall, the impression is fostered that the opinions of female staff were not a priority for the ministry, and thus the stage was set for Ferguson's problematic behaviour to continue.

Consequent to the ministry's inquiry into complaints about Superintendent Ferguson, the ministry temporarily suspended him, and then transferred him to a management position in one of their head offices where he would not directly supervise staff on a day-to-day basis. This strategy has also been used by the ministry in dealing with other 'problem' managers.

6. Not all of the women discussed in this research have made formal complaints. Many of the incidents described have been revealed subsequent to the grievances of Diana Hooper, Nora Diamond, and Karla Preston.

CHAPTER 6. Responding to, and Ending, Discrimination and Harassment

1. The four major victims are correctional officers Nora Diamond, Diana Hooper, and Sharon West, and cook Karla Preston.

Pursuant to her harassment, Sharon West, who had been a casual officer, resigned from the Jail in 1992.

Diana Hooper, a full-time classified officer, went on medical leave in late 1992. She subsequently went on long-term disability, and did not return to work at the jail. Her stress arising from discrimination and harassment continued to be aggravated during the hearings before the Grievance Settlement Board of Ontario, and during the lengthy period of waiting for the arbitration decision. As of August 1997, she told me that her doctor was of the opinion that she could never return to work at the jail, but, when the decision on the case came down, she might be fit for occupational retraining.

Nora Diamond, a casual correctional officer, continued to work at the jail during the Grievance Settlement Board hearings in 1994–5, and for over a year afterwards. Her work attendance was interrupted owing to medical leaves arising from the discrimination and harassment. Despite her having a medical certificate, the Ministry of Correctional Services failed to renew her contract at the end of March 1997, thereby terminating her entitlement to medical-related unemployment insurance as a source of income. Nora Diamond has grieved this revocation of her contract.

Meanwhile, casual cook Karla Preston continued to work at the jail. As documented earlier, her hours of work were severely reduced from what they had been prior to the complaints, and she was ostracized by many of her colleagues.

2. The major findings of North American and other literatures have been discussed in Chapter 4. For research concerning Australia, see Farnworth (1992), and for a commentary concerning New Zealand, see Hanson (1993).

3. This case also exemplifies how management staff at an institution could easily discriminate against certain women – that is, by only calling them when they know that the women will not be available to take the call. Meanwhile, no such discrimination would be apparent in records. On the contrary, the records could show that the women were called just as frequently, or even more frequently, than men.

4. For example, one anonymous University of Toronto Press reviewer of this manuscript suggested that harassers could be instructed to do their next 100 hours of overtime at their regular rate of pay. The reviewer further suggested that – to preclude the government using this as a cost-cutting strategy – the difference between the regular and overtime rates of pay be donated to a charity agreeable to all concerned.

5. OPSEU's final submission to the Grievance Settlement Board gives several specific examples of supervisors disciplined by the ministry for harassment who were transferred to other institutions and subsequently assumed supervisory positions (see Symes 1995, 48–9).

6. In September 1996, the Ontario government announced its intention to close fourteen jails in small towns, and replace them with much larger 'superjails' and refurbished detention centres (housing over 1,000 inmates each). The initial and subsequent government announcements also indicated its openness to having a far greater involvement of the private sector in corrections, including in the operation of the new institutions (The *Ottawa Citizen*, 6 February 1997, A3).

7. An important and allied component of such social scientific research would be an inquiry into the views of male guards themselves, and especially of

those perceived by women as discriminatory and harassing in their behaviour. How do they perceive the reactions of women? And, for those subject to investigatory procedures, how do they perceive these inquiries and their outcomes? Research could further examine how male officers who offend women are perceived, and responded to, by their more progressive male colleagues.

Overall, while the literature frequently presents surveys identifying male attitudes and stereotypes with respect to women, questions such as these have not yet been investigated in any great depth.

8. The ministry's failure to renew Nora Diamond's contract in March 1997, subsequent to the Grievance Settlement Board hearings and her related, medically approved absences from work, also demonstrate the ministry's limitations in providing support systems for women.

9. This occurred, for example, with the election of a Progressive Conservative government in Ontario in 1995. The government withdrew commitment to the Employment Equity programs of previous governments in favour of a modified 'Equal Opportunities' policy. Yet, as we have seen, the Employment Equity policy by no means precluded arbitrariness and discrimination in hiring.

CHAPTER 7. Conclusion

1. *Bradwell vs. Illinois* 16 Wall 130, 141 (1873).

2. See, for example, the vitriolic attacks by Christina Sommers (1994) on various forms of feminism.

3. These debates become all the more complicated in Canada as 'quota' systems here are, in fact, rare. Yet opponents of various programs designed to facilitate the advancement of women and other marginalized groups often attack them *as if* they did involve quotas. This occurred, for example, when the Progressive Conservative Party attacked Ontario's Employment Equity' program when they were in opposition during the early 1990s. Although the Employment Equity program did not impose any quotas, it was far more difficult for this to be explained than for the opposition to make their single-charge attack. Once elected in 1995, the Progressive Conservative Party had set the stage whereby it was a relatively straightforward task for them to abolish the Employment Equity program, and to replace it with their own weaker policy of 'Equal Opportunity.'

4. On the situation at Mount Cashel Orphanage in Newfoundland, see Harris (1991); and on those at St Joseph's and St John's Training Schools in Ontario, see Henton with McCann (1995). On allegations of harassment and

discrimination at the Political Science Department in the University of British Columbia, see McEwen (1995); and for discussions of harassment and gender politics in Canadian universities more generally, see Emberley (1996). Overall, despite the currency of harassment issues in Canada, the major forum for discussion continues to be the media, and much research remains to be done. In 1998, for example, *Maclean's* magazine was a major source of information on sexual harassment in the Canadian military.

5. I am thinking here of situations commonly described by those who feel overwhelmed by the emphasis on sexual improprieties – including fathers who are wary of bathing their female children, university professors who no longer close their office doors while having discussions in their offices with students – and even one male friend who no longer felt comfortable having a woman perform oral sex on him, because it might involve her adopting a position that could be interpreted as demeaning!

EPILOGUE: The Arbitration Decision about the Wakefield Grievances

1. The arbitration decision contains the real names of the grievors and of other individuals at the Wakefield Jail, and the real name of the jail itself. In order to be consistent, however, and also bearing in mind the preference of two of the three grievors to maintain a low profile as well as the social scientific perspective of this book, pseudonyms are again used in this epilogue (with the exception of the names of public figures, namely Leah Casselman, president of the Ontario Public Service Employees Union, and Bob Runciman, solicitor general and minister of correctional services in Ontario). The three members of the Grievance Settlement Board (real names) are vice-chair N. Dissanayake, T. Browes-Bugden, and M. Milich. Their decision was unanimous.

For those unfamiliar with the arbitration process, it may be helpful to know that this form of dispute resolution comes into play only in a unionized setting (options available to victims of sexual harassment in non-union settings include employers' internal complaint procedures, complaints to human rights commissions, and civil actions). Arbitrators draw their powers to derive remedies from several sources. One is the collective agreement between the employer and the union, which governs the terms and conditions of employment for members of the bargaining unit. Arbitrators also draw from the power to interpret and apply other labour legislation, including employment standards and human-rights legislation. In addition, arbitration decisions are informed by those of the courts.

Arbitration boards are authorized to make orders that will remedy the

situation that gave rise to a successful complaint. In carrying out their mandate arbitration boards must fashion remedies in such a way as to ensure the
full and final resolution of the dispute (Cornish and Lopez 1994, 123).

In practice, the role and scope of arbitration boards differs in different
jurisdictions in Canada, and can also vary over time within any given
jurisdiction (for example, arising from legislative changes, and from those
negotiated into collective agreements). Beyond this, there are also varying
opinions about the functions of arbitration, and specifically with respect to
sexual-harassment issues. As Cornish and Lopez (1994, 123) explain:

> There are two competing interpretations of an arbitrator's proper role.
> Arbitrators dealing with sexual harassment have tended to see their role
> as that of 'judge' or 'reader' whose function is confined to the strict
> reading and application of the collective agreement terms. A more ex-
> pansive interpretation sees the arbitrator as 'labour relations physician.'
> This second view recognizes the arbitrator's function as including the
> role of an industrial relations policy maker who is influential in the social
> developments in the relationship between the parties.

A full discussion of the legal complexities involved in arbitration is beyond
the present scope. Later in this epilogue, however, we do briefly discuss
some legal issues relevant to the grievance from the Wakefield Jail (e.g.,
concerning the power and role of arbitration boards with respect to the
disciplining of harassers). It is pertinent, though, to call attention to the
basic issue identified by Cornish and Lopez (1994, 123–4), and to voice our
agreement with their recommendation.

> Arbitral reluctance to do what some interpret as rewriting the collective
> agreement is similar to the initial judicial reluctance to adopt expansive
> remedies in human rights and *Charter* cases because of a belief that it was
> usurping the role of the legislators. The Supreme Court of Canada had
> to admonish judges to overcome this reluctance as they were charged
> with ordering strong and positive remedies.
>
> In order to properly address the issue of sexual harassment in the work-
> place arbitrators must embrace this more expansive role. Like judges, arbi-
> trators will fail to carry out their contractual and statutory mandate if they
> continue to rely on traditional remedial orders such as declarations and
> cease and desist orders. These sorts of orders inform parties on what they
> are not to do without providing them with affirmative instruction on what
> to do.

For discussions of the legal concepts of sex discrimination and sexual harassment in Canada, and analysis of the various issues involved in responses to related complaints, see Aggarwal 1994; Bartholomew 1993; Cornish and Lopez 1994; Duclos 1993; Hughes 1994; and Kilcoyne 1994.

2. *Robichaud v. The Queen* (1988), 40 D.L.R. (4th) 577 (S.C.C.), pp. 582 and 584. Emphasis in original.

3. For a very informative analysis of employers' liability for sexual harassment of employees, with discussion of *Robichaud* and other relevant cases, see Aggarwal 1992, 181–234.

4. See the Appendix, which presents the Workplace Discrimination and Harassment Prevention Policy.

5. Cases cited by the Board include:

> *Kotyk and Allary v. Canadian Employment and Immigration Commission and Chuba* (1983), 4 C.H.R.R. D. 1416, 83; C.L.L.C. at 17,012; aff'd (1984) 5 C.H.R.R. D. 1895; 84 C.L.L.C. at 17,005

> *Bell v. The Flaming Steer Steak House Tavern Inc.* (1980), 1 C.H.R.R. D. 155 (Ont. Bd. of Inquiry)

> *Cuff v. Gypsy Restaurant* (1987), 8 C.H.R.R. D. 3972; 87 C.L.L.C. at 17,015 (Ont. Bd. of Inquiry)

> *Robichaud v. The Queen* [1987] 2 S.C.R. 84; 40 D.L.R. (4th) 577; 75 N.R. 303; 8 C.H.R.R. D. 4326; 87 C.L.L.C. at 17,025

> *Re McKinnon*, unreported decision of the Ontario Grievance Settlement Board, 905 A/92 (Gray) at 29

> *Re Chan*, unreported decision of the Ontario Grievance Settlement Board, 1990/90 (Dissanayake) at 45

> *C.U.P.E. v. O.P.E.I.U.* (1982), 4 L.A.C. (3d) 385 (Swinton), at 404-405

6. Karla Preston had also grieved that the reduction in her hours as a cook was a form of reprisal, but the Board did not support this. Nor did they support the contention that she had been subject to intimidation and unduly harsh criticism of her work following her complaint.

7. Some other complaints by Diana Hooper were deemed 'unfounded' by the Board. Specifically, her belief that one of her colleagues was trying to 'crank up' inmates and turn them against her was rejected.

8. Diana Hooper felt that these and other actions by Lieutenant O'Reilly constituted sexual harassment of her (see Chapter 4 of this book for examples of her experiences, and Chapter 5 for a description of his behaviour more generally). But the Board did not support her in this. The Board

members' argument was that O'Reilly generally operated in a 'dictatorial fashion,' and Nora Diamond had noted that male officers also felt harassed by him. In the Board's words (Dissanayake et al. 1997, 65): '[Mr. O'Reilly], the evidence suggests, did not always follow the policy. On several instances, he shirked his responsibilities. His behaviour was clearly inappropriate and not professional. However, that conduct did not constitute sexual harassment of Ms. [Hooper] or any other woman. It was simply a case of a poor and inappropriate work performance by a supervisory member of staff.'

9. The reader might ask: why did the union not file a 'union' grievance, and in so doing, confront policy issues more directly? The answer is that a 'union' or policy grievance would not provide remedies for each of the three women. In order to have a possibility of getting financial compensation for hours lost, and the possibility of a new job, the women had to file individual grievances.

10. *Canada Post Corporation v. Canadian Union of Postal Workers* (1983), 11 L.A.C. (3d) 13 (Norman), explicitly referring to the *Canadian Human Rights Act*, R.S.C. 1985, c. H-6.

11. Fudge provides some explanations of why arbitration procedures historically have been less than successful in engaging and transforming gender relations in the workplace. For example, she observes that, '[b]ecause grievance arbitration is conceived of as a private dispute resolution mechanism bounded by the collective agreement, arbitrators are unlikely to develop innovative analyses of, or remedies for, the problem of sexual harassment in the workplace' (1991, 128). She goes on to argue that '[i]nstead of deferring to the idea of private contractual relations and managerial prerogatives, arbitrators must be prepared to invoke our public commitment to equality to challenge the gender hierarchies which inhere in the privacy of the workplace' (131). Aggarwal (1994, 78) similarly points out that 'employment discrimination (including sexual harassment) is not just a private dispute between the parties to the collective agreement. Rather, it raises a broader issue of public policy and general concern.'

Cornish and Lopez provide insights on why arbitration boards (and other adjudicative bodies) have traditionally been narrow in their response to sexual harassment, and slow to apply systemic remedies. As explained by them, one basic problem has been adjudicators' 'failure to understand the systemic conditions which produce workplace harassment' (1994, 96). In other words, the complexity of gender-related social interactions and prejudices in the workplace and in society more generally, as well as the complexity of the workplace culture itself, have often gone unrecognized. As Cornish and Lopez further observe, this lack of understanding has been compounded by the rarity of arbitrators' exposure to sexual-harassment issues. Of those cases involving sexual harassment that have come to arbitration in Canada, they have far more typically involved harassers' grievances about penalties to which they were subject by the employer, than they have victims seeking redress (114). These observations by Cornish and Lopez are strongly borne out in research conducted by Aggarwal (1994). Of the 71 sexual harassment-related cases brought to arbitration in Canada between 1977 and 1993, and studied by him, 63 were brought by the harassers. And, of those 8 cases involving victims of sexual harassment that went to arbitration, only 2 were successful (76).

At the same time, and as discussed by Cornish and Lopez (1994), some legal developments have occurred that should encourage arbitrators to more directly examine the broader picture of sexual harassment and discrimination, as well as to engage systemic issues, and apply systemic remedies. Of particular note here is the decision of the Supreme Court of Canada in the *Action Travail des Femmes v. Canadian National Railway Company* (Canadian National Railway Co. v. Canadian Human Rights Commission) [1987] 1 S.C.R. 1114; 87 CLLC 17,022; 8 C.H.R.R. D/4210. In this case, a human-rights complaint filed with the Canadian Human Rights Commission alleged that the Canadian National Railway Company had systematically impeded the hiring and promotion of women, and that discriminatory practices were occurring, including sexual harassment. In providing remedies, the Human Rights Tribunal ordered systemic remedies, and specifically the introduction of an employment-equity program. In supporting this decision, the Supreme Court noted that (*Action Travail*, at 1143) 'such a programme will remedy past acts of discrimination against the group [of women] and prevent future acts at one and the same time. That is the very point of affirmative action.'

Legally, explain Cornish and Lopez (1994, 112), one of the very significant aspects of the *Action Travail* case is that it means that 'employers and unions can be ordered (after a finding of discrimination) to implement employment equity programmes even in the absence of proactive employment equity legislation.'

Turning more specifically to the arbitration process, Cornish and Lopez again note the 'inability of arbitrators and many workplace parties to adequately understand the problem and therefore the solutions' (113). In their view, the remedial approach of arbitrators with respect to systemic issues has been even more constricted than that of human-rights adjudicators and 'arbitration remedies for sexual harassment are still in the developmental stage ... [D]isappointing decisions continue to dominate, particularly in the area of poisoned work environment' (113, 116). In part, this cautious approach has stemmed from the view that sexual harassment was not arbitrable unless the collective agreement contained anti-discrimination or anti-harassment provisions (although grievances could potentially be pursued under health and safety clauses). Yet, even when anti-discrimination and harassment provisions have existed (as in Ontario), arbitrators have tended to take the view that issues such as sexual harassment were more properly the preserve of human-rights commissions and other adjudicative bodies, where the powers to apply systemic remedies were clearer. When sexual-harassment cases did come to arbitration, arbitrators continued to rely primarily on individual remedies.

In Ontario, the likelihood of systemic remedies being applied by arbitrators took a major step forward in the 1990s with amendments to the Ontario *Labour Relations Act* to 'both clarify and expand existing jurisprudence' (Cornish and Lopez 1994, 124). Specifically, section 48(12)(j) now provides arbitrators with the power 'to interpret and apply the requirements of human rights and other employment-related statutes, despite any conflict between those requirements and the terms of the collective agreement' (*Labour Relations Act*, 1995 S.O. 1995, c.1 Schedule A).

In layperson's terms, this amendment means that arbitrators more clearly have the power to take actions consistent with broader legislative provisions, including the *Human Rights Code*, the *Canadian Charter of Rights and Freedoms*, and occupational health and safety and employment-equity legislation. In turn, arbitrators more clearly have the power not just to remedy individual wrongs of the past for individuals, but also to make systemic orders that will help to prevent similar problems from arising in the future.

In short, arbitral imposition of systemic remedies in the past has been impeded by a lack of exposure to, and awareness of, systemic issues concerning sexual harassment; by a more restricted interpretation of arbitral jurisdiction than was perhaps necessary; and by the perception, and reality, of legal constraints. Following from the *Action Travail* decision, the incorporation of anti-discrimination and harassment provisions in the Ontario collective agreement, and amendments to the Ontario *Labour Relations Act* some of the traditional legal restrictions have eased. The decision of the Ontario Grievance Settlement Board to apply systemic remedies in the case of the Wakefield Jail reflects the board's willingness both to recognize the systemic nature of discrimination and harassment, and to make use of the legal powers available to it.

12. Strangely, the Grievance Settlement Board did not elaborate on its rationale for ordering an affirmative-action plan. It is likely that the board was

following the precedent set in the *Action Travail* case discussed in the previous endnote. The union's final submission had referred to this case, and particularly its endorsement of the establishment of a 'critical mass' of women as the previously excluded group. Justice Dickson C.J.C.'s commented (*Canadian National Railway Co. v. Canada* (CHRC) (1987), 40 D.L.R. (4th) 193 (S.C.C.), at 214):

> [A]n employment equity program helps to create what has been termed a 'critical mass' of the previously excluded group in the workplace. The 'critical mass' has important effects. The targeted group eliminates the problems of 'tokenism'; it is no longer the case that one or two women, for example, will be seen to 'represent' all women ... Moreover, women will not so easily be placed on the periphery of management concerns. The 'critical mass' also effectively remedies systemic inequities in the process of hiring ... Once a 'critical mass' of the previously excluded group has been created in the work force, there is a significant chance for the continuing self-correction of the system. Specific hiring goals ... are a rational attempt to impose a systemic remedy on a systemic problem.

13. There are several reasons for arbitrators' reluctance to penalize harassers. The first is arbitrators' belief that 'the decision to discipline an employee is best left to management as part of its management right to control the structure and operation of the workplace' (Cornish and Lopez 1994, 121–2). In short, they defer to management and their prerogative in disciplining employees (Fudge 1991). Thus, while arbitrators are slow to order employers to penalize harassers, in the majority of recent cases where harassment has been proven, and management discharged the harasser as a penalty, arbitrators have upheld this penalty in responding to grievances by the dismissed harassers (Cornish and Lopez 1994, 117). A second reason for arbitrators' reluctance to penalize is the fact that penalties (e.g., ordering an apology) are, by definition, punitive rather than remedial in nature, and thereby conflict with the compensatory thrust of the arbitration process (121).

Recent legal developments in Canada have extended the powers of some arbitrators to impose non-traditional – and specifically disciplinary – remedies. For example, the collective agreement between the Municipality of Terrace (in British Columbia) and C.U.P.E., Local 2012 provides that '[i]n cases of sexual harassment, an Arbitration Board shall have the *power to transfer, discipline, or levy a financial penalty against the harasser and the employer*' (quoted in Aggarwal 1994, 73, emphasis in original).

This tendency of expanding the disciplinary powers of arbitrators seems likely to continue. Even if one agrees – as we do – that arbitrators should have the power to penalize harassers, however, important questions arise about when, and under what circumstances, the ultimate power of dismissal should actually be used. As Cornish and Lopez strongly argue (in their discussion of the tendency for arbitrators to support an employer's decision to dismiss a harasser), dismissal per se does little to counter the broader problem of sexual harassment and may give the misleading impression that the problem has actually been dealt with. Indeed, dismissal, in the absence of other strategies for dealing with sexual harassment, may do more harm than good. In the words of Cornish and Lopez (1994, 118):

> Discharging harassers and having that discharge endorsed by arbitrators does send a message to the workplace that certain forms of behaviour will not be tolerated. However, it also sends the wrong message about the causes of sexual harassment and does little to actually change the work environment. The discharge of a sexual harasser eliminates the immediate problem of that individual harasser while failing to address the root of the problem.
>
> The removal of an offensive individual does not remedy the harm caused by that individual nor does it address the working conditions which permitted and encouraged the individual to be a sexual harasser.

A further problem with dismissal as the primary response, note Cornish and Lopez, is that it may be perceived as too harsh a penalty, and 'may expose the complaintant to censure within the workplace which further serves to discourage complaints being made in the first place' (118). They conclude that '[t]here may well be circumstances where the harasser's conduct is so unacceptable that discharge is appropriate. However, it should not be the standard response. Further, discharge should not be the arbitral way to express strong aversion to the practice. In the context of harasser grievances, that should be expressed by strong remedial conditions attached to reinstatement' (118).

14. Both Fred Ferguson and Pat O'Reilly attended the first day of the Grievance Settlement Board hearings, and were granted party status. But Mr Ferguson did not subsequently attend. Mr O'Reilly attended regularly, and participated on his own behalf in the proceedings.

15. As noted earlier, Superintendent Ferguson had already been penalized when the ministry suspended him without pay, and transferred him to a position in one of their head offices without supervisory responsibilities. As also noted earlier, the ministry had penalized Lieutenant O'Reilly by suspend-

ing him without pay for 3 days. His colleagues deftly juggled the schedule such that O'Reilly would not work the regular hours but did work overtime. Although O'Reilly lost 24 hours pay, he was able to work 24 hours of overtime during the same pay period, and was paid for the equivalent of 36 hours of work (time-and-a-half). The women understandably were of the opinion that O'Reilly had 'beat the system.'

16. As will be discussed, the media coverage also proved stressful for employees of the Wakefield Jail.

17. For example, Karla Preston participated in a video made by the union for educating colleagues on sexual harassment and discrimination.

18. Let us reiterate, however, that all of the women have been consistently very supportive of this research and book, as they hope that it will assist others facing discrimination and harassment. Nora Diamond's and Diana Hooper's wish to avoid media publicity was an important factor in the decision to use pseudonyms in this book.

19. For an examination of the length of time taken in labour arbitration in Ontario more generally, see Picher and Mole (1993). With the total time from the beginning of the hearings about the Wakefield Jail on 14 October 1994 to the release of the board's decision in November 1997 being just over three years, this case falls at the longer end of the spectrum. Given the variety and complexity of the issues involved, the lengthiness of the process is understandable.

20. The information that follows is derived from conversations with the grievors and union officials, and media reports.

21. In another media article, the former minister was quoted as saying that the jail system is so sick 'it has to be stopped' (Brennan 1997b, A3). The stimulus to this particular comment was a report that '[s]taff at Ontario jails have been downloading pornography, including child pornography, from the Internet so often the corrections ministry has cut off their routine access' (A3).

On this occasion some harsh words were also attributed to the then minister of correctional services, Bob Runciman (a member of the ruling Progressive Conservative Party, and who, it will be recalled, first raised the issue of harassment at Bell Cairn Staff Training School for correctional workers in the Ontario legislature when he was opposition critic in 1992). The newspaper reported 'Mr. Runciman said this is just more proof that the staff at Ontario's 45 adult correctional institutions present a greater problem than the inmates. "There are more problems with the staff than the inmates," he said.'

The minister is also quoted as commenting that: '"It has been a very difficult work environment for as long as anyone can remember ... We are looking for some direction on how we can turn this thing around.'" Here Mr. Runciman was alluding to a study in progress by the consulting firm of Coopers and Lybrand 'on ways to deal with what the Minister called the "corrections culture."' As Mr Runciman elaborated: 'Broadly speaking it looks at the culture and the problems we've had in the system over the years. The attitude of staff, the managers, the relationships between management and union ...' (A3).

Mr. Runciman's comments also provoked ire at the jail, with some correctional officers arguing that their employer should be sued.

The report later produced by Coopers and Lybrand (*Ministry of the Solicitor General and Correctional Services: Culture and Human Resources Review*, April 1998) was hard-hitting. It delivered a trenchant critique of management practices, noting, for example, the tendency to deny problems, and to make excuses for not addressing issues. The report further noted that 'many of the union's grievances are valid, and yet management has not acted appropriately' (47).

Although the report did not specifically address gender issues the consultants did spotlight 'harassment' as one of the major problems identified by members of focus groups as detracting from a positive working environment (35). However, as none of the questions posed in the survey component of the research directly explored harassment, the consultants were unable to state the extent of the problem. They instead recommended further 'mining' of their survey data to 'determine the real extent to which harassment [is] present' (36). As has been argued earlier in this book, such survey analysis alone is insufficient in portraying the nuances and complexities of discrimination and harassment. It is to be hoped that the ministry will take a more holistic approach in assessing the extent of problems of discrimination and harassment.

References

Abramajtys, Joe. 1987. Unpublished Investigation of Officer McCallum's Murder and SPSM Policies. Michigan Department of Corrections.

– 1982. Unpublished Summary Report of SPSM Labor Relations Project. Michigan Department of Corrections.

Aggarwal, Arjun P. 1992. *Sexual Harassment in the Workplace*. 2nd ed. Toronto: Butterworths.

– 1994. 'Dispute Resolution Processes for Sexual Harassment Complaints.' *Canadian Labour and Employment Law Journal*, 3(1), 63–93.

Alpert, Geoffrey P. 1984. 'The Needs of the Judiciary and Misapplications of Social Research: The Case of Female Guards in Men's Prisons,' *Criminology*, 22(3), 441–56.

Alpert, Geoffrey P., and Ben M. Crouch. 1991. 'Cross-Gender Supervision, Personal Privacy, and Institutional Security: Perceptions of Jail Inmates and Staff.' *Criminal Justice and Behavior*, 18(3), 304–17.

Anon. 1982. 'Women Correctional Officers in Canadian Provincial Institutions.' Unpublished table. Distributed by the Ontario Ministry of Correctional Services.

Arbour, The Honourable Louise, Commissioner. 1996. *Commission of Inquiry into Certain Events at the Prison for Women in Kingston*. Ottawa: Canada Communication Group.

Avebury Research and Consulting Ltd. 1992. 'Competition File Review.' Report prepared for the Ontario Ministry of Correctional Services.

Bartholomew, Amy. 1993. '"Achieving a Place for Women in a Man's World": Or, Feminism with No Class.' *Canadian Journal of Women and the Law*, 6(2), 465–90.

Beattie, John. 1977. *Attitudes towards Crime and Punishment in Upppper Canada, 1830–1850: A Documentary Study*. Toronto: University of Toronto, Centre of Criminology.

Beirne, Piers, and James Messerschmidt. 1995. *Criminology.* New York: Harcourt Brace.

Bennett, Katherine. 1995. 'Constitutional Issues in Cross-Gender Searches and Visual Observation of Nude Inmates by Opposite-Sex Officers: A Battle between and within the Sexes.' *The Prison Journal,* 75(1), 90–112.

Benson, Margaret. 1971. *Admissions to the Provincial Correctional Centre for Women in Ontario.* Toronto: Elizabeth Fry Society.

Binken, Martin, and Shirley Bach. 1977. *Women and the Military.* Washington, DC: Brookings Institute.

Bowersox, Michael S. 1981. 'Women in Corrections: Competence, Competition, and the Social Responsibility Norm.' *Criminal Justice and Behavior,* 8(4), 491–9.

Breed, Allen F. 1981. 'Women in Correctional Employment.' In *Women in Corrections,* 37–44. American Correctional Association Monograph Series #1. Maryland.

Brennan, Richard. 1997a. 'Harassment Case Reveals "Horrible" Jail Culture: Tribunal Blames Ministry Inaction for "Poisoned Environment."' *Ottawa Citizen,* 12 November, A5.

– 1997b. 'Porn-surfing Prison Staff Lose Web Access: Internet Scandal Gives More Proof That Staff Present More of a Problem Than Inmates, Corrections Minister Says,' *Ottawa Citizen,* 22 November, A3.

Britton, Dana M. 1995. 'Sex, Violence and Supervision: A Study of the Prison as a Gendered Organization.' PhD Dissertation. University of Texas at Austin.

Bronskill, Ann. 1980. *Female Correctional Officers in the Ministry of Correctional Services.* Ontario Ministry of Correctional Services.

Campbell, Monika. 1990. 'Information Paper – Employment Equity Program.' Ministry information sheet. Ontario Ministry of Correctional Services.

Canadian Panel on Violence against Women. 1993. *Changing the Landscape: The Final Report of the Canadian Panel on Violence against Women.* Ottawa: Supply and Services.

Caron, George. 1981. 'Female Correctional Officers in Adult Male Correctional Institutions.' Professional Project on Human Resource Management. Ottawa: St Lawrence College and Correctional Service of Canada.

Caron, Roger. 1985. *Go Boy! A Lifetime behind Bars.* Toronto: McGraw-Hill Ryerson.

Commission on Systemic Racism. 1994. *Racism behind Bars. The Treatment of Black and Other Racial Minority Prisoners in Ontario Prisons.* Interim Report of the Commission on Systemic Racism in the Ontario Criminal Justice System, Toronto.

– 1995. *Report of the Commission on Systemic Racism in the Ontario Criminal Justice System.* Ontario: Queen's Printer for Ontario.

Cornish, Mary, and Suzanne Lopez. 1994. 'Changing the Workplace Culture through Effective Harassment Remedies.' *Canadian Labour and Employment Law Journal*, 3(1), 95–129.

Correctional Service of Canada. 1975. 'Reality Is Now.' *Discussion*, 3(3), 7–10.

– 1980. 'Women as Correctional Officers.' Pamphlet. Ottawa.

– 1992. *Towards Equal Partnership: Report on the Conference for Women in CSC.* Ottawa: Correctional Service of Canada.

Crouch, Ben. 1980. 'The Guard in a Changing Prison World.' In Ben Crouch (ed) *The Keepers: Prison Guards and Contemporary Corrections,* 5–45. Springfield, Illinois: Charles C Thomas.

– 1985. 'Pandora's Box: Women Guards in Men's Prisons.' *Journal of Criminal Justice,* 13:535–48.

Deaux, Kay, and Joseph Ullman. 1983. *Women of Steel.* New York: Praeger.

Dissanayake, N., T. Browes-Bugden, and M. Milich. 1997. *OPSEU v. The Crown in Right of Ontario (Ministry of the Solicitor General and Correctional Services),* 5 November. Toronto: Grievance Settlement Board, 3155/92, 643/93, 656/93, 2168/93.

Dowrich Management Services and Key Learning Group Inc. 1995. *Building a Partnership for Change: A Report on the Evaluation of the WDHP Policy Training.* Ontario: Ministry of the Solicitor General, Ontario Public Services Employees Union, and Management Board Secretariat.

Duclos, Nitya. 1993. 'Disappearing Women: Racial Minority Women in Human Rights Cases.' *Canadian Journal of Women and the Law,* 6(1), 25–51.

Emberley, Peter C. 1996. *Zero Tolerance: Hot Button Politics in Canada's Universities.* Toronto: Penguin.

Employment Equity Program. 1990. 'Ministry [of Correctional Services] Profile.' Unpublished manuscript. Ontario: Human Resources Secretariat.

Employment Systems Review Task Force. 1994. *Open Minds/Open Doors: Report of the Employment Systems Review Task Force.* Ontario Public Servants Employees Union, and the Ministry of the Solicitor General and Correctional Services. Toronto.

Epstein, Cynthia. 1981. *Women in Law.* Garden City, New York: Anchor.

Ericson, Richard V., McMahon, Maeve W., and Don E. Evans. 1987. 'Punishing for Profit: Reflections on the Revival of Privatization in Corrections.' *Canadian Journal of Criminology,* 29(4), 355–87.

Farnworth, Louise. 1992. 'Women Doing a Man's Job: Female Prison Officers Working in a Male Prison.' *The Australian and New Zealand Journal of Criminology,* 25(3)278–96.

Foucault, Michel. 1977. *Discipline and Punish: The Birth of the Prison.* New York: Pantheon.

Freedman, Estelle B. 1981. *Their Sisters' Keepers: Women's Prison Reform in America, 1830–1930.* Ann Arbor: University of Michigan Press.

Fudge, Judy. 1991. 'Gender Issues in Arbitration: An Academic Perspective.' In William Kaplan, Jeffrey Sack, and Morley Gunderson (eds), *Labour Arbitration Yearbook 1991*, 119–31. Toronto: Butterworths – Lancaster House.

Graham, Camille G. 1981. 'Women Are Succeeding in Male Institutions.' In *Women in Corrections*, 27–36. American Correctional Association Monograph Series #1. Maryland.

Griffiths, Curt T., and Simon N. Verdun-Jones. 1994. *Canadian Criminal Justice.* 2nd ed. Toronto: Harcourt Brace.

Gross, George R., Susan J. Larson, Gloria D. Urban, and Linda L. Zupan. 1994. 'Gender Differences in Occupational Stress among Correctional Officers.' *American Journal of Criminal Justice*, 18(2), 219–34.

Gruber, James, and Lars Bjorn. 1982. 'Blue-Collar Blues: The Sexual Harassment of Women Autoworkers.' *Work and Occupations*, 9:271–98.

Hansen, Her Honour Judge Inger. 1993. *Report of the Bell Cairn Centre Inquiry.* Ontario Ministry of Correctional Services.

Hanson, Pleasance. 1993. 'The Integration of Women into Auckland Maximum Security Prison.' *Criminal Justice Quarterly*, 4:26–8.

Harris, Michael. 1991. *Unholy Orders: Tragedy at Mount Cashel.* Toronto: Penguin.

Harrison, Deborah, and Lucie Laliberté. 1994. *No Life Like It: Military Wives in Canada.* Toronto: James Lorimer.

Hartel, Lynda J., and Helena M. VonVille. 1995. *Sexual Harassment: A Selected, Annotated Bibliography.* Westport, Connecticut: Greenwood.

Henriksen, Sheila. 1993. *Harassment and Other Forms of Discrimination in the Workplace. Report on a Survey of Female Employees in the Ontario Region of the Correctional Correctional Service of Canada.* Ottawa: Correctional Service of Canada.

Henton, Darcy, with David McCann. 1995. *Boys Don't Cry: The Struggle for Justice and Healing in Canada's Biggest Sex Abuse Scandal.* Toronto: McClelland and Stewart.

Horne, Peter. 1985. 'Female Correctional Officers: A Status Report.' *Federal Probation*, 49:46–55.

Hughes, Patricia. 1994. 'The Evolving Framework of Sexual Harassment.' *Canadian Labour and Employment Law Journal*, 3(1)1–31.

Hunt, Jennifer. 1986. 'The Logic of Sexism among Police.' Paper presented at the American Sociological Society Meetings, New York, August.

Hunter, Susan M. 1986. 'On the Line: Working Hard with Dignity.' *Corrections Today*, June: 12-13.

Jacobs, James B. 1981. 'The Sexual Integration of the Prison's Guards Force: A

Few Comments on *Dothard v. Rawlinson.*' In *Women in Corrections*, 57–85. American Correctional Association Monograph Series #1. Maryland.

Jurik, Nancy C. 1985. 'An Officer and a Lady: Organizational Barriers to Women Working as Correctional Officers in Men's Prisons.' *Social Problems*, 32(4), 375–88.

– 1988. 'Striking a Balance: Female Correctional Officers, Gender Role Stereotypes, and Male Prisons.' *Sociological Inquiry*, 58(3), 291–305.

Jurik, Nancy C., and Gregory J. Halemba. 1984. 'Gender, Working Conditions and the Job Satisfaction of Women in a Non-Traditional Occupation: Female Correctional Officers in Men's Prisons.' *The Sociological Quarterly*, 25:551–66.

Kadar, Marlene. 1983. 'Sexual Harassment: Where We Stand; Research and Policy.' *Windsor Yearbook of Access to Justice*, 3:358–74.

Kanter, Rosabeth. 1977. *Men and Women of the Corporation.* New York: Basic.

Kilcoyne, John. 1994. 'The "Politics of Policies": Responding to Sexual Harassment on Campus.' *Canadian Labour and Employment Law Journal*, 3(1)33–59.

Kissel, Peter J., and Katsampes, Paul L. 1980. 'The Impact of Women Corrections Officers on the Functioning of Institutions Housing Male Inmates.' *Journal of Offender Counseling, Services, and Rehabilitation*, 4(3), 213–31.

Klofas, John, and Hans Toch. 1982. 'The Guard Subculture Myth.' *Journal of Research in Crime and Delinquency*, 19:238–54.

Lafontaine, Edward, and Leslie Tredeau. 1986. 'The Frequency, Sources, and Correlates of Sexual Harassment among Women in Traditional Male Occupations.' *Sex Roles*, 15(7/8), 433–42.

Lewis, Stephen. 1992. Letter to Ontario Premier Bob Rae (Report on Findings as a Temporary Advisor on Race Relations), Toronto, 9 June.

Lovrich, Nicholas P., and Mary K. Stohr. 1993. 'Gender and Jail Work: Correctional Policy Implications of Perceptual Diversity in the Work Force.' *Policy Studies Review*, 12(1/2), 66–84.

Mann, William E. 1967. *Society behind Bars – A Sociological Scrutiny of Guelph Reformatory.* Toronto: Social Science Publishers.

Marron, Kevin. 1996. *The Slammer: The Crisis in Canada's Prison System.* Toronto: Doubleday Canada.

Martin, Susan. 1980. *Breaking and Entering: Policewomen on Patrol.* Berkeley: University of California Press.

Marvy, Leonard. 1995. *Final Submission in the Matter of an Arbitration Under the Crown Employees Collective Bargaining Act Before the Grievance Settlement Board Between OPSEU [Grievors' names] and The Crown in Right of Ontario (Ministry of Correctional Services – Employer).* Ontario Ministry of the Attorney General, Legal Services Branch, Management Board Secretariat. November.

Maschke, Karen J. 1996. 'Gender in the Prison Setting: The Privacy–Equal Employment Dilemma.' *Women and Criminal Justice*, 7(2), 23–42.

McEwen, Joan. 1995. *Report in Respect of the Political Science Department of the University of British Columbia.* Vancouver: University of British Columbia.

McMahon, Maeve W. 1988. 'Police Accountability: The Situation of Complaints in Toronto,' *Contemporary Crises,* 12:301–27.

– 1990. '"Net-Widening": Vagaries in the Use of a Concept.' *British Journal of Criminology,* 30:121–49.

– 1992. *The Persistent Prison? Rethinking Decarceration and Penal Reform.* Toronto: University of Toronto Press.

– 1996a. 'La répression comme entreprise: Quelques tendances récentes en matière de privatisation et de justice criminelle.' ['"Control as Enterprise": Some Recent Trends in Privatization and Criminal Justice.'] *Déviance et Société,* 20(2), 103–18.

– 1996b. 'Critical Criminology and the Problem of Power,' *Chronicles/Xponika [Greek Journal of Criminology],* 9:1–20.

McMahon, Maeve W., and Richard V. Ericson. 1984. *Policing Reform: A Study of the Reform Process and Police Institution in Toronto.* Toronto: Centre of Criminology, University of Toronto.

Meyer, Herbert, and Mary Lee. 1978. *Women in Traditionally Male Jobs: The Experience of Ten Public Utility Companies.* Washington, DC: Government Printing Office. Department of Labor, Employment and Training Administration.

Ministry of Correctional Services, Ontario. 1983a. 'Historical Perspective in Corrections.' Unpublished manuscript.

– 1983b. 'The Affirmative Action Program.' Briefing note of the Ministry of Correctional Services.

– 1992. *Chronology of Events: Bell Cairn Staff Training Centre.* A collection of memoranda. Toronto: Ministry of Correctional Services.

Morton, Joann B. 1981. 'Women in Correctional Employment: Where Are They Now and Where Are They Headed?' In *Women in Corrections,* 7–16. American Correctional Association Monograph Series #1. Maryland.

Nallin, Judith A. 1981. 'Female Correctional Administrators: Sugar and Spice Are Nice but a Backbone of Steel Is Essential.' In *Women in Corrections,* 17–25. American Correctional Association Monograph Series #1. Maryland.

Oliver, Peter. 1985. *Unlikely Tory: The Life and Politics of Allan Grossman.* Toronto: Lester and Orpen Dennys.

Oliver, Peter, and Michael Whittingham. 1987. 'Elitism, Localism, and the Emergence of Adult Probation Services in Ontario, 1893–1972.' *Canadian Historical Review,* 68(2), 225–57.

Ombudsman of Ontario. 1977. *A Report on Adult Correctional Institutions.* Ontario: Ministry of Correctional Services.

Outerbridge, William. 1979. Unpublished interview. Oral History Project of the Ontario Ministry of Correctional Services.

Owen, Barbara A. 1985. 'Race and Gender Relations among Prison Workers.' *Crime and Delinquency*, 31(1), 147–59.

Palango, Paul. 1993. 'For Whom Bell Cairn Tolls.' *Eye Weekly*, 18 February, 7.

Petersen, Cheryl B. 1982. 'Doing Time with the Boys: An Analysis of Women Correctional Officers in All-Male Facilities.' In Barbara Raffel Price, and Natalie Sokoloff (eds), *The Criminal Justice System and Women*, 437–60. New York: Clark Boardman.

Philliber, S. 1987. 'Thy Brother's Keeper: A Review of the Literature on Correctional Officers.' *Justice Quarterly*, 4(1), 9–37.

Picher, Michel G., and Ellen E. Mole. 1993. 'The Problem of Delay at Arbitration: Myth and Reality.' In William Kaplan, Jeffrey Sack, and Morley Gunderson (eds), *Labour Arbitration Yearbook 1993*, 3–43. Toronto: Butterworths – Lancaster House.

Podrebarac, George R. 1984. 'Policy on the Assignment of Male and Female Correctional Officers.' Memorandum sent by Deputy Minister Dr. G.R. Podrebarac on 30 March. Ontario Ministry of Correctional Services.

Price, Barbara, and Susan Gavin. 1982. 'A Century of Women in Policing.' In Barbara Price and Natalie Sokoloff (eds) *The Criminal Justice System and Women*, 399–412. New York: Clark Boardman.

Riemer, Jeffrey. 1979. *Hard Hats: The Work World of Construction Workers*. Beverly Hills, California: Sage.

Roach, Kent. 1995. 'Canadian Public Inquiries and Accountability.' In Philip C. Stenning (ed), *Accountability for Criminal Justice*, 268–93. Toronto: University of Toronto Press.

Rustad, Michael. 1982. *Women in Khaki*. New York: Praeger.

Sakowski, Marie H. 1985. 'Women Guards in Canada: A Study of the First Women to Work in a Federal Penitentiary for Male Offenders.' *Resources for Feminist Research (Women and the Criminal Justice System)*, 13(4), 52–3.

Shawver, Lois, and Robert Dickover. 1986. 'Exploding a Myth.' *Corrections Today* (August), 30–4.

Sommers, Christina Hoff. 1994. *Who Stole Feminism? How Women Have Betrayed Women*. New York: Simon and Schuster.

Stan, Adele M. 1995. 'Introduction: Feminism and the Culture of Sexuality.' In Adele M. Stan (ed), *Debating Sexual Correctness: Pornography, Sexual Harassment, Date Rape, and the Politics of Sexual Equality*, xix–xlviii. New York: Delta.

Stanley, Kay. 1992. 'Barriers.' In *Towards Equal Partnership. Report on the Conference for Women in CSC*, 3–4. Ottawa: Correctional Service of Canada.

Stenning, Philip C. 1995. 'Accountability in the Ministry of the Solicitor General of Canada.' In Philip C. Stenning (ed), *Accountability for Criminal Justice*, 44–73. Toronto: University of Toronto Press.

Stewart, Ron L. 1995. *Special Report of the Correctional Investigator Concerning the*

Treatment of Inmates and Subsequent Inquiry Following Certain Incidents at the Prison for Women in April 1994 and Thereafter. Ottawa: Minister of Supply and Services.

Strange, Carolyn. 1985. '"The Criminal and Fallen of Their Sex:" The Establishment of Canada's First Women's Prison, 1874–1901.' *Canadian Journal of Women and the Law,* 1:79–92.

Symes, Beth. 1995. *Written Submissions on Behalf of OPSEU in the Matter of an Arbitration Under the Crown Employees Collective Bargaining Act Before the Grievance Settlement Board Between OPSEU [Grievors' names] and The Crown in Right of Ontario (Ministry of Correctional Services – Employer).* Toronto: Eberts Symes and Street, Counsel for OPSEU. November.

Szockyj, E. 1989. 'Working in a Man's World: Women Correctional Officers in an Institution for Men.' *Canadian Journal of Criminology,* 31(3), 319–28.

Taylor, Brenda 1986. 'No Place for a Lady? Female Security Staff in Male Prisons.' *The Correctional Review* (Correctional Service of Canada), 1(1), 51–3.

Walters, Stephen. 1992. 'Attitudinal and Demographic Differences between Male and Female Corrections Officers: A Study in Three Midwestern Prisons.' *Journal of Offender Rehabilitation,* 18(1/2), 173–89.

– 1993. 'Changing the Guard: Male Correctional Officers' Attitudes toward Women as Co-Workers.' *Journal of Offender Rehabilitation,* 20(1/2), 47–60.

Westley, Laurie. 1982. *A Territorial Issue: The Study of Women in the Construction Trades.* Washington, DC: Centre for National Policy Review.

White, Martha. 1975. 'Women in the Professions: Psychological and Social Barriers to Women in Science.' In Jo Freeman (ed), *Women: A Feminist Perspective,* 227–37. Palo Alto, California: Mayfield.

Wright, Kevin N., and William G. Saylor. 1991. 'Male and Female Employees' Perceptions of Prison Work: Is There a Difference?' *Justice Quarterly,* 8(4), 505–24.

Zimmer, Lynn. 1982. 'Female Guards in Men's Prisons: Creating a Role for Themselves.' PhD dissertation, Cornell University.

– 1986. *Women Guarding Men.* Chicago: University of Chicago Press.

– 1989. 'Solving Women's Employment Problems in Corrections: Shifting the Burden to Administrators.' *Women and Criminal Justice.* 1(1), 55–79.

Zupan, Linda L. 1992. 'Men Guarding Women: An Analysis of the Employment of Male Corrections Officers in Prisons for Women.' *Journal of Criminal Justice,* 20:297–309.

Index

abuse, as 1990s issue, 132
Affirmative Action Program, 22, 28, 144–5
Aggarwal, Arjun P., 196–8n. 11
arbitration, 60; boards, 193–5n. 1; decision, 193–5n. 1; powers of, 199–200n. 13; process, 151, 193–5n. 1. *See also* Grievance Settlement Board Australia, gender-based discrimination and harassment in, 111
authoritarianism: of Fred Ferguson, 94–5; of prison management, 6–7, 16

Basher, Hedley, 17
Beauchamp, Kerry, 65; micro-inequities, 68; property defacement, 77; reprisals following complaints, 105
Bell Cairn Staff Training Centre, 184–5n. 8; authority of staff, 48; as case study, 32–54; complaints, 37–9, 42–3; discipline protocols, 41; 'gang-rape' allegations, 8–9, 35–6, 47; harassing telephone calls, 39–40; incidents at, 11–12; policy significance of operational issues, 113; rowdyism as policy issue, 112; scandal at, 8–9, 49–54; security staff, 39–41;

sexual harassment recognition, 41–7
Breed, Allen F., 99
Bronskill, Ann, 182n. 4
Building a Partnership for Change: A Report on the Evaluation of WHDP Policy Training, 53–4, 121–2

Canadian Auto Workers, 91
Canadian Charter of Rights and Freedoms, 28
Canadian Labour Congress, 91
Canadian Panel on Violence Against Women, 91
Casselman, Leah, 91, 153
casual employees, 26; vulnerability of, 64, 90; Wakefield Jail, 57–8, 103, 104
Chronology of Events: Bell Cairn Staff Training Centre (Correctional Services), 10–11, 36, 43–4, 50
Code of Behaviour (Bell Cairn), 45–6
Collective Agreement, 60; Article A.1, no discrimination/employment equity, 91–2, 138; Article 27, sexual harassment, 92, 138, 139–40
community-based programs, 23
community services orders, 23
complaint investigation process, 59–60, 87

complaints: advice of Preston's
    doctor, 101; consequences of, 90,
    104–9; emotional strength required,
    101–2; and women, 100–4
conflicts: between union members, 91;
    at Wakefield Jail, 56; women in the
    workplace, 131
Contentious Issues Unit, 49
Conway case, Supreme Court of Can-
    ada, 31
Coopers and Lybrand, report on the
    culture in corrections, 201–2n. 21
Cornish, Mary, 147, 194n. 1, 196–8n.
    11, 200n. 13
correctional officers: code of solidar-
    ity, 102; inherently female aspects
    of tasks, 63; insecurity and isolation
    of, 5; observations by Micheline
    Pelletier, 106–7; social status of, 5;
    stereotypical perceptions, 63; wo-
    men as, 25–6; women's access to
    tasks, 31–2
Correctional Service of Canada, 60,
    113; conferences for female staff,
    10, 129; surveys of discrimination,
    110
Correctional Services of Ontario. *See*
    Ministry of Correctional Services
Couglan, Dan, 20
criminal offences, 83, 133; assault, 76
cross-gender supervision, 30, 74

Davis, Bill, 22
deputy minister, and Bell Cairn, 8–9,
    46–7, 49
Diamond, Nora, 64; casual employee
    and promotion, 124–5; complaint
    procedures, 104; correctional offi-
    cer, 59–60; feelings following discri-
    mination, 87; and Fred Ferguson,
    94–5; grievance, 60, 97, 190–1n. 1,
    192n. 8; grievance decision, 140–1;

142, 145–6, 148–9, 150–1; harassing
    telephone calls, 81; lack of support
    for, 65; micro-inequities, 67–9;
    offensive and sexist comments to,
    78–9; property defacement, 77;
    reprisals following complaints,
    105–6; Westbury transfer incident,
    95, 97; and work schedules, 71
differential assignments, 70–4, 85
dispute resolution, 117
'divide and rule' tactics, against wo-
    men, 128–9
documentation, of incidents at Wake-
    field Jail and Bell Cairn, 11–12, 13
Don Jail, matrons in, 18

earnings, of women in Correctional
    Services, 25
employees. *See* casual employees;
    unclassified employees
employer, liability of, for sexual harass-
    ment, 138
Employment Equity Policy and Plan,
    24–5, 92
Employment Equity program, 28,
    192n. 127; operational issues as
    barriers to women, 113
'Equal Opportunity for Women in
    Ontario: A Plan for Ontario', 22
equity issues: Correctional strategies
    toward, 29–31; female probation
    officers, 20–1; government policies,
    28–9; hiring and promotion, 127;
    and management, 108

fear of reporting, 89–93
fear of reprisals, 47, 54; from com-
    plaints, 90, 102–3, 104
female correctional officers: historical
    data by Bronskill, 182n. 4; introduc-
    tion of, in prisons for men, 4, 18–19,
    19t; relations with male inmates,

61–2; Wakefield Jail, 57. *See also*
Diamond, Nora; Hooper, Diana;
Jackson, Melissa; Pelletier,
Micheline; Poirer, Kathy; West,
Sharon
female probation officers, 20–1, 36–9
feminist movements, 131–2
Ferguson, Fred, 59; and dispute over
work schedules, 71; gender issues,
95; grievance decision, 139, 141,
147, 148; harassment of Karla
Preston, 77–8, 82, 94–5, 101; human-
rights complaint against, 95, 189–
90n. 5; lack of support for women,
65; offensive and sexual comments,
77–9, 94; sexual harassment, 94;
transfer of, 85, 110
Fischer (acting IC), 71
Fudge, Judy, 146, 196–8n. 11

Gagnon, George: hostility toward women, 65; unwanted touching of, 83
'gang-rage' allegations, at Bell Cairn
Staff Training Centre, 8–9, 35–6, 47
gender-based discrimination and harassment, 14, 69–70; as 1990s issues,
130–4; differential assignments,
70–4, 85; hiring and promotion,
124–9; holistic approach, 61, 135,
143; hours of work, 70–3; responses
and penalties, 115–20; task allocation, 70, 72–4; at Wakefield Jail, 11,
58, 70–4, 108–9, 110; women's feelings following, 86–8. *See also* sexual
harassment; Workplace Discrimination and Harassment Prevention
policy (WDHP)
gender-based problems: recognition
of at Bell Cairn, 41–7, 48; and *Report
of the Bell Cairn Inquiry*, 50. *See also*
Wakefield Jail
gender related issues: and hidden

nature of prisons, 9, 135; as policy
issues, 112; and Workplace Discrimination and Harassment Prevention
Policy, 99–100
'glass-ceiling,' 74
Grievance Settlement Board, 11, 101,
120; decision, 136–7; imposition of
systemic solutions, 142–5; individual
grievances, 139–42; legal foundation
of decision, 137–9; members of,
193n. 1. *See also* arbitration
grievors: emotional upheaval of, 150–1;
media coverage, 149–50; public as
unsympathetic, 149–50; reaction to
grievance decision, 146–51; women
from Wakefield Jail, 11. *See also*
Diamond, Nora; Grievance Settlement Board; Hooper, Diana; Preston, Karla
Guelph Reformatory, 17

Haines, Superintendent, 103
half-way houses, 23
Hansen, Inger, 49–50, 138; recommendations, 186–7n. 22
harassers: penalties, 119; supervisors
as, 117–18; transfer of, 118–19
harassment prevention, government
policies, 28–9
Henriksen, Sheila, 60, 118, 120
hiring and promotion: arbitrariness
of, 126–7; barriers to, 26–7; and
casual officers, 103, 124–5; limitations on, 24, 75, 85; of women,
124–9
holistic approach, to sexual harassment and discrimination, 61, 135,
143
Hooper, Diana: exclusion from certain
assignments, 73–4; feelings following
discrimination, 87–8; female correctional officer, 57–60; grievance

decision, 141–2, 145–6, 148, 151; harassment by O'Reilly, 69; health, 190–1n. 1; hostility toward at Wakefield Jail, 65; on Gerry Kennedy, 66; liaison with colleague, 80, 116; and Maurice, 101; speculation and rumours about, 80; unwanted touching of, 83; Westbury transfer incident, 95, 97, 104; work schedules, 71. *See also* Ferguson, Fred.

Horne, Peter, 62

Human Rights Code, 28; poisoned environment under, 33

human-rights complaint, against Fred Ferguson, 95, 189–90n. 5

impediments to reporting, 89–93, 109; at Wakefield Jail, 102–4

incarceration pursuant to 'alcoholism,' 18, 181n. 3

Incident Reports, for minister, 185n. 14

Independent Investigations Unit, 49, 58–60

Institutional Management positions, women in, 25

investigators: gender-based discrimination and harassment, 115–17; Wakefield Jail, 59–60

Jackson, Melissa: differential assignments, 73; exclusion from certain assignments, 74; harassing telephone calls, 81; micro-inequities, 68; property defacement, 77; work schedules, 71, 72

Joint Management-Union Assessment Team, 143–4, 153

joint management-union ventures, 93; *Open Minds/Open Doors*, 24; and reality of culture of Wakefield Jail, 109

Kadar, Marlene, 91

Kennedy, Gerald (Gerry): attack on Micheline Pelletier, 84; excluding women from assignments, 74; hostility toward women, 64, 65–6

Kingston Prison for Women, 178n. 5, 6

Labour Relations Act, 198n. 11

lack of knowledge: about correctional officers, 5; about penalties imposed, 118; about procedures for complaining, 102, 104

lack of support: for complaints, 90; from unions, 90–1, 102

La Forest, Hon. Gerard V., 137

Lalonde, Francis, 79; and Fred Ferguson, 94

Laroche, Lieutenant: grievance decision, 140; harassment, 68, 72; and Diana Hooper, 101; hostility toward women at Wakefield Jail, 65; objectionable behaviour list, 96; offensive and sexual comments, 79; unwanted touching by, 83, 84

legal foundation, Grievance Settlement Board's decision, 137–9

legal rights, 28, 133

Lopez, Suzanne, 146, 194n. 1, 196–8n. 11, 200n. 13

male correctional officers: abusive behaviour of, 44; fury at grievance decision, 152–3; hostility toward women, 64; hostility to training, 122; lack of support for women colleagues, 64; offensive behaviour of, 58; reprisals, 105–7; sexual harassment at Bell Cairn, 36, 42–3; traditional views of, 65–6; working with female inmates, 3

male culture: excluding women from,

85; need for change in, 112; of prisons, 61–3; at Wakefield Jail, 64–6, 83, 85

male inmates: and female correctional officers, 61–2; in Ontario provincial prisons, 188n. 9

Mallon, Lieutenant, harassment, 68

management: condoning of abuse, 103; employer's liability for sexual harassment by, 138; exacerbation of problems, 93–100; impact of definition of problems, 48; as impediment to reporting harassment, 14, 93–100; managers as harassers, 100; ongoing problems, 108, 110; reprisals following complaints, 105, 107–9; strategies for change, 112; women in, 19, 25, 58; women's access to work, 64. *See also* training; Workplace Discrimination and Harassment Prevention policy (WDHP)

Mann, William E., 16–17

Marron, Kevin, 5, 6

matrons, in Ontario prisons, 17–18

Maurice (correctional officer), and Diana Hooper, 83, 101

media, and workplace issues, 131

media attention: and criticism, 6; events at Wakefield Jail, 149–50; everyday life of prisons, 6; and male officers, 152–3

micro-inequities, 66–7; at Wakefield Jail, 67–9

military orientation, prison management, 16–17

Ministry of Correctional Services, 7, 12; and backlash at Wakefield Jail, 153; betrayal of female staff, 95; disjunctures between rhetoric and reality, 31–2, 109; Employment Systems Review, 24–5; gender discrimination in hiring and promotion,

126–7; grievance decision, 139–40, 141; and harassment prevention, 32–5; lack of communication in, 118–19; as male dominated, 22; policy significance of operational issues, 113; response to events at Bell Cairn, 47–9, 50; systemic problems, 51, 134

Murray, Patricia, 64–5; exclusion from certain assignments, 74

New Zealand, gender-based discrimination and harassment, 111

oath of secrecy, correctional officers', 5

offensive behaviour, of Wakefield Jail male colleagues, 58, 60–1, 96–7

offensive and sexual comments, 77–9, 85

Office Administration Group, women in, 25

Ombudsman of Ontario, on women working in prisons for men, 23, 31

Ontario, Government of. *See* Collective Agreement; Ministry of Correctional Services

Ontario Crown Employees Grievance Settlement Board. *See* Grievance Settlement Board

Ontario *Human Rights Code*, 28; poisoned environment under, 33

Ontario Ministry of Correctional Services. *See* Ministry of Correctional Services

Ontario Parole Board, female appointments, 21

Ontario Public Service Employees Union, 11–12, 109; and backlash at Wakefield Jail, 153; Employment Systems Review, 24; and safety of Karla Preston, 153; training of Wake-

field Jail staff, 122–3; women in, 91.
See also Collective Agreement
Open Minds/Open Doors (Employment
Systems Review), 24
operational matters: impact on women's occupational equity, 114;
inmate privacy and female officers,
114; and management, 48; recognizing, as policy issues, 112–15
O'Reilly, Lieutenant Pat: gender-
related issues, 87, 99–100; grievance
decision, 141–2, 147–8; harassment,
68–9; hostility toward women, 65;
objectional behaviour list, 98–9; occurrence report, 97; pornographic
movie incident, 100, 108, 141; sexual
propositions, 81; unwanted touching by, 84; Westbury transfer incident, 95, 97; work schedules and
women, 71

Palozzi, Dina, 8, 33. See also deputy
minister
participant-observational analysis, 121,
122
'passive cover-up,' of incidents at Bell
Cairn, 36, 49
patriarchal assumptions, of unions, 91
Pelletier, Micheline, 26, 109; aggressive
attack from Kennedy, 84; discrimination and abuse, 66; observations
by, 106–7; work schedules, 72–3
penalties: for discrimination and harassment, 117–20; grievance decision,
145–6; under Code of Behaviour,
45–6
perpetrators: transferring of, 119; at
Wakefield Jail, 110
persistent harassment, dismissal as
penalty for, 119–20
Philip Conway v. Her Majesty the Queen,
31

Poirier, Kathy, 26; offensive and sexual
comments directed to, 79
poisoned environment: grievance
decision, 138, 139–40, 141, 143, 146;
Report of the Bell Cairn Inquiry, 50–1;
under Human Rights Code, 33;
Wakefield Jail, 13, 56, 83, 84–7
police, occupational subculture of,
102
police investigation, Bell Cairn, 49
policy issues: liquor consumption at
Bell Cairn, 38; and management, 48;
procedures for staff, 115
political accountability, 36, 49
political scandal, about Bell Cairn,
8–9, 35–6
pornographic movie incident, Wakefield Jail, 100, 108, 141
power: of Fred Ferguson, 94, 103; gender imbalance, 52
Preston, Karla: casual cook, 58–60,
125; complaints initiated, 100; divide
and rule tactics, 128; feelings following harassment, 86–7; grievance,
60, 190–1n. 1; grievance decision,
139–40, 142, 148–9, 150; harassment
by James Randell, 102, 103; micro-
inequities, 67; reprisals following
complaints, 105; safety at Wakefield
Jail, 153; teasing and insulting of, 77;
unwanted touching, 83; work schedules, 72. See also Ferguson, Fred
prison culture: authoritarian, 6–7; and
change, 111; systemic problems, 51
prison guard subculture, 63, 75
prisons: as form of punishment, 178n.
3; hidden world of, 4–6; 178n. 3;
macho culture of, 14; occupational
world of, 5
probation and parole officers: and
harassment at Bell Cairn, 36–9;
women as, 19–21

Probation and Parole Services, women in, 25

procedures: and change, 111; policy component of, 115

Procedures [for] Disruptive Course Participants, 41

Procedures for Residents Causing Problems Outside of Class, 41

Progressive Conservative government, Employment Equity programs, 192n. 3, 192n. 9

Provincial Inquiry (Bell Cairn), 49; limitations of report, 50–1; terms of reference, 50

public culture, flashpoint issues of 1990s, 132, 133

public information, lack of, 49

public knowledge, of correctional officers, 6

Public Service Alliance of Canada, 91

racial harassment, 185–6n. 16

Rae, Bob, release of documents concerning Bell Cairn, 9–10, 36

Randell, James: grievance decision, 139; and Karla Preston, 102, 103; sexual propositions by, 81; unwanted touching by, 83; and Sharon West, 101

rape, as 1990s issue, 132

rehabilitation programs, 23

Report of the Bell Cairn Inquiry, 50–3

Report of the Royal Commission on the Status of Women, 22

research: on female correctional workers, 9; on impediments to reporting, 89–93; need for, 6–7; on women working in prisons for men, 55–6, 61

Robert, Joe, 71; attack on Nora Diamond, 84, 103; hostility toward women, 65

Robichaud v. The Queen, 137–8

rowdyism, 36–41, 45; as policy issue, 112

Royal Commission on the Status of Women, 22

Runciman, Bob, 35, 201–2n. 21

security staff, Bell Cairn Staff Training Centre, 39–41, 45–6

Senior Management Group, women in, 25–6

sexual harassment, 74–82; as 1990s issue, 132; allegations of at Bell Cairn, 8, 35–6; brought to arbitration, 196–8n. 11; equating experience of men and women, 51–3; holistic approach, 61, 135, 143; insidiousness of, 75–6, 105; legal definition of, 139; ministry's initiatives, 32–5; offensive and sexual comments, 77–9; reluctance to complain, 60; speculation and rumours, 80–1; teasing and insults, 76–7; telephone calls, 81; unwanted and sexual touching, 82–4; unwelcome intrusions and sexual propositions, 81–2; vulnerability of women to, 52. *See also* gender-based discrimination and harassment; Wakefield Jail

sexual improprieties, 193n. 5

Sinclair, Don, 16, 17

Smith, Superintendent: grievance decision, 140; and pornographic movie incident, 108

social education, 53

Social Programs Administration, women in, 25

social status, of correctional officers, 5

speculation and rumours, about women's sexuality, 75, 80–1, 116

Stan, Adele, 132

Starr, Patricia (Patti), on sexual abuse
    at Vanier Detention Centre, 184n. 7
Stenning, Philip C., 135
strip joint incident, 95, 141
strip searches, 30–1; incidents, 178–9n.
    6
'superjails,' 154, 191n. 6
supervision, by male officers of female
    inmates, 177n. 1
supervisors: as harassers, 117–18;
    ongoing problems at Wakefield Jail,
    107–8; reprisals following com-
    plaints, 105, 107
support systems, for women, 127–9
Supreme Court of Canada, 194n. 1;
    *Action Travail des Femmes v. Canadian
    National Railway Company*, 197n. 11;
    Conway case, 31; cross-sex supervision,
    31; *Robichaud v. The Queen*, 137–8
Symes, Beth, 11, 136, 150
systemic problems: harassment, 115;
    hiring and promotion, 127; Ministry
    of Correctional Services, 51, 111–12,
    134; as organizational, 135
systemic remedies, 134–5, 196–8n. 11;
    imposition of by Grievance
    Settlement Board, 142–5, 153
Szockyj, E., 67

teasing and insults, as sexual harass-
    ment, 76–7
telephone calls, sexual harassment, 81
Temporary Absence program, 23
Toronto West Detention Centre,
    correctional officers, 177n. 1
traditionally female occupations: Wake-
    field Jail, 57; of workers in prison
    for men, 4, 16
training, 120–3; and education about
    discrimination and harassment, 123;
    grievance decision, 144

unclassified employees, 25–6
unions: conflict between members, 91;
    lack of support for women, 90–1,
    104; and women's issues, 91
United States: gender discrimination,
    70, 111; sex as flashpoint issue, 132;
    women working in prisons for men,
    21–2, 55

Vanier Detention Centre for Women,
    184n. 7; correctional officers, 177n. 1
victim-offender reconciliation pro-
    grams, 23
victims: fear of retaliation, 47; leaving
    Wakefield Jail, 110; on trial, 116

Wakefield Jail: as case study, 56–61;
    closure, 154; dearth of women at,
    64; everyday culture of, 109; fear of
    closure, 104, 123; grievance deci-
    sion, 137–42, 151–3; ministry
    investigator, 59–60; as poisoned
    environment, 13, 56, 83, 84–7, 137,
    139–40; problems with penalties,
    117; rhetoric and everyday reality
    in, 32; sexual harassment at, 13, 58,
    76–82, 85; staff, 11, 26–7, 57; train-
    ing function of management, 122–3;
    women hired at, 124–5; work sche-
    dules and women, 71–4. *See also*
    grievors; management; Workplace
    Discrimination and Harassment
    Prevention policy
Wallace (correctional officer), 95
WDHP. *See* Workplace Discrimination
    and Harassment Prevention policy
    (WDHP)
*Welcome to Bell Cairn Staff Training
    Centre*, 41
West, Sharon: casual correctional
    officer, 58, 125; complaints by, 60;

exclusion from assignments, 74; feelings following harassment, 88; hours of work, 70; lack of support for, 65; and O'Reilly, 99, 103; propositions from Randell, 81, 101, 103; resignation from Jail, 88, 190–1n. 1; sexual harassment of, 83–4; speculation and rumours about, 80–1; on working conditions, 64

Westbury transfer incident, 95, 97–8, 104

Windsor, Mike, surveillance of female staff, 80

Windsor, Ontario, grievance, 189n. 2

women: and complaints, 100–4; employed at Wakefield Jail 1980s–1990s, 57; hazards in traditional male occupations, 6–7; in management, 19, 25–6, 58; matrons, 17–18; in probation and parole, 19–21; trivializing physical intrusions on, 115–16; in unions, 91; working in isolation, 58; in the workplace, 130–1. *See also* women working in prisons for men

women's movement, 131–2

women working in prisons for men, 3–4, 9; comparative figures, 29–30; co-workers as largest problem, 61; growth of, 183n. 8; history of, 16–27; lack of recourse for, 93; limitations, 24–7, 30–1; mistreatment as paradigmatic, 13; United States, 21–2

Workplace Discrimination and Harassment Prevention (WDHP), 13, 29, 33; complaints under, 100; and conflict with confidentiality, 48; evaluation of, 121–2; and management, 94, 106–8; persistent harassment, 85, 119–20; poisoned environment, 138; retaliation after complaints under, 72, 105–9; text of policy directive and guideline, 155–75

Workplace Harassment Unit, 49

workplace issues, and women, 130–1

zero tolerance, 133; workplace discrimination and harassment, 54, 92–3

Zimmer, Lynn, 21, 62–3, 66–7; role of unions, 90–1; sexual harassment, 75